Anti-Matter
Poems for the Manic Nihilist

Jeremy Void

Other books by Jeremy Void

available at www.lulu.com and www.amazon.com and all other online retailers

Fiction

Derelict America

Nefarious Endeavors

Sex Drugs & Violence: Incomplete Stories for the Incomplete Human

Nonfiction

My Story: The Short Version

Postal Prose: The Musings of a Tortured Soul, For Sure

Postal Prose 2: My Shadow Hates Me

Poetry

Smash a Lightbulb: Poetry for Lowlifes

Just a Kid

The Lost Letters

An Art Form: The Crass Poetry Collection

The TR*TH

My Psychedelic Suicide

A Crime of Passion

Shattered Illusions

The SkullFuck Collection

Erase Your Face

I Need Help

A Crass Philosophy

Pre-Apocalyptic

Breaking News

Spoken word albums by Jeremy Void
available at www.bandcamp.jeremyvoid.com

Absurd Nihilism

Word Vomit

Irrelevant Discourse

Anti-Matter
Poems for the Manic Nihilist

Jeremy Void

Anti-Matter: Poems for the Manic Nihilist

Copyright © 2017 by Jeremy Void

All Rights Reserved

No part of this book may be reproduced, scanned, or distributed in any print or electronic form without permission. Please do not participate in or encourage piracy of copyrighted materials in violation of the author's rights. Purchase only authorized editions.

ISBN Number:
978-0-578-19831-6

ChaosWriting ^{Press}

It's a Mindfuck
www.chaoswriting.net

To Stephen Audsley

You will be missed

Categories of Cataclysmic Scales

Jeremy Void is not responsible in the event of spontaneous corruption upon reading this book

Manic/Depressive Monuments
— 1 —

Decomposed Compositions
— 43 —

Exponential Interpretations
— 127 —

Revolting Sensitivity
— 169 —

Hysterical Resolutions
— 231 —

Esoteric Demonstrations
— 299 —

Jaded Delicacies
— 357 —

Table of DisContents
—— **435**

x

Manic Nihilism/Absurdism/Call It Whatever You Want It Makes No Difference in the End
An Introduction

You see
I just happen to like
pointing out all the
absurdities ironies and flaws
that life undergoes through
day after withering day
Just because I'm saying
it's absurd ironic and
flawed
does not mean
I'm rendering it a negative reproach
but I'm only
approaching life's horror
through an obscure scope
shining light on the many ways in which
life people and the like
partake in tomfoolery
of the loony-tune variety
following trends
blending in
just being a human being

seen through a shattered lens
I just happen to find humor in
foolish behavior
squirrelly, labor-intensive, utterly sensitive,
duly pretentious attitudes of
the phony, godlike parasites that
leech off of competition like
a miniscule shit actively
being sucked back in
to a butthole as wide and large
as the shimmering moon
of a thousand stolen dreams
seen through the deeply twisted
minds of anonymous breeders alike
the kind that have guts so wide
it devours my conscious mind
eats my brain through a shriveled-up
IV that pumps TV into my blood
almost like it's a drug
        you know the type/

Or maybe you're just too uptight
to appreciate the small things
in life
to disempower your commercialized views
to honestly admit to yourself
I AM POWERLESS OVER EVERYTHING
——AND MY LIFE WILL NEVER BE
——MANAGEABLE
so giving up seems like quite
a feasible avenue to take
because if you're out of control
there's no reason to hone in on it
any more than focusing on a zit
that just can't be popped
Fuck the Lot of You

if I'm honest enough with myself to
call all my friends TWATS
and say the hell with power
because we live in an insidious wet dream
that constantly streams
sex and violence and ruthless crimes
that good people do in
a socially acceptable manner
Glad I'm not one of those fascist fucks
preaching ANTI-HATE
when instead I can drop that hypocritical cliché
and just promote LOVE
saying Love Your Neighbor
and Keep Your Stupid Opinions
to Yourself
Because in the end
the hate-monger will
hate you all the same
it makes no difference to them

It Begins

Brace Yourself

www.chaoswriting.net

Manic/Depressive Monuments

29

i'm 29 today & i swear in a year i'll go out like hunter s. thompson, or at least that <u>was</u> the plan, but i slashed out my 30-year-old suicide pact when i became old enough to grasp that i got at least another 40 years to go & millions of more roads to explore & hundreds of more people to annoy, more buttons to find, more levers to crank, more words to abuse, more truths to disuse; so i'm 29 years old & i think i've got some more living to do....

Vindictive Arrogance

One moment I'm determined to tear everyone down; the next moment I'm concerned I might have torn someone down.

One moment I'm brutally blunt; the next moment I'm brutally second-guessing my previous transgressions.

Was it something that I said?
Truly, I meant you no harm.

I can assure you my arrogant and cocky demeanor are only as a result of an overall dissatisfaction with self—give myself a moment to cool off and reflect, boy I might stake my head to the ground, slug me in the eye socket with a long, steel club with a nail jutting out the top.

Everyone hates me—well fuck em anyway!
Everyone hates me—I feel guilty and ashamed
borderline psychotic, bold and indecisive, a prick with a conscience—see that's me.

And I'm proud

And I'm self-loathing

And I'm sure
but so unsure that I might seem like a different person.

Don't need to worry about me being two-faced, either
because I'm only twofaced to those I don't like >>>
and yet I don't like anyone;;;;
so you see, I'm in a bit of a bind …

But please like me anyway, it's free of charge
just please let me into your heart …

so that I can tear you up from the inside
that's all I really want in the end…………….

Artistic Expression

I like to write

>I like to share my writing

I like to create

>I like to share my creations

I like to think

>I like to share my thoughts

I like to talk

>I like to share my voice

Sober-X

Why do I do this to myself? Take an icepick to the center of my head—see what makes me tick. Now my brain is bleeding; it's gruesome and grotesque. Just split my head in two. Chop it up like an orange and suck out all the juice. <u>I'm sober now</u>! Those three words, in that order, leave behind a nasty tinge in my mouth. I'm sober now, and yet   and yet I seek other means of destroying myself. I don't drink, I don't smoke, nor do I snort lines or ram a spike in my arm. But still I feel rather depleted. This is just no way to live.

I'll be moving on soon. Another ten years and I'll be 40, and then 50 do the math. Another town another state another nation—but it's all the same in the

end: the fastest, most precise way to make my head feel like it weighs a thousand tons,,,, do the math.
I'm lost in a hopeless dream the walls are breathing and I'm climbing the cliff to the tippity top of my skull which shatters when I grip just one bone—just one frikken bone.

It's hopeless I'm hopeless. It's hopeless you're hopeless. We're all hopeless/ One step forward, fifty steps back. Why bother going forth when one step means the bricks crunching cracking breaking apart with a cataclysmic quake of sorts.

I read something about gratitude a little while ago///something I wrote myself. Five or six years ago. It said professing gratitude for anything would be dishonest. Five or six years ago. Today I might lie—tell you what you wanna hear all the time….

I'm tired. Aren't you?

Tied to Remorse

For the past week or so (a month?), I've had this feeling of emptiness just festering inside of me. Maybe it's due to hunger, maybe dissatisfaction, maybe something or another, I don't know. Either way, it's killing me when I'm alone. There is just no hope….

I don't know

Maybe I'm just hungry
I don't know
I don't see the point anymore
I don't know

I'm gobbing on realism
gobbing on ideas
I'm gonna get the kills in
maybe surrender to my ideals

but I won't

Maybe I'm just horny
I don't know
I don't see the point anymore
I don't know

I'm just a loaded, misguided leper
aiming to break the sky
Complete with a self-destructive lever
maybe someday I'll see the whys

but I won't

Maybe I'm just lonely
I don't know
I don't see the point anymore
I don't know

My friends all come & go
Some days I let them stay
My worldviews are beginning to explode
Try to make me see it another way

but I won't

Maybe I'm just broken
I don't know
I don't see the point anymore
I don't know

Burn Out

I can't find the right words to say what I'm feeling. Usually I'm on a roll, but today self-doubt has taken its toll. I hate my face, the way it smirks when I'm all alone, sneers and growls and I feel oh so cold. I get energetic and wild and I do what I please. I get frenetic and shy and I can't do anything. Boxed in—intense energy holding me stiff; too much of it makes me hate existence. I burn out from time to time, I'm only human. It's times like these when I just wanna die. This past week I wrote almost twelve pieces: two were stories and ten were poems. But it's all garbage, I know now; I'll pile it up and douse it with gas, light a match and let the flame do the rest. I'm sorry if we ever spoke, I'm sorry I got to know ya. I'm losing a dream of the past that's gotten too mean, and now I'm suffering and slipping and sinking into a pit that's way too deep. Do I care only so others will care, or do I care simply because I'm a caring person? It's pointless anyway, throw caution to the wind; your right and wrong just don't seem fit for a person like me.

Safe House

It's in my dreams
where I find comfort
It's in my thoughts
where I find ammunition
It's in my voice
where I find protection
It's in me
where I find reprieve

Fake

Take off your makeup
and show us
who you really are

You got:
        <u>pumps</u>
        <u>pushup bras</u>
        <u>wonder bras</u>
        <u>plastic dolls</u>

Take off your plastic
and show us
who you really are

You got:
        <u>eyeliner</u>
        <u>lip shiner</u>
        <u>one-liners</u>
        <u>two-faced liars</u>

Take off your masks
and show us
who you really are

You got:
  yoga pants
  spray on tans
  disco bands
  horny frats

Take off your paintjobs
and show us
who you really are

You got:
  blue balls
  spandex pants
  eyes of lust
  rejected much

Unhinge your chains
Remove your veils
Let down your hair
Take off your costumes
and show us
who you really are

because all I see
are a bunch of fakes

Existential Angst

Some days I feel like I'm walking on a treadmill, just trundling through life, traipsing through existence. I'm a mere nonentity. I don't exist except in my own head. I'm a figment.

People Places & Things

I hang out with
    broken people
I frequent
    broken places
I play with
    broken things
Maybe it is I
      who is broken

A Rebel's Paradise

Okay, so we live in squalor, surrounded by bitter rebels, because today everybody is rebelling, today everybody is a rebel, today rebellion has become a trend, and today there is nothing to rebel against—or maybe there is. Maybe that is in fact what we have to rebel against: the fact that there is nothing to fight for anymore, all our problems solved by the Beatniks, by the Hippies, by the Punks, by the Nazis, by the Black Panthers, by the Taliban, and by the Feminists too—can't forget about them.

I think about how everybody is rebelling. I think about it as I walk through a new city on my way to meet new people at a new place to drink new coffee and everybody I pass has new hair and new clothes and new piercings and new tattoos and everyone who looks at me in my filthy rags are thinking he's a freak, he's a cretin, he's a birth deformity—a defect wandering in a rebel's paradise.

Back up. It's open-mike night....

That's right! I'm walking to the coffee shop to read my introspective period piece about how I'm a diseased freak and I hate my existence with every last ounce of breath I have left as I choke down another cigarette and sit in the back of the bar drinking myself to death but not with alcohol but with coffee but with water but with everything the rebels are not in fact drinking and they call me a freak cuz I'm not fighting with them, so I must be the problem I'm not the solution so I must be the problem I'm delusional for seeing hope in a backwards world and I hate the fact that I see hope and it's burning like crisp coals inside my head and my heart explodes and I sit down and cry ... on the stoop leading up to the church. I skip the open-mike and sit here instead, that's right; I sit here and cry, and people sneer and mutter, Religion is for fools, for freaks, for brainwashed geeks, for mindless drones, you're a recovering Catholic aren't you? a rehabilitated Jew?—no Jews ain't that bad, as long as you don't believe in the second-coming of Jesus Christ....

Back up. I'm at the coffee shop. Wearing my leather jacket that says HATE down the sleeve. I'm an angry person and I hate myself for being so angry for being so mean—can't tell you how many friends I've lost for being so disturbed, I'm a jerk ... and I sit in the chair, no I sit on the table, no I sit on the roof, and I stand up there and say, Hear me roar hear me bite hear me ...... uh ...... HATE???? Let me hate let me hate let me hate—cuz it's only me that I hate, it's not you it's me, I wear my heart on my sleeve and my heart is drowning in hatred and why doesn't it say LOVE on my sleeve? you're asking me. Because to me love is heartless....

So back at the open-mike. The black poet reads about being a struggling black American poet. The gay poet reads about haters in this day who look at him

the wrong way. The Muslim says that white people think Muslims are terrorists. I hear the feminist say, Why doesn't a man stand up for women's rights? The black says, Why doesn't a white person stand up for black people? The gay says, I agree. Straight men never stick up for me.
I stand up there and say: I'm a straight white American male and I hate you all....
And they hate me back.

And I don't fit....

And I walk the streets and they sneer and shout and hate me and I don't know where my home is. We live in squalor and squalor is shit....

The Crazy

What's the point?

                I bring the crazy outta people!

What's the point?

                I bring the crazy outta people!

But why????

                Because I'm disturbed.
                Because I say disturbing things....
                Because I do disturbing things///
                Because I'm an abstract thinker?
                              Because my head is over here

while the rest of the world
lingers right here   right fuckin here....

I'm alone   alone   alone
lonely brooding fuckedup annoyed irritated
so fuckin   irate
clouding my judgment
you're an ugly cunt
you're a nuisance to my life
you lie you lie you lie
while I clean up the mess you left me with….

Crawl into a void crawl into me babe
I hate life I hate living I hate you babe
Die with me I'll die with you die die die
Kill fuck & conquer is the way
Running outta time and all I've gotta say is

RELATIONSHIPS????

Save me the trouble

because there ain't no point….

        I bring the crazy outta people!
            sodomized w/
             a soldering gun

Love & Death

I hope you die, not because I'm mad, but because I love you. Well, I at least hope one of us dies. I hope I die soon. I wanna die. I want you to kill me. I'm a bastard and I don't deserve to live. No. Fuck that. I don't know how to live.

Today or Nothing

Tomorrow's gonna suck
so I guess it's
today or nothing/
I can't get enough
of the morning sun
of when midnight comes
Tomorrow's gonna suck
so I guess it's
today or nothing/
Gonna have some fun
cuz time is running out
Tomorrow's gonna suck
so I guess it's
today or nothing/

Harmful Determination

I used to drink, today I think, and then I sink. When once I took another shot even though I was far beyond reason, today I push for another hour of sleeplessness; one more minute one more second one more night one more day my conscious is expanding my reach on abstract thinking is enhancing my mind is opening wider and I'm staring down down down into a black hole and now I'm forced to skirt the edge of the pit as it grows larger and larger and I'm stepping farther and farther backwards until I reach my limits, my back hits the edge of my skull and there's just no place to go but down downward flailing and plunging deeper and darker into a large and bleak nothingness that grows wider and bleaker and there comes the stones at the bottom of my plunge, the hole is coming to a drastic end, the fall has almost reached its massive conclusion, I see the stones coming, rising, coming closer, and closer, the bleak nothingness all around my floundering self rushing past my field of vision like smudged black paint, the paint is peeling, I'm screaming, kicking, thrashing, trying to avoid the inevitable which is only seconds away. . . . . . .   I brace myself for the oncoming collision;;;;   and there it comes, and there I go, and there comes the madness that has been waiting around the corner all along, waiting for the floor to drop, my legs to flop, my arms to claw at space and nothing and nothing there it comes—yeah, that! So here goes nothing….   I'm determined and my determination is usually rather harmful to my well-being;;;;   but if I could only stay awake for one more hour. <u>Just one more hour</u>—I'm almost there…. **Splat!**

Pushed!

I've had a very shitty night involving some very shitty interactions with some very shitty people, so I apologize for my brashness here. But listen very closely, as I make myself clear:

When you push me far enough, the truth always comes out giftwrapped in a brashness that may very well resemble a brick getting dropped on your head. I can only take so much. I vent once I vent twice I hate this prick who coexists as my friend. But here's the kicker: I don't take so kindly to being ignored controlled twisted or pulled. You leave me with this livid decision to make, which is: *Should I stay or should I go?* Because if I stay I might very well lose control of my own tongue which I typically keep locked in place inside my mouth. Push me once push me twice but on the third time I won't act so nice. Sure it's just a reactionary device, this desire to tell you to shove it fuck off and eat me right; just cut me from your life and I will not regret saying goodbye, because all our past interactions left me feeling so alien and lost. I wonder where did it all go wrong?... You were never my fuckin friend to begin with! So let's stop pretending and just cut our losses….

Into My Heart

The best way to win
my heart:
Make yourself
unavailable
Gimme the slightest advantage
and you'll never see me
again
        guaranteed

Baby

You make me jaded, baby!
                              and I hate
                        the way you hate
                            and I love
                        the way you love

So you better stay away
or I might just break
                      <u>down</u>

I'm breaking down!

HOPE

I see hope///
I'm sorry that you don't....

Misunderstood

I don't understand people. Don't understand how to interact with them. Why do I even bother trying? Their ways are so foreign to me. Like I'm an alien from another planet. Like I have fins growing out of my back and long feelers sticking up from my head and webbed feet that slap against the ground as I walk. They look at me like I'm some kind of freak, when all I really want is to be human just like everybody else.

Untitled Poem

i write to express
i create to digress
i guess you cud say i'm blessed
Blessed to be less than
the rest
& for that i regress

Lonesome Loathing

It's raining/
I sit here
saddened &
alone
drained by
utter exhaustion
It's not that I can't sleep
It's just that I don't see the use
I'll just wake up tomorrow
into another sequel and remake
of another wasted existence
which I thought I had
left behind me
And yet this self-depreciation
seems to be
my only true friend
in the end
It's the only thing
that has yet to abandon me

Unpredictable

Don't burst my bubble

                                        or I might just bust your head

Why Do the Good Always Leave Such Feasible Scar on Our Hearts?

The fun ones die young
The boring ones get old
dedicating their lives
to corporate black holes
The few that run loose
and wild and free
get shoved behind bars
forced to shovel up trash
on the side of the street
The few that live rigidly
make millions and die
with five cars six kids
and a debtless existence
and spend eternity in an
eternal prison
Whereas the few that kick
and thrash
crash & burn
go nowhere but a hole
hollowed out by a slave
who wanted to stay young
for a little too long

Racing Thoughts

I am running—mentally >>>

My feet just haven't caught up yet.

A Hopeless Cry

I'm not all right
I can't fight it anymore
I can no longer deny
        what I know
        I've gotta do….

I surrender

Insanity Is In

Going Out Is Hopeless
Staying In Is Hopeless
I'm Broken and Devoted
to Destroying Myself
I'm Self-Destruction Run Wild
a Running Riot I Aim High
I Fall Low and I Seek
— *wait for it* —
I Seek to Be the Best
I Pretend to Be the Worst

I Frolic in Debauchery
Like Fraudulent Robbery
Like a Playpen for
the Sick and Disorderly
the Disturbed Who Are
Nothing Like Me
They Hate Me
and I Hate Them
I'm the Least Bit Disturbed
If You Compare Me to the Masses
I Think I'm Sane
But in Radical Comparison
I'd Give My Left Nut
for a Brand-New Brain
a Brand-New Heart
One That Doesn't Erupt When
You Break It Down for Me
Ever So Gently....

Mental Oppression

Ever had your mind feel like it was hit with a tire iron, thrown at the wall, stomped on, crushed into a ball, stuffed into a canyon, and shot to the other side of the world, and now Chinamen use it as their own special coffee table? I know I have.

Control

I lost control. My biggest fear is losing control. I lost control. My biggest fear is being imprisoned in one's own body but lacking the ability to think or move. On Auto-Pilot. What if something else took over? what if something else burrowed into my skin and took over? Hypnosis—stay away. What would happen if I gave in and instead thought of it less as somebody maneuvering me but as riding in a car with somebody else driving and you're just going along for the ride? Sit back and enjoy the ride! Keep your hands and feet inside! I don't want to lose control, I don't want to be maneuvered—so I take pills and submit submit submit. It's so easy to let them to let them to let them control you from somewhere else. Sit back and enjoy the ride! I don't want to lose control. I don't want to be a puppet. I don't want to be someone else's tool. I want to lose control—to lose control to lose control. I want to be driven and motivated and driven by motivation and forced to speak in certain ways and use certain mannerisms and dress in certain fashions and fathom nothing because I don't need to think I don't need to I don't need—I want to lose control! Force me to submit!!! I dont want to lose control. I want to, I want to control.... I lost control!...

Timeless Indecisions

Sitting in a still room
From my phone comes
acoustic strumming melody
and
        Patrik Fitzgerald's
soft, sweet voice, soothing

I'm alone, I lick the beast on the nose
my mind like a dead weight
who needs it
              anyway

my body like a couple tons
of concrete   keeping me suspended
in space

I'm alone, lonely   a loner with
no sense of time
no depth: my wings having fallen
to the wayside/
a child suspended
a delinquent having grown up
to become something out of this world
a baby bat upchucked through
the funnel of light
          of thoughtless radicalism/

a fantastic dream
elastic it seems
A spider spins its web
hit with a mistletoe
it fumbles to death
          falling through time

My wingspan epic
I fan the demented walls of wisdom
on a mission from some silver deity
                in the clouds
so self-righteous in its brooding
a loose leaf I tear the pages
from Kafka's latest manuscript
          see no evil hear no evil
Sartra mocks me
in black clothing   I'm
philosophy run wild
a relentless yearning I churn
my brain into miniscule notions

So bored
        so hopeless
Oh lord
        I think I'm broken/

The clock sits up on the wall
like an ill-advised sphere
waiting for the bungee to give
        to just give a little
tick tick—the second hand churns
around me
filling me with tormented lies
I feel my heart burning
I look around the room
for the smallest kernel of truth
The brunette sitting to my right
turns to me and says:

        "Hey, I'm talkin to you!"

Misplaced Rage

Gimme a baby to punch
a dog to kick
a midget to flatten
a bug to swat
or a gimp to knock down
Gimme someone smaller weaker
and overall meeker
and I'll beat beat beat them
because I got reamed
by someone so much meaner
than me\\\

Fire-Starter

I'm not a fire-starter anymore
well not like I used to be
        anyway
Today it's more like
I'm a fire-thinker
a fire-waiter watcher observer
I don't wanna start fires
anymore
but I will
light the fuse
and watch the whole world
go bloom
But I'm not a fire-starter anymore
well not like I used to be
        anyway

Just Swell!- - -☺

My whole life is disheartening. Every glimmer of hope that comes to me is quickly replaced with a shiny sliver of rope tied like a noose, complete with a wooden sign that says: HERE, TRY THIS!
It's like I'm slowly being dragged into Heaven over ruts and stones and abrasive dog shit and I'm almost there, so close, just over this tall mound of manure and you have arrived. But once I reach the top, the Devil is standing there laughing and shaking his head and saying: "I was just fucking with you; you're really in Hell! This was just the first round of a very long series of torture you are going to have to endure for the rest of your stay here…." And then, suddenly, he gets all serious, looks me square in the eye,

and says: "Sucks to be you! don't It!"

no such thing

i dont believe
in luv
becuz i fall
in luv
way too often
& history
has taught me
time&time again
that there is
just no such thing
as luv

On Gratitude

It's hard to feel grateful cuz i feel unworthy. I'm almost as disgusted with myself as i used to be when i was using. My life seems unmanageable & my writhing mind is what seems to overpower me. But i'm gonna try to find something to honestly be grateful about. No i'm fucked up. Anything i think of—from money to friends—seems like something i'm wasting, so i'd be dishonest if i were to profess gratitude for it.

Everybody

Everybody is making judgments about me that are not true.
Everybody is saying things about me that contradict one another.
Everybody is claiming that they know me when they really don't.
Everybody is ostracizing me for crimes I never committed, for thoughts I never
   had, for words I never used, and for ideas that aren't even mine///

and the irony of that is, everything everyone has ever said about me I have already said about myself, and all the different self-administered putdowns are just mere contradictions to one another, and that's the reason I can never decide, it's the reason I'm so confused all the time, it's the reason I hate my own reflection, it's the reason I hate my face and my shadow cuz one day my face and my shadow are going to overpower me like everyone else had, and then one day I'll be king of the hill, standing tall above everyone else, higher than anything could ever reach in its own diminishing state of disrepair; but I'm much too scared to conquer it on my own, and soon I won't be afraid, and soon I won't be afraid, and soon I will not be afraid but it's way too late for that anyway, because the moment I lose all fears I will leap straight for the stars … but I know the only direction I'll ever go, the only direction I <u>can</u> ever go, the only direction I ever <u>want</u> to go, is straight down like a tumbling barrel of bricks and I'll be plunging and picking up speed as the rumbling barrel of bricks bumps and tumbles and quickens its menacing pace as I'm taken for a ride in this runaway barrel that barrels downhill like a plowing snowball traversing the fierce slope with rapidly increasing speed and the barrel is blundering and hitting ruts and bumps and then there's a slope up ahead coming at me faster and faster but the barrel keeps hitting the downward skid and there comes the slope and the barrel dips and rolls straight upward and is launched higher than anyone has ever been;;;;   and there I am: the self-hatred is gone….

Collateral Damage

Losing sleep over
        over
        over——what??

Losing my mind because of
        because of
        because of——what??

Is this trouble
    these troubles
Are these struggles
    a manic brain
    propelled by
        insanity
worth the strain
the utter propulsion
a biting pressure
a nagging burden
tumbling
        I'm tumbling through
        into
        downward to——where??

A downward plunge

It's a useless struggle
a futile tug
    of
        war
ripping
        I'm ripping down
the concrete floor
        flipping out
I'm so belligerent & loud

Life always kicks me down
      & out
      I'm too hard on myself
maybe

maybe
Maybe my heart is scarred
maybe
Maybe it's scarred for life
maybe
Maybe God is just bringing down
   the sky
maybe
Maybe He
   She
      or It
                      or Something That Isn't
ME
      Maybe my life is just insipid
& maybe

& maybe

& maybe I don't have a single honest bone
in my entire tortured body
Oh My Tortured Soul
      I'm alone but I'm trying
      I'm sold on convictions &
I'm crying

& I tell you

I'm trying to lie
      I'm Trying To Lie
           I'm trying to L-I-E

I'm trying to dye
my own hair
        purpleorgreenorpink

I mean
I need an escape route I need to run away from you I'm afraid & I'm scared of you
I'm afraid & I'm scared
    I'm afraid
    &
       I'm
                      !SCARED!
of you
of   everything
of my own reflection
as I stare at the slants
& slashes
        in the shattered glass

that I smashed up in my dream
just to awaken the next day
with thin gashes
crisscrossing my hands & feet

Please oh please
oh please won't you just
look at me
Just look into my eyes
&
        I guarantee

you'll hate me
       I think
you'll think I'm a bad man
        I believe

(I believe in Nothing)
you'll be happy to see me

die
    dead
        dying
            death
                I'm dead & I'm
gone

to the tornado
of my devious thought
process

just like a
        bastard
            snapping turtle
flipped on its back
stomped on
        CRACK!
by the fat man
        in bright red & glittery
        high heels
        that ride up his shins
like a hooker in jeans

You've sold me on your
wisdom
of
the mentally retarded
        I'm surfing a mental swale
        of thoughts destroyed
You've sold me on your   My best friend named Loyd
had kicked me in
my no-no parts

before the night had
departed
& left me there retarded
my image chipped & charred by
the beaming headlights cutting me in half
down the center
       split in two
as the clock ticks another sinister
second
ticks another menacing minute
tick tick ticks as the hour dawns
on us
leaving us divided &
weak
leaving us wretched &
diseased
Going Nowhere Fast
We're all just freaks
to the crowned cretins
in charge of civilization
       for the time being
&
the hour looks too bleak to me
I'm just too meek to be

I'm holding on
       life is sometimes too hard
I'm holding on
       life is sometimes too hard
           it's just too hard for me

I'm holding on
    to the blade of the knife
holding on tight
     tight as a vice

afraid of the fall that
                is behind me
                            afraid of the rise
                                      that looms bright & big
                              in front of me
afraid of you for
putting me through the wringer
like you did one day
      some day
      <u>any day</u>
                EVERYDAY
                        everyFUCKINday
                        it's always the same fuckin shit
I'm so sick of it....

To think I used to play with broken girls
today they play with me
      I used to rob people
          today they rob me

After all the shit I survived
I only survived to be
a victim to all your stupid fuckin lies
      so this is bye
         this is bye
              this is Goodbye/

You see I'm

at war
   with
      myself   all the time
I destroy my mental health
I destroy my family's wealth
You sell me self-destruction by the gallon
You sell me

just sell me anything
that takes me away
from here
    straight to
        cloud
        9
& I swear I'll never
go home
        again
I'll just never ever go back
          I'll never have to
          as soon as the kick
          sets in

& it brings me right back
to where I started

I'm losing sleep over
      over
        over——whatever you got
I'll take it down
I've lost it

I lost my mind
Aren't you proud

Dynamite

My heart is like dynamite.
When it gets too hot it
    explodes!

lost

I'm feeling so alone
worthless
hopeless
broken
deserted
left for dead?
and kicked to the curb;

and what's worse
I seem to have
nobody who cares enough
to feel this pain with me
which only makes me
feel
just that much more alone

Anxious Qualities

Something about today ... I don't know what it is exactly …… my veins have been buzzing rapidly and I'm starting to lose control of my mind and I can't seem to slow down my extended reality any more than I can stop the progression of time and I seem to be stuck in a flutter of anxious derailments and the train is veering tipping leaning swaying angling angling angling rolling and tumbling and twisting and fumbling quickly crashing thwacking smacking bashing the whole cart shattering on a wall of jagged rocks and ……… you know! ... my veins just won't stop buzzing and it's simply driving me insane....

a drug called life

waiting for the drugs to kick in
this drug called life
they say it will kick in eventually——
————but when??

No Misgivings

Living life to the fullest means taunting death and orbiting gloomy scenarios like a fragile moon exploding soothing hymns down the spiral of life's mad design. I walked the plank and forfeited the ocean beneath a sun that can't shine oblivious, wretched decisions under a sky so scorned it makes the reaper seem shy and bored like a tapestry of fantastic gatherings of a lacerated force running with the blind and torn children of a night so alone it makes the world seem scarcer and for that we all show no remorse.

Down the Tubes

A few weeks ago
I had lost a friend to
the clutches of addiction;
he took a bad hit
his friends & family
all took a bad hit.
He was a really good kid/
too young to die
too stubborn to live,

now surfing a sea of daisies—
maybe they got heroin in heaven
maybe not
<u>   would one even need it</u>?

I picture the impact of
my own untimely death
on the people who care about me.
How would they take it
if I simply
threw my life down
the tubes?
my parents, my friends, people
I worked with at some time
in my tumultuous life///

Everyone leaves at least a scratch
on life, some scratches more fierce
and brutal than others,,,,
some people more sensitive to certain
scratches than others.
Every day I live, the scratch gets bigger
and stronger, and then I
simply drop dead one day,
leaving people with a thick and deep
wound for them to live with—
to mend as tears dance mournfully
down the sides of their faces.

I don't wanna die
until I'm at least one hundred and five.
I don't want my life to be
thrown down the tubes,
leaving in my wake a wound
for people to have to bandage up ...
in my ugly passing.

<u>It's just not gonna happen</u>.

What with my history I'm
lucky to be alive anyway.
What with my history I
should be six feet underground
by now surfing a sea of daisies.
But I'm not;
I'm alive
living my stolen life
and I choose to live it
till the day that I die >>>
      because others weren't
        as lucky as I....

Is this love?

I hate you
but I need you
& I want you
so I believe you

standing out in the rain
I'm cold
& I'm tired
& I wanna go home
& spend the duration of the evening
curled up in a warm bed
all alone
without you there
but you're here
now
& your lingering stare

delivers me
to cloud 9
shrouded with emotions
that I regret ever feeling
in the first place

I know it's a lie
I know you're just playing a game
I know it I can see it in your eyes
but I'm so desperate for a body
for a unified bond of sorts
that I'll just buy <u>anything</u>
that you sell me
        a spell cast with tears
        dripping
        & bleeding
        locked in a fearful castration

& I find that I'm
lost in your mesmerizing glare
I feel dejected from
the lion's lair
ejected through the roof
but at least the moon won't reject me
he's up there & I'm down here
& I stare up at the stars
& I scream >>>

that I hate you
but I need you
& yet I want you
so I believe you even though
I know the truth
I know it all too well
I've been here before
different day same exact shit

different day same-old story
different day dripping with insidious morphine
like the kind of bad dream
that never fuckin ends
& yet I'm shriveled & I'm
sick\\\

the rain now falls to a drizzle

the cold is calling my name
calling out to me
calling my name
my body overheating
with remorse

your touch feels like a bee sting
when I needed you the most

& now I'm bleeding tears

a gutted heart for all the
cheerful leers
that pass me by
when I walk home
at the end of the night

the rain dies out
& I'm falling
plunging into your arms
only I fall straight through
they were never there to begin with
it was just a dream
& to think
I believed your lies
that you would catch me before

I died///

Beat the Devil

Where were you
when I needed you?
You said you'd be there
for me
to wipe up the blood
to scrub away the tears and
to catch me when I
plunged
But when I fell the only thing catching me
was the cold hard truth
and the brutal reality of
a nowhere boy's fate
and a nowhere man's destiny
and a putrid future waiting for me
straight down the line
like a solid brick wall
and blood will drip
and tears will fall
and I will collapse
into your arms but the gutter
will always catch me first
I feel I like I deserve
worse
But your desertion only
served
to show me that
I can't count on nobody but
myself
and when the blood
comes gushing
and the tears start
rushing
and I find that I'm

plunging
down
down
down
a downward backslide
through a decrepit side
of this conniving universe
hopeless and disturbed
eating dirt and rain and running for
my life which is worthless
I'm the only one
who can save me
and this hatred grows stronger
through my soggy, swollen eyes
I beat the devil
I cheated this level
I defied the rebels and their fledge
lings who always chant no
when the rebels demand it
to be so
I will deny my crimes of hellion glory
stories that glorify all that
will rectify my horrorshow existence
hate   is all that is left
inside
<u>Let the machineguns roar</u>!

Decomposed Composition

Caustic Reality

I'm alive
or am I dreaming
stuck in a twisted nightmare
am I scheming
SCHEMING to be more
than what I am and this
this
this
this is reality such a beaten aspiration

I pray to the sun
it brings us light
I pray to the moon
a futile shape that sits and looms
it spins and shines
but that's it that's all that it does
except for the red rash
dicing my brain with sadistic ambitions

I pray to the earth
is this a dream
it must be—for nothing's real

a shattered world
a plastic girl flirting with me
when I crest the battlefield
she speaks of real evil
& I can see it in her plastic eyes
I look left I look right and
it's all the same in the end
more fakeness parading around
like I'm in a stolen wet dream

Is this real
if I can touch it
then it must be
if I can throw it
then I must know it
I must know something is too ill-fit
to be in this tormented world
but that someone is me
A Bleeding-Heart Conformist
A Right-Wing Hippy
A Conservative Punk Rocker
A Sympathetic Nazi?
no sympathy for the filthy
only empathy
it goes way over my head   anyway
painting the sky with ambient wonders
am I dreaming   or did I
just see a cat spooning a frog
a spider with twentytwo legs
seventeen shoes
and a giant talking head that spews LIES
through its hairy eyes
<u>a senseless thing that it is</u>

This reality
THIS reality

THIS REALITY
You wouldn't know real
if it stomped on your foot
took a jagged spiketoothed shark
out for a romantic ride down under
and rode the seven seas on a driveby shooting
godsent >>> to destroy
and you were hit by a ricocheted bullet
and to think you knew
KNEW
that today wasn't the day to go swimming
but defying reality
you decided to push your luck
and there you are
choking down blood in the middle of
the ocean———FUCK THAT SUCKS

Am I alive
dead
breathing
obeying physics
I mean it's the law   right?
Disobey & you might fall
SPLAT
dead men tell no tales   unless
this isn't real
this   isn't   real
IT'S NOT
and I'm lost surfing an epic swale
through my wretched head
as the earth of a fallen dream
almost as though
touched by an angel itself
——the angel of death   that is
evaporated on the thinnest wisp of smoke
thin enough to eat like flat bread pizza

a puff & a flash
just dissipates and it's gone

Sorry ladies but I'm taken

just dissipates and it's gone

Sorry sir but those drugs are mine
        you owe me/

just dissipates and it's gone

Is this a dream or a beaten omen
trying to warn me about the upcoming
apocalypse the world is on the brink
of nothingness
and I ride my skateboard through
swindled lanes
of pure hatred
nihilistic and disturbed I ollie over barrels
filled with toxic waste—well that sounds real
———but wait there are rabid porcupines
frolicking amid the filth
and if you were to hit one hard enough
with a twisting, winding stick
its innards would turn to candy
before your very eyes
Trust me it's no lie
and then we can all have a feast till our
teeth fall out

Is this real?
Or am I somewhere else....

My Void

Step into My Void, join my hand why won't you/// I'll show you a world you never knew existed….

I'll tear away your veil, I'll hand you my mask, and together we'll march through the shade of nothingness, going nowhere and expecting less—no hope is all you'll find here, a futureless chaos that will lift you up and make you high,,,, just the two of us.

We'll dance on glass floors that loom high over a bleeding city, a beaten world; we'll boogie as bombs blow holes in the universe—up here it'll be just you and I going closer to my black hole.

A vacuum winding beautiful spirals to paint filthy backdrops that glow vacantly, like a ghostly desert. Walk with me as I show you the pure bliss that My Void has in store. Watch as the whole world goes to hell around us.

But here in My Void everything will be fine…. Step into My Void and I'll show you something magical—something you could never have imagined, not even in your wildest dreams. Babe, it'll be pure emptiness, a jaded wasteland, a lustful sort of nothingness that's so nihilistically sound….

I'll show you the meaning of life/

You'll realize it don't mean shit….

I'll show you the reason to live/

You'll realize it's just a moot point.

Step into My Void and you'll never be the same again….

Experimental Poem

```
And the poem begins

itisfastpaced but   s o m e t i m e s   slows down

thenpicksupspeedand  p
                     l
                     u
                     m
                     m
                     e
                     t
                     s  to the ground
it can be                            it can be
manic                   t            depressing
                        h
it could start a riot   e
            it could install order
                        w
                        r
                        i
                        t
                        e       j
                        r'      o
                        s       b is to provoke
bring the 5 senses <<< meaning <<< emotions
to life———that is soundsmelltouchtaste and
                       H E A R I N G
Dammit, I meant sight   ʌʌʌʌʌʌʌʌʌʌʌʌʌʌʌʌʌʌʌʌʌʌʌʌʌʌʌ
```

You are loved

(or) Journey to the End of the American Dream

> "All the world cannot be wrong / It must be me I don't belong."
>
> — "Did He Jump" by the Zounds

THE ROAD TO RUINS
SHOOTING
LOONYTOON PHILOSOPHIES
THROUGH
LOADED LOWRIDER SLOGANS

THE WORLD IS BROKEN

I broke it

WITH A ROLLING SHARKTOOTHED HAMMER
THEY TRIED TO SLAM DOWN A
SLAPSTICK FINE
JUST HIGHFIVED THE GHOSTS IN THE SKY
AND JAMMED LOADS OF REDTAPE
DOWN MY GAGGING GULLET
AS A WAY TO GET ME TO
BEHAVE
THEY JUST NEEDED ME TO
    BEHAVE
THE REDTAPE WAS NEATLY
SNIPPED AND TAPERED AWAY
SO AS TO DISPLAY
A DERELICT D.J. SKIPPING AND SCRATCHING
ANOTHER MINDLESS TRACK ABOUT
BLOWING LINES OF COCAINE OFF OF
SAINT NICK'S RIPPLING RIBCAGE

you are loved,
THEY TOLD ME   ON THE FIRST DAY
I WAS BORN
happiness is only
an arms length away,
THEY HAD PROMISED ME

AND I BELIEVED THEM TOO
SOUGHT RELIEF ON A DAY-TO-DAY BASIS
BUT ALL THAT THAT RELIEF HAD EVER GOTTEN ME
WAS A CHARRED & CRISPY LIP
AND A NARROW SPIKE THAT RAN FROM
ONE SIDE OF MY ARM TO
THE OTHER- - - - - - - - -COMPLETELY PUNCTURING
MY PREVIOUSLY STAGGERING VEINS
AS IT PUMPED ME FULL OF ____
(((well wudnt you wanna know)))
I COULD CHOOSE BETWEEN
      uppers
         downers
            screamers
               laughers
                  & ____
                     yodelers??
OH GOD DID THEY MAKE ME
   || yodel ||
I WOULD BE YODELING all   night- - - - - -long///
JUST STRAIGHT YODELING
as tho i was A mere WOLF
howling at THE shimmering MOON ____

ONLY
REPLACE THE MOON w/
      ALL THOSE MISERABLE BILLBOARDS
      LOOMING IN THE SKY
      WITH ALL THEIR MISERABLE SLOGANS

   & clichés
   ADVERTISING A BROKEN SOCIETY
     in bed
   THAT ALWAYS SEEMS TO MAKE ME
   CRY in dismay
        AT THEIR OUTRIGHT
        DISPLAY
          OF SHEER POSITIVITY

ALL THEIR FILTHY, ROTTEN LIES
ALL THEIR CHEAP AND CHEESY LINES
THAT ONLY SERVE TO ALIENATE ME FROM THIS
DEGENERATE WASTELAND
  happiness??
  what happiness?
  in the end we/re all just
    born to die
anyway/
THE SOONER YOU GET IT THROUGH
THAT THICK SKULL OF YOURS
THE SOONER YOU CAN GO OUT THERE
   AND LIVE YOUR TOTALLY HOPELESS
   LIFE
FOR A CHANGE >>>>>>
        becuz that is where
        i find my <u>own</u>
        liberation/
          thru hopelessness
          despair & degradation

NOW I FIND THAT I'M FEELING
RATHER LIBERATED FROM THE SAME-OLD
  BORING
   MESSAGES
THEY COOED DELICATELY

TO ME AS I SLEPT IN BED
AT NIGHT
WHEN I WAS ONLY A CHILD
AN IMPRESSIONABLE
LITTLE CHILD

  AND TO THINK IF I ONLY KNEW
  THAT I WAS JUST GONNA DIE
    soon
I MIGHT HAVE HAD
MORE OF AN OPPORTUNITY
TO LIVE MY LIFE THE WAY I
DESIRED TO

AND I WAS VERY SUGGESTABLE
    TOO
of course

SO I WENT AFTER THAT
<u>DREAM</u>
the dream THAT GOT ME
FEELING
LIKE A
  TOTAL fuckin **_FREAK!_**
  OF NATURE
IN COMPARISON TO
THOSE THAT THE DREAM HAD WELCOMED
EASILY
WITH OUTSTRETCHED, BECKONING ARMS
   I MEAN IT'S KINDA HARD
    TO NOT COMPARE YOURSELF
    TO THOSE WHO GOT IT
    TO THOSE WHO JUST GOT
    ALL THE RIGHT
    MOVES
    ALL THE RIGHT STUFF WHATEVER
    YOU WANNA CALL IT

                    BECAUSE THEY WERE EVERYWHERE
                              <u>ARE</u>
                              everywhere
                    I LOOKED
                    IN MAGAZINES ON TV AND IN MOVIES TOO
               YOU NEVER SEE
                    <u>my</u> people
                    IN THE PICTURES
               YOU NEVER SEE
                    <u>my</u> people
                    ON BILLBOARDS LOOMING OVER A LARGE
                    EXPANSE
                    OF HIGHWAY
BUT THEN
WOULD YOU REALLY WANT TO??
SEE ONE OF US GAPTOOTHED FREAKS
LOOMING OVER THE LONG, WINDING STREET
ALMOST AS IF WE WERE GODS
TO ALL THE MANY DRIVERS
JUST PASSING US BY
          yeah fuck that!!!

hit me over the head w/ a rainbow
why doncha
& make it count
**   make it last**
i want to <u>feel</u> the surge of glitter
as i overdose on peace & love & happiness

am I right?

                         — — — —

SO NOW
ON THE SECOND DAY

OF MY RATHER- - - - - - - - - - - - - - -DISJOINTED DREAM
OF OBLIVION MEETS MEDICALLY PRESCRIBED
ORGASMIC DEVICES
I USE TO
STIFLE MY RIFLE   JUST pump&pump&pump
UNTIL IT EXPLODES IN MY HAND AND I
SUDDENLY FEEL REAL DIRTY FROM
THE SHEER ACT OF JACKING THE THING OFF
            in the first place/
MEETS
MORE MONEY THAN PLASTIC CAN BUY|||
ALL OF WHICH ADDED UP EQUALS PRECISELY

A FLOCK OF WINGED PIRATES
I CAME ACROSS ON MY JOURNEY
TO THE END OF the american dream

AND THEY WERE ALL
JUST SO HUNGRY TONIGHT
IN THE PROCESS OF
RUMMAGING ANGRILY
THROUGH THE DEAD MAN'S LUGGAGE

I USUALLY RUN FROM SUCH THINGS
— — —A GIGANTIC BRIEFCASE FULL OF
FALSE HOPES &
SHATTERED DREAMS
        run for cover
        & dont you dare come out until
        the coast is   CLEAR FOR TAKEOFF >>>
BUT TODAY I DID THE
UNTHINKABLE AND
    JOINIED IN
I MEAN IT'S ONLY PLASTIC
in the end

——————SO CURRENTLY I
HOLD IN MY HAND A SHATTERED SKULL
THAT RIGHTFULLY BELONGED TO
THE MAN
WHO HAD LIVED PEACEFULLY
AND QUIETLY
ON JUPITER'S CROONING RUINS
BUT WHO WAS EVENTUALLY
FOUND OUT ABOUT
BY THESE LOOTING MUTANT PIRATES
WHO HAD GANGED UP AND
BASHED IN HIS HEAD WITH PADLOCKS
ON THE END OF CHAINS
ON THE END OF LONG BILLYCLIBS
ON THE END OF AN american FAG
WHO WAVES RESTLESSLY
AT ALL THE CUTE YOUNG BOYS WHO PASS HIM BY
ON THE STREET
AND THEY ALWAYS WAVE BACK
     maybe a bit
     reluctantly though
BUT STILL THEY DON'T KNOW EXACTLY WHAT
THE WAVING fag REALLY IS
         hes queerbait   thats what
         yea   bait those queers ya faggot

BECAUSE IF THEY DID IN FACT KNOW
THAT HE ONLY WANTED TO GIVE THE BOYS
A POKE IN THE BUTT is all
THEY'D WISH HIM THE SAME FATE AS
THE MAN ON JUPITER
WHO IS SIMPLY INTENT ON
        SUING THE SHIT OUTTA
THOSE WINGED PIRATES WHO JUST LAST YEAR
BROKE THE OZONE'S UNFOLDING VERTEBRA
IN HALF

IN ORDER TO **make** PEACE
AND SPREAD IT TO EVERY SINGLE STATE
ACROSS THE ENTIRE GLOBE
    unite & destroy! THE PEACE ENFORCERS SANG
    BRASHLY

AND TOMORROW THEY'LL **BURN**
the american fag
YOU'LL SEE
    JUST TO MAKE AN EXAMPLE OUT OF
    HIM

        — — — —

SO NOW I'M ALONE AND I
SCAN THE SKY FOR SOME ANSWERS
I NEED HELP/
    I NEED HELP/
        I REALLY NEED HELP >>>>>>
JUST WALKING DOWN THE SIDE OF
THE BUSTLING HIGHWAY
    IN HEAT
I FEEL SO BROKEN AND BUSTED
SO DISGUSTED AND HOMELESS
WANDERING THIS HOPELESS ROAD
DESPERATE FOR RESOLUTION
SCANNING THE SKY FOR A SOLUTION
PANNING THE STARS
    <u>THE STARS</u>
I PRAY!
    I PRAY TO GOD FOR
DELIVERANCE
SALVATION
SERENITY
    JUST ANOTHER WAY TO ESCAPE   THE VICIOUS TUG
    OF DESPONDENT RELATIONSHIPS

OR FOR THAT MATTER
ANYTHING HE'S WILLING TO PRESCRIBE ME
IN MY TIME OF DESPERATION
FOR AFTER ALL
    im not at all picky
    about what i end up getting
I MEAN REALLY I JUST NEED <u>SOME</u>THING
    ANYTHING
        GIMME WHATEVER YOU GOT
FOR PETE'S SAKE

BUT THE ONLY ANSWERS
I EVER GOT
    SPANNING THE FACE OF
THE GREAT BIG LOOMING
BILLBOARDS
    ARE THE SIMPLEST CLICHÉS
LIKE
happiness is only
an arms length away

BUT
    ALL THAT'S IN FRONT OF ME
    AND ALL THAT'S BEHIND ME
IS MILE AFTER MILE OF
SHIMMERING OPEN ROAD
SO DEVOID OF HOPE
        THE SUN BEAMING
        THE HEAT OVERWHELMING
ALL OF MY SENSES

I CAN'T BEAR THE PAIN   ANY LONGER
I CAN'T STAND THE DESPAIR
THAT COMES UP BLOOMING LIKE
    A BLOODY NAPKIN

Hope

        hope

                hope

& happiness

                        & hope

                                    what the hell does that
                                            even mean??
                                  ive honestly never heard
                                 of such a radical concept
                                            in all my life

BECAUSE RIGHT HERE & NOW
NOTHINGNESS   SEEMS TO BE
THE ONLY THING I CAN EFFECTIVELY
        TOUCH
WHEN I EXTEND MY
REACHING ARMS
OUT IN FRONT OF ME

I HOVEL BENEATH THE SUN
ALLOWING THE DESPERATION I FEEL
TO EMBRACE
               MY EMBERS
FOREVER &
       EVER
AS CARS THAT CAME FROM NOWHERE
       AND THAT ARE GOING NOWHERE
RUMBLE PAST///

Nihilism Is Everything
said he

Everything I own is broken. Everything I touch breaks. My life is like a maze, winding through backrooms that collapse when … when … when I'm rattled like loosely woven bees roaming through my hair///

I lost alotta crap today. It's crap because I couldn't care less, and I do care, feeling quite depressed, as if a big, bulgy dog stands over me swatting my nose on the head with a rolled-up newspaper.
Only it isn't a newspaper at all—it's a chew toy, and it squeaks via connection///

Am I making a connection?

Sometimes I think I'm dyslexic, or maybe I'm schizophrenic, or maybe even obsessive to a compulsive nature///

I'm rattled by that, too!
But it doesn't matter///
       Nothing Matters

and it rattles me like a crude anorexic that people give a shit more than they're worth/
cuz I care that maybe I'll learn a thing or two bout what it means to live in a zoo, where ghouls & goblins dab diseased goo on their hands and tell me to bend over and touch my feet.

See, I'm a nihilist, but a broken nihilist, a nihilist who won't amount to nothing cuz the sheer concept of pure annihilation rubs me like a cock and I'm rearing to explode.

And I'm rattled by that!

A dilapidated man once told me that what goes out must come back in and I said, Dude don't you got it the other way around?

He looked at me then, with these two eerie, weasel-like eyes, the kind of eyes that you know belongs to a man who knows nothing about nothing, the kind of man who uses double negatives like I just did

and I realized then
as a swindled thought withers and dies
as a universe dissipates and cries
as a world lives retardedly high
as a knife feels nice and right
against my itchy eyeball

that the future seems rather caustic when you've got a head the size of a peanut, a mind the size of a buffalo, and a brain that's relentlessly suffocating against the incessant pressure of a sacred fart that rattles off into the sky/

And that rattles me, goddammit!

United We Divide

Today's a good day. It is—keyword: **is.** Tomorrow is a day. Yesterday was a day that happened to me—or I happened to it. But today, right now, is a good day—or moreover, good night….

That's what you say when she goes to sleep; you say goodnight, and then you rack the phone in the cradle because it is not a good night. You tell yourself you're a liar—you lied to your daughter, you lied to your mommy, your sister, your girlfriend and your wife.

You sit on the fringe of indecisions. A shimmering tantrum is brewing. You can hear the banging from below, the banging from above, the riffraff of biting nerves you bite your tongue.

I look in the mirror.

Goodnight, I whisper; you hear the thunder.

Good morning, I sing, as the blundering storm comes a-brewin.

Good day! You slam the door in my face. It connects with a reverberating echo, a surging release >>>

I cum.

I'm cumming.

Don't hold back; don't look back.

Knock knock!

Who's there??

Crack!!!

I release my snapping fingers as I brace myself for the calm. You're calling my name, he's calling my name, she's balling on the floor. Today was a good

daaayy.

Kick a hole in the glass. A knife's edge feels tight and moist.

Tonight was a good, dot dot dot

night.

I'm swollen I'm bright I'm alive I'm scared of the, dot dot dot

night stop || night stop———STOOPPPP!!!

Knock knock knock!

Who is it?? you shout. I make my way to the door.

There I am, there you are >>>

The mirror roars, rumbling and pouring.

And I think I might be
... falling?
        No, not me.

I look behind me///there it comes.... You look behind me///there I come....

I'm cumming I can't stop // I'm cumming I can't stop....

I hate myself I love myself I hate myself I love myself/// I'm falling to my knees gushing instant relief; I'm gushing instant relief///
The mirror stares at me. So Instantly Gratified. Is that what they're calling it these days? SO INSTANTLY GRATIFIED....

I look at my fist. It smokes and smolders like a loaded gun.

I watch the smoke rise.

I look at the mirror. You stare at me.

I look at my fist.

You stare at me.

I look at my fist I look at myself. I kiss my knuckles on the lips, and the mirror explodes into dust >>>>>>

I bow my head and cry///

Broken Sunshine

Swimming in darkness/
The sun blazes bright on the waves
as I tread the nowhere wakes of existence
the world blissful & exquisite
I see the shattered moon as it pours thru
the ozone layer looking massive &
untamable
I squander the nothingness but but but
there's just so much light to bask in
and yet yet yet
floating nowhere & hovering over no one
it all seems way too heavy to hold
too mild & cold
It all explodes in my gut
and I just won't let go….

The Genius in Failure

I'm not apologizing
for you guys
but for the sake of
the lukewarm sky
of another diluted failure
I tried to decide but
derailed another lucid railroad
of devalued hopes and
seizures
The tangy lizard
felt miserable when

the sasquatch of a fallen tree
brought elusive soliloquies
to be sung and wrung out
by the towering panther of
another maddening anthem as I
ring my fist and rack my brain
just plain **thwack** it
on the crumbling bricks
that come in rolling leisurely
through zigzagging deviations
of clustered lily pads rolling
and swaying
across a star-speckled flame
Bury the hatchet
Hatch a flaccid stillborn infant
It will grow up to be
great
but not famous

The baby's a madman with
artistic design
Hear it cry
for a paintbrush
for a pad of
paper and a pen to
scope its visions with
Listen to it shout
but don't respond just listen
Just watch but don't react
Focus when you deduct
the artistic infant with
a world brimming with Nazi
critics and
fascist editors

I'm not apologizing for the
ways in which I spread my
pedantic lies and alibis
I will not apologize/
for the baby was raised
in a world
devoid of thought
headless
clueless
       not very lucid
too exclusive

This
ruthless muse
is running around
plastered across
the televised blue
Just plug in the tube and watch it
dilute
The baby cries
but nobody listens….

Breaking Down

I was taking a chance now. I was knocking on that door. I was stomping up those stairs. I was barging into that room——

—but she was gone….

I had it all planned out. I would confess to her just how I felt.

I was down on the street, panting. Where had she gone?? She'd said she was home. We'd broken up about three months ago, and she had wanted me back but I had said no. And then yes. And then Yes! And Then YES!!! so I hurried to her place but she was gone, and I was alone. Cold and alone. I walked home, beneath a sudden shower from up above, like a black cloud was following me there.

When I arrived back at my apartment, drenched, I pushed open the door and everywhere I looked there was dynamite. Everywhere! Strapped to the wall. Stacked on the floor. Piled high. Enough to level an entire city block.
And there she was, holding the plunger which was sticking out of a box, with a thin wire weaving its way outward and branching off and threading its way beneath the sticks.

Oh shit!

She smiled. I said No——

And she pushed down on the plunger.

Before the biggest blast I could have ever imagined, I remembered why we had broken up in the first place....

Horrorscope

Thunderous soliloquy
Branded by adventure that has yet
to reach the trees of
ominous bright green lights
It's a horrorscope
is what the papers said
I read it on a milk carton
I built a bridge
in my own mind
Linguistic psalms

A glowing yellow tongue
Searching for fun in the mirror
that brings about
devout menacing phantoms
like a clout wanton dynamic
We the People
We the Freaks
We the Crazy
Built a restrospective reality
where the hotshots
and the idols
and the wannabes and the fakes
and the leeches and
the creeps
and the lurkers and the jerks and the
queens
get left with dirty diapers
dirty dishes
dirty floors and dirty sinks
dirty walls and
all those dirty things
We the People
We the Freaks
We the Crazy
Live in a wary world
We fill our blaring nerves
with bitter spurts of
joy
like a nuisance to deploy
We live to annoy
or at least that's what
the papers said
when I read all about it
in my horrorscope

I begin to notice

I begin to notice
I begin to notice
I begin to notice
I begin
        to ponder
the world beneath a
dayglow fog
It's a Wednesday night
I look out the window
speckled with dust
the great big bottom
rising into stardom
I'm riding the broken pony

I begin to notice
something wasn't quite right
My dissipating life
is rumbling at the edge of the knife

I begin to notice a hole
in my head in my brain
in the wall I'm going insane
I step on through
The floor of the jungle is
cracked
I'm razzle-dazzled by the horse's saddle
galloping between trees
the golden smog a rolling fog
jumbled I'm so hungry

Wait!   Stop!   Hold on|||
Hit the roiling ground with two tons of
mounded-up toilet paper wadded

and left for waste
Rummaging through the demented rubbish

I begin to notice
the hopelessness in the sky
I tried to say hi to you last night
but the haunting glare
radiating from behind your eyes
between your dilapidated stare
has made me go blind
and I can dishonestly say I'm scared
of what your mind has decided
in just a few seconds of

I begin to notice
the hope on the ground
I step into the hole
I fall
into the
bottomless hope, clawing
The walls are ribbons
my name is clipped
the numbers are scrolling
as I'm pulled farther and deeper
into a nowhere existence
where I hang my head
and let go >>>

Open me up and spit me out
I begin to notice
the hole of eternity
is broken and scattered

I begin to notice
I know nothing but
the clattering of thoughts——

Come Be Androgynous with Me

Blitzed
on
manic bliss
my mind a maze of
seething adrenaline
zipping through delicate tubes
just itching to
erupt
       and I think I'm wasted
                         a- -gain

I sit
       No I stand
       on the edge
of erratic indecisions
    I plant ticking
manic
time bombs that
punch destructive holes
through idle minds
      like
      hydraulics
ripping down dangerous structures
      of deluxe   enterprises
But then what structure isn't corrupt??

It's a derelict system
a corrupted world we live in
From Broken Homes
        From Polished Roads   of death
Descendants of a Nuclear Plastic
just thumbing through
          the oh so delicious signs
        of a thrown-out afterlife

So we ride the beast till we die
Shake the plates of a broken sphere
            Dance on damaged planes
Stamp fierce crevices
                into   a sickness of sorts
so twisted
and conniving
       we live like
       livid dreams

Running till our feet give out
Jumping   we jump and scream and holler
     Flick a severed hand
     and cast diabolical
nightmares   all across the land

<u>deep inside a sold-out hole</u>
<u>intertwined with a broken soul</u>
<u>amid a series of lifeless dribble</u>

We paint vivid, trickling landscapes
of utter blackness and
deterioration
across winding windows packed with
              glitter and
              worthless identities
              sold by the dozen
                    Just pack it stamp it and
                    cash it in/
(I mean   it's only worth your soul >>>
no big deal
    in the grand scheme of things)))

And then the ever-sought-after
American dream

springs into focus
        vaporizes
        like a fading   notion

in the process destroying
your once-cherished
        pair of speckled
        rose-colored glasses
that you take with you
to bed at night
so as to awaken you

to a civilized nightmare

that I dreamed would

someday
one day
   <u>any</u> day
embrace me forever/

so that I can surrender all hope
and for the next millennium drift
far
far
away
        into a dying sky
        overtaken by a lucid
        resolve
fit for a king // fashioned for a loser
so that for once I can

dissolve into the nothingness
Uncle Sam had promised me
on the day I was born

I can't sleep

1.
Fuck Me Silly with a German-Toothed Tiger Watching Us Make Woopy on a Bed of Straw in a House Made of Dolphin Hides That Looks Out Over a Devouring Blue Sky and an Ocean That Laps and Churns Relentlessly at the Defiant Sandline as You Scream Your Own Name in Latin and the Receiver of Such Delinquencies Punches You in the Eye for Your Urgent Ignorance That Comes Out Squawking and Meowing You All the Way to the Moon

2.
In the Throes of the Nothingness Is Typically How It Goes When You're Down and Out with Nothing but a Working Mouth That Screams Get Me Out of Here Before I Break My Back Climbing Down the Ladder into Your Mysterious Indecisions That Tickle My Insides with Stolen Logic Like Dental Floss

Fixer-upper

Add a bit of something. Add a bit of everything. Add a bit of nothing. Add a bit of anything—anything   ANYthing you've got and I'll drown my sorrows with waves of tortured anguish, dive deep into gallows of tumultuous tremors that'll swallow me whole. Burrow my head in a plastic bag, fly the zip line—it's my only lifeline—lock it down, now bound to a diminishing, finishing, lavishing, blasphemous, celebratory, bashful plunge that'll grapple my heart and tackle me to the ground. Why take one when I can take two?? Why take two when I can take three?? Why take three when I can take it all???? Now I'm tethered to the grindstone. Bondage and leather binds me to an ebbing nonexistence; I lost my head. I lost my heart. I balled up my soul and hurled it across yards of filth. Don't cash checks that you can't afford to relinquish—I can't afford to relinquish, I can't afford to relinquish, I can't afford to let me down….

Glittered Romance

The windows
I stare through
They caress my face
with glitter

I listen for the morning
It comes with a throbbing
aching
pain
in my heart

The daytime is
bright and
vicious
deliciously coy
I stare at the
hourglass

The minute hand
rounds
the surface of
the frying pan
Then comes
the hour hand
I'm broken and

immature

About a Boy

The boy stands in the shadows. Sirens blare. He waits. A flux of red and blue. "Hey, you!" He runs. Behind him, men in full uniform. He lunges over a fence. Hits the street. Go go go >>>

A cruiser pivots and plows. He goes. Comes to a T. Cuts left. A cruiser meets him. Slides on the slick, wet road. He dodges. Another cruiser barrels. He rolls. Cruiser after cruiser careen. He pivots. A cop takes out his legs. He's down, hands behind his back. He's cuffed. A cop drags him to the cruiser. Tosses him in. The door clicks shut, and they're off….

In the cruiser now. He watches lights flashing by. He watches cars in a blur. He watches. He watches watches watches …
      as his whole life ebbs away///

Darker Things

    I just happen to enjoy the darker things in life….

    So fuck your colors! we'll bask in the moonlight.

tantric excursions

delving thru tabloidic nighmares i dabble with hocus-pokus schemes. the monologue of a hopeless soliloquy fumbling thru plastic dreams i seek fantastic fabrications a drastic disaster of an evening. i'm seeing frightful stars, going too far, living like large insects tittering down withered, wasted dead ends. bending extensions gleaming proud these insidious cloud plowing nuclear holes thru stone walls i'm headless idle & deadly but get to know me i'm gentle enough to distrust until you rub my led and i'll be ready instead. a portrait of a tethered revolutionary i carry rods of light across a silvery sky that turns to gold every time i churn the pedals of my broken bicycle/moped/rowboat/bloatedbuffoon. the evening reeks of boredom and loose bellybutton piercings and shiny, smooth earrings penetrating demonic bearings where i go when the chips turn rotten like the burning wanton fuse soothing a surge of trickling blues i tie the holy noose around the sun and watch the jolly earth ripple it's fun. wound like two tons of coiling snake skin i dip my legs deep into pond scum and lick the mutated toad on the mouth we make out on my front porch and gloat proudly about the odd connection between the two of us but then sob softly when the chains of romantic misadventure come abruptly unlatched before the whole wandering crowd floats upward into the sky and gets lost in and absorbed by a high-strung, strung-out delusion it's so insipid the way i lose sleep over it the way i lose minutes beside it the way i'm simply wired to be the final cat to pound the **snooze** button before the day unravels with cherry bomb explosions and toy soldiers in black launduray emerge from the roiling fog and in the distance i watch the battle of battered toddlers as they fight to own fight to consume fight to distill fight to reuse perhaps reissuing the haunted stone which tumbles out of reach. at last the triumphant one mans his throne and bellows the anthem of the day that refuses to get started....

Untitled Poem

I lost my soul in a dream
What it is
and what it should be—
two separate entities
that make me jittery and
confused
blue in the face as I howl
up at the simmering sun
and wait for the darkness to envelope
all of these insidious creatures
Reality cracks down like
a guillotine
locking me in its cutting bite
and I walk the streets at night
watching my shadow as it drifts
and sways trailing my being from
a distance
So adrift
I feel like everyone
on earth is dead
The air cold and frightening
The moon bold and illuminated
My world lost in
a fantastic paradise
I think about devilish schemes
seeping through the cracks
of a lightning invasion
where thunder thwacks and wallows
and the rain swallows me up
I have no place to go
no way to turn
no time to burn
no life to yearn

When I dreamt about magic
my tongue got stuck
between my teeth and my brain
felt like two-tons of
roiling cement and my world
shriveled up
inside my heart—a fierce force of flashing
striking stabbing slashing
brash and tactical forks of thrashing
light
The thunder feels hollow
The rain feels blank
My heart vaporizes as
my hopes dissipate
Jaded I awaken to
a world stricken with
nothing but
nothing but
nothing but nothing
and I'm thrumming my fingers
on my legs
my knees are bumping
and I'm trying to burn away
the seconds turn to minutes
turn to hours
the secondhand churns
and I learn that escape
isn't what it used to be
I feel elusive and afraid
My mind blank my heart empty
and my heartbeat trembles
with agitation
I fidget with the minute hand
and wait for it all to
STOP
What's the point when

you sold your soul
to the man in your dream
and all you got in return
is a festering, enveloping emptiness
that never seems to leave
Time movement space distance
radius weight
it all seems so irrelevant when your heart
is in a permanent state
of erratic desolation
When you're just so vacant
but all the rooms are
full

Never have I ever

The world
is a rather wakeful
habitat
that can seem like quite
the lonely place
when you just don't know
where it's at

It's a Friday night
I sit on the infected
jungle jim
The bars are giddy with
color
the sun
explosive & delightful

I can hear music
coming from
a different world
Ain't it such a
delirious plight
when you're sitting all alone
on the moon
at the stroke of midnight
as billowing asteroids zoom
straight past you
with glittery voices
bubbling right outta the flittering
ozone layer

like
a burning turd

And I find that I'm
dissipating
fast
in the center
of all the madness
that shrouds me like
a single evaporating tear
which taints my face
like the soft & curious touch
of a newborn
man or woman
He/she whispers soft, rhythmic
hateful rants to me
at night before they go to
sleep
in their bulbous cribs

And I find that I'm
standing

on center-stage
Don't know my cue
          my line
the next right thing
for me to do

I'm loaded on
absolutely nothing
That's right
I'm a sober cheetah
The only thing I take
are flashing lights
which clatter against
my diminishing skull

A heavy bassline
now rattles
the levitating floor
of a universe I saw
glimmering
on a big, shiny screen
Now I'm stranded
in my own head
It's where you'll find me
when I'm dead
straddling
my own bloody eyeballs
watching as
I'm immersed in
thoughtful gibberish

A loaded gun
pressed gently
against my head
feels kinda like
purple

& green
a delicious blend of nothingness
that shadows the
fading night

A waking fit
A sleeping zit
The grime behind my eyes
is like a mutation
of my mind's own
deviating thought process

Wow a galactic
gigantic
practicing frantic
is absolutely dazzled by
the craptastic show that
features
1,000 teenage mutant
glittery princesses
holding hands as they
march off
into the sun's devouring
maw—

It's a bad day
to be ugly/
      if you ask me

Don't go into the light!

Your house is burning
Your house is burning
Your house is burning
      <u>My</u>   house is burning
Your house is burning
Your house is burning
Your house is burning
      <u>My</u>   house is burning

I'm trembling through channels
      thru channels
          thru channels
              thru channels
of
      lightning
striking biting radioactive uniting

a decrepit
      par   adise
We see the night sky blemished with stars and other delightful frights
that bite into our heads like
a brain in a vise

trippin
   I'm tumbling and   I'm   falling
                                            off!

Don't let go of the truth
strangle it like
      a superb being
be one with it
behold its wonderment
but just don't let go   or

       you'll find
      you are just as blind
     as the numbest bystander
      who stands in line
       falls in line
       comes on time
        and leaves
      <u>behind the times</u>

and when he does
when she runs
when it lunges
  through hoops of turbulence

       he always says
       GOODBYE

               Good <u>bye</u>!

That is why
  I tell you lies/
That is why
  I watch you cry/
That is why
  I see no reason **WHY!**

I might fall behind
but you are outta line....

So you see

when it's all over and done
when it's all come and gone

when the world dissolves
in putrid parasites

                        I look up at the sky
                        and say goodbye

                                                  Good   <u>bye</u>!

                        and walk off into the night

                                                  Good   <u>bye</u>!

all because:

Your house is burning
Your house is burning
Your house is burning
          <u>My</u>   house is burning
Your house is burning
Your house is burning
Your house is burning
          <u>My studio flat is burning</u>

I'm a long way from home///

I'm slowly learning the ways
      of
            the world
I'm burning through cigarettes
I'm burning through brain cells
I'm learning to burn
      learning to burn
          learning to burn
Will you join me in a <u>burn</u>??

Be me
        I'll be you
Be you
                but don't be me

We're fucking now
    you & I
cumming together
like astronauts
a single being
unified in the most sacred of acts
through lust we react
through love
       we walk away   <u>JUST WALK AWAY</u>

departed
    you & I

We hate each other
       unified
       by
a single act of   a sinful infraction

a deranged deterrent

It all boils down
to just one thing:
       to a solitary noose
       to a royal excuse
       to a solidified truth
I'm rolled and I'm loose
losing control of
                themotherfuckinnoose

It's useless anyway   because:

Your house is burning
Your house is burning
Your house is burning
        <u>My</u>   house is burning
Your house is burning
Your house is burning
Your house is burning
        <u>My</u>   house is burning

Just Killing The Boredom With A
    glorified
    pleasure-ridden
    heathen-stricken
    never ending
    indecisively driven
practically nonexistent

universal reality >>>>>>

Insomnia

Sleep on it. Meditate on it. Do backflips over it. Run circles around it. Fire-bomb the moon. Kiss an Indian chimney sweep. Light a match, chuck it into your past, and watch as you make history ... uh ... **burn!!!** Try to tell a wise old man that climate is a lie. Explain to a naïve little child that the truth is buried in the sky. Climb Mount Everest, stand on the summit, and pluck the sun from outer space, kinda like taking a bite of a chain of Fig Newtons stuck together at the root, each link so explosively sound. Sleep on it. But why??—I've got way too much to think about....

Taking Flight

The turquoise hawk swoops through the mountainside like a galloping zebra, its wings **whoosh**ing lightly but with bold confidence as it soars between trees, and its body arches slightly as it starts its gentle ascent over the green-as-spinach hilltop, all the while in the back of its airborne mind it remembers its mother the green and orange fox squawking in its ear before it took off: DO AS I SAY! DO AS I SAY!!! The rebellious hawk skittered across the floor of the hut on eight tittering legs like that of a spider as it reached the door and burst through, spreading its wings as wide as ever and taking flight up through the blossoming leaves, all the while hearing in the back of its mind the squawking fox balk loudly: DO AS I SAY! DO AS I SAY!!! Presently the hawk peers downward and sees a fierce-looking deer zipping and zanging past trees as fast as tumbling volcanic rock. The hawk whistles kind of like a catcall at the dashing deer; the deer slows to an abrupt halt, looks up at the hawk, and the hawk touches two crisp talons to the top of its skull, and with that the deer offers a validating smile of bone-crushing sincerity then kicks the dirt and vanishes into the tree line faster than the turquoise hawk can swerve around the approaching tree. But just in time it serves the wheel a hard right, pushes the pedal to the grindstone and manages to bypass it so fast he can barely hear the **crrraack!** of the tree branch snapping in half….

Untitled Poem

Trickling
Crowds
Shrouded
Shivering
Delirious
Sensational
Deranged

Ashamed
Motoring
Echo
Supersonic
Flatulent
Riffraff
Plantation
Electronic
Malfunction
Mathematical
Dysfunctional
Lewd
Pompous
Zigzag
Hydraulic
Wiggle
Descending
Mammoth
Spiderwebbing
Ferocious
Entertaining
Nuisance

Looking into it

I'm looking into it
past
    present
        future
over-analytical mental annihilation
I'm peering too far into
the scope of a shattered lens
I'm looking into it

perhaps without enough conviction
lacking the proper volition
my mental ammunition sustaining attrition
I'm looking onto the eye of
a magnified
a mummified
     a sexually solidified
a traumatized
series of über lies
past
   present
      future
rendition
of a feline superstition
caught in a net wielded by
a whimsical drag queen
in thigh-high combat boots
I stuck out my neck and
all I was left with was
a telescope that indicates all the blisters
and the boils
that spot my brain///

Untitled Poem

adeliberate   pulse

poundsinside   my   neck

like   viking mucus

running   throughhoops   like

mountainmen

        seperateme

from   the   crowdedlem mings

shootingstarsbeyondthe   sky

    fumbling

      downthe

scope of   the

rifle

beat my wife

find a lover

destroy my life

give birth toanother

yesI'm   quite disturbed

buttherearethings you know nothing

a bout

correctmeif   I'mwrong

playmychords

     my- - -   - - -cords

broke

        atthesoundof   your

unlordly   voice

flick   a   match   and   throwit

intoa   puddle

ofbubblinggas

full   throttle

hitthebrake   and   slam

                theconvertiblethrough

ashimmering,silverwall

pluck the throttle

I'mouttatime

                movingfast   through

                rampant   disasters

thebackwardsflowingocean

watch me as I   disintegrate

        shatterme please

shatter my   wholeentire   life

                        killme   please

watch   me   as I die

diedie   I'mdying

throughthe   mazeof   massproduction

ashimmering   tire   deflated

                                zeroedin

yesI'm   quite disturbed

but it's   tooearly   togo

berserkon

                            themindsofallthe

lurkersin   thedark

disturbing   yesitis

                                        ImeanI'monly   30

Oblivious Discontentment

I noticed something wasn't quite right. I stared out the window at the lashing flames that whipped and thrashed and devoured everything in sight. *What the hell is wrong with this picture?* I mused, as the window exploded and broken glass assaulted me head-on, nipping and stabbing exposed skin. I stood there and mulled over this new development, trying so hard to figure out the root of the problem.

With a cataclysmic **crunch!** a large maple tree snapped in half leaving only a crude-looking stump in its passing, and with that my whole house shook and the lights flickered and the room went suddenly dark, the only light coming from the shuddering fire outside the broken window.

Should I call someone, maybe?

"Wendy!" I yelled.

"What?" rasped my wife from upstairs.

"Are you seeing this?"

"What?"

"Outside, honey. Are you seeing what's happening?"

"I'm sleeping! You woke me up."

"Sorry, honey. Go back to bed. It's not that big of a deal, anyway."

I could feel the fire singeing the hairs on my head; I rubbed my chin. *Hmmm....*

Something didn't feel quite right, was all I knew....

You & I
and Anyone Else Who Wants to Join Us on Our Ride

Anyone wanna walk with me
beneath the beaming moonlight
bright as a knife, crisp as a rifle
through the daylight strife, as pigeons fight and frolic
and ravens prop sharp talons
on the flesh of the fallen
Anyone wanna cruise with me in stolen cars
down streets glazed in oil
down broken lanes of razorblades dull as chocolate
Anyone wanna dance with me
on the Fourth of July
as flaming rockets explode and disperse beneath
the blazing stars of the black beyond
just look for O'Ryan's Pocket
filled with odds and ends as we drop dead
onto the bloodied grass beneath us
beaten by vandals who sport
cans of red spray paint in their ugly maws
and we could watch the boats take off and the jets
sail the seven skies like missiles on a kamikaze crash course through
hell & beyond, and we'll bomb the ozone layer with
rubber bands and knives, with candy apples and shotguns
let's celebrate the demise of the ones we love
and celebrate the lives of the those that we hate
and we can discuss why our fate seems broken as we throw
painted darts into flying targets that whizz and buzz
too far over our heads to reach
and we'll make sure to
hawk loogies on the passersby down below us
Anyone wanna come with me
and we'll fuck atop dead bodies of rotten men
the kinds we murdered ourselves

and laughed as they bit the bucket
Anyone wanna help me blow up the TV screen
throw the radio down seven flights of stairs
we'll charge onstage and murder celebrities
with a swift stroke of our hair
we'll double over and puke out our own guts
get drunk on goblets of piss
smoke moldy organs through massive glass pipes
made of that shiny substance lining the windows of churches
and then shatter it like the past
and the present
and everything in between
In dreams I'll see to it that you know who I am
but I won't know you
guess you could say I'm a hopeless romantic
with violent intentions, who wants to see the world turn upside down
and watch as life turns inside out
and I'd much rather give life to the badmen on TV
than watch the perfect people always succeed
and I'd most definitely prefer to watch as
sociopathic homosexuals suck each other to death
than see another set of shiny white teeth
Anyone wanna join me in a nasty rendition
of "Ring Around the Rosy"
as we dance around the bloody fountain
spewing red lines of human waste
singing and chanting because
only in death will we be stopped
for we're just a bunch of
murderous enchantments set on destroying ourselves
Anyone wanna kiss me on the moon
take an express flight to the sun
and perish as everyone remembers
the man that I'd become
Anyone wanna meet me on Saturn
we'll surf the crisp ring of flames and plasma

that surrounds this forgotten planet
Trust me it'll be loads of fun
Lust for me/
Want me/
Search for me/
Kill me,   please
before I kill you
because I want to do it, too.
Anyone wanna lie beside me in a coffin
and wait for the maggots to eat us alive
we'd befriend some parasites
as we chow down on dirt just to stay alive.
Life/
Death/
Anyone wanna die with me????
because I wanna die with you….

Can't Take the STRAIN

We've all got our problems/
Everyone Is Number One….

> *Standing in a crowded room*
> *in a packed stadium*
> <u>faces like numbers</u>
> <u>haunt you till the day</u>
> <u>that you die</u>

We've all got our problems/
Everyone Is Number One….

Let me dream if I want to

I'll blow your mind
with sincerity
I'll show you dreams
of disparity
Before I'm through
you'll be straddling fairy tales
like racing midgets
on a quest to be the best
like the rest
and dissolve in
asbestos
like the ones
with chimney-tall
heads
with buffalo-wide
faces
and a singular eyebrow
that raises all the right
questions

Just like yesterday we sailed
the seven layers of
consciousness
we attach the drip
to our fuzzy heads
and our mutated minds
immersed with diluted
fantasies
float away on a strand of
magically prancing
rainbows damaged on
bland commercialism
      Just another day at the office
      it was
and yet

there was that day
of bold eroticism
floating up up up until
the tedious merchant
of a lenient heritage
bought us all takeout
and we mainlined the
entire menu
It was just a
wacky sensational
thing of a dream
of a dream
of a nagging queen
that surrenders the sun
to a boisterous scene
and for that we all
fade away into dreams

everything I need to say
in only a few words

How could I say everything I wanna say in only a few words what if I was a giant and I could catch the sun in my hand what if the moon was really a giant chunk of bologna and there's a giant man who nuzzled his way into the meaty chunk and sleeps there nightly but during the daytime he surfs the fiery slaps of a roiling sun what if I had eyes on the back of my hand how do I say everything I wanna say before I die before I die before I die have you ever felt so alive that you knew you were really dying you were dying watch out cuz I'm alive I'm alive im aLiVe I was born to die bread to lie beaten raw and stabbed with an upside-down knife

round&round&round

acting is living
doing = death
dying is surviving
& survivors die!

Document, Recovered

This is a joke
spoke the madman
The broken globe
sits on damaged axles
Practice the fragile excuses
The caustic muse meets
the beat of a shaven feline thief
We run wild and free
Beat on the brat
till he beats on me
I hold the shovel
keep digging my hole
keep prodding my soul
I lose sleep to the planes
of the unknown

The Show Must Go On

Sitting amid
a mass of commotion
Deliberately woven
A series of
broken tears
Pondering a
fluid laundry shoot
Cue the blasphem
y like
a deranged poodle
Loosely damaged
Challenged by a
rabid woman
Change the channel
Tune it till
we're completely immersed
with earsplitting feedback
Terrorized by
laughing yacks
Listening to
the battered cats
of a crafty dream
Saw
the claws
in half
Reaching through
an elusive sea
Bringing forces of
evil to a T
Bought by me
Sold by she
A disheveled prostitute
was

he
Surrender the sword
of a discordant future
and strum those
lordly power chords
before the bystanders
simply
get too bored
to care
anymore
Sold to you
by
a raucous hoard of
raccoons lunging
through
an expanding bungee cord
Bouncing
It bounces
Bouncing
I pound
my idle heart
back into motion
however devious the
manifestations of a runaway
locomotion
happens to be
In any case
I'm find that I'm
bound by
six different strings
that when plucked
a different tune
sounds delightfully
harmoniously
weaving its way
through

a televised lounge
where the band
onstage
chimes in with
their very first song
of the night

A Pet Called Projection

Don't think things about me
that are not true
or I might just do
the very same for you///

Like looking at myself
through the eyes of a stranger
I'm confronted with insidious insight
        everywhere I go it seems at times
        I'm just so
        delirious and bright
        delighted to never have
        gotten to know you
            right?
which causes me to lash out
and destroy
        my fellow parasites
like a leech
on a shopping spree

So my solution is simple:
Annoy the civilized classes
Delusional I know
I'm just a spoiled rich kid brat

You see
I wear my heart on my
pant leg
don't you know it
and sometimes I might drop it
    SPLAT
    [oh no, not again]
               (it's happening to me again
                & again)

I'll kick it around like
a soccer ball
     you'll see

Will you gimme the first-place prize
for stomping the heel of my boot
into the center of
this deformed vital intestine——
    that which shall not be named
        but shunned
        but shunned by all
        and stunned and mauled
cuz it ain't worth a damn
anyhow
I'm just so enthralled
by this worthless relinquishing
of surgical disasters
    one after the next
You're Up Now
it's chowtime
        Why bother getting out of bed
        when the planet that you live on
        is constantly tipping and turning
        like a spastic in a fit

So next time you see me on the street
please don't project
onto me
things you'd never realize
or be accustomed to
in your short-lived lives
Don't make me out to be
who you want me to be
cuz I'll probably just disappoint
or maybe I'll surprise
cuz I'll try to do it
    anyway
    you'll see
but only if you're worth the strides

which is something I will determine
on my own time

A Method to My Madness

There is a reason as to
why I am
the way I am
    today/

A busted-up reason
like a loose lugnut
rolling crude spirals
in front of a group of lewd woman
who are always on the prowl for
a couple of
hunky dudes with a few hundred
loose screws rolling and wobbling

inside of their clogged arteries/
        their boggled hearts
twisted and
mangled——

It all starts with a heart....

My mind is rather lopsided right now
        just so you know/
like bounding sailboats
loosely driven
by a slew of Neanderthals
dropping hatchets on the
hub
        <u>land a hoe</u>
        <u>land a whore</u>
        <u>man the oars</u>
        <u>as we rock its core</u>

and my core is rather rocked all right....

But you see
there is a method
to my otherwise conniving
decisions that I've derived
from a broken sky
dotted with rotting clouds///

See if you know me
I probly screwed you
or I fucked you
or maybe even made sweet sweet love
to your number-one cousin
        with a heart so neat

I came a perfectly fashioned
line of nefarious ribbons that
ripped holes beneath this planet's
hydraulics system >>>

A heart so neat that
I made sure to
store it on ice
when I took it out for
a stroll
        one fine summer evening

as you slept soundly in your
banana
peeled for a queen
and I thought of her
of her succulent breasts
so voluptuous and creamy///

I thought too of the way her tongue felt
when I pressed it
between my thumb and pointer finger
and <u>yanked</u> it
with everything I had
in me at the time
        which was much less than nothing/
        I can assure you of that

Now planning to hock your cousin's heart
for a pack of Pall Malls at the store
I lost it on my way to

the epic Chess match
where strangely enough
Pawns
seemed to rule over the entire flock

with a mildewy thumb pressed
in outwardly flowing blood
and they sent
their Kings & Queens
out to fight their battles
for them/
just to be cut down
one by one >>>
        How Do You Like Dem Apples!

and I said to the ring leader
dawning a pinkish tutu
around his wiry arms:

"How much for a frozen heart?"

                "It's frozen, huh?"

"No it <u>was</u> frozen/
    Now it's broken."

                "Broken you say?"

"Yes, quite broken."

                "How so?"

"I stole it from a foxy heartache."

                "I see," said the
                      golden pawnbroker

who I suppose looked like a
flamingo/
and he held up his right hand
and I watched as he

stretched and wiggled his
fingers
        like the legs of a spider

                "I like em broken."

I smiled
to let him know
I was listening

                "Yes, broken is good."

still wiggling his fingers
around

still smiling to keep him
going

                "Yes, indeed."

He stopped wiggling them
and looked at me with
these grimy, shapeless eyes

A stare I had seen before
somewhere in a withering dream
so cold and eclectic

He stopped
Looked me dead in the eye
Stopped
Nodded softly
and sincerely
and with my guard distracted
by the sincerity of it all
his hand shot straight out

like a bazooka blast
zeroed in on my chest cavity
and tore a path straight through
which took him to the cage
that kept
my beating heart in shackles

His cold, flat grin
faded into an ironically pale half smile
that caused my skin
to derail/

and out came his hand
holding a red and bloody vessel
with a beat that seemed to be
<u>ebbing</u>
        fast
He said to me then

                      "But yours——

                    But yours is even more broken!"

with the accent of
a mad Russian on TV
        his laughter filling the stadium
        like two tons of bony icicles
        dropping all at once >>>

and with that
my knees gave
my body started to bend
and fold
and then collapse
        and my eyes imploded
when my swollen head

clunked against the
fractured concrete
                    beneath me/

and I knew
right then and there
that I was dead....

And now you see
The connection that bridges
this incorruptible gap
together is thus
forever
           And now you see

Flight

The feather
of an angel
caresses my
ignorance
Blessed by
intuition
instinctively
diluted
I remove
my wisdom
from the
whole of the
image

Untitled Poem

Thunder
crash
Lightning
thrash
Windows
shudder
Trees & leaves
flutter
Roof
quake
Pot brownies
bake
Stomach
ache
Walls
gyrate
Floor
undulate
Mind
falling into place/

Staggering to the Blues

A ruckus of a night
Romping to the light
Stocking through layers of
demented foresight
The trembling basslines
Fumble with their insides
Blunders and allies
Crabwalks and swaggers
Soothing beggars crumble
into the onslaught of noise
The world blackens with insidious
back alley freaks
Trapdoor nuns, backwoods sluts
A world overrun with drinks and drugs
Drunks and addicts frolic with
gay dementia
Fermented grapes and carrots
Misshapen rabbits
Musketeers sold on the wine of tears
The shadow people walk the line
The subconscious minds
come out to play
They say that they know this tune
Cuz tonight you and I
are staggering to the blues

Untitled Poem

Colors brightening
words aligned
the crosshairs thrumming
pitches of sublime

I kneel on stony crevices
I watch the roosters frolic
in dirt and pine and crumbling sand
as the antelope drinks the wine

It's a perfect Tuesday night
my mind lit up and full of life
I watch the pigeons as they fight and plummet
I say down with the system down with the sky

Sifting through dreams

I mount the ledge
bound the dredge
see through wanton wrecks
of mountainous pirate ships
rummaging over stony
shores like
gory throes rampant
with waste
Disgrace the mad endeavors
shiv the feverish levers
throw caution to
the thunderous phantom

prowess
Damaged by power
corrupted by
nuclear theatrics
Blackened cherries
Smothered fairies
frolicking
Release the wary eye
let it shy away from the
sky slivered with retro laser
beams
slashing slits in the polluted
stream of conscious
I stare at the ozone
layer
watch as it unfurls greatly
proud to be a legendary
cretin sucking predators dry
by tattered swirls
of devious matters
like a feather waxed by
years of fulsome severance
By December the switchblade
curls gently down the winding
spine of the defiant bat's
nefarious prey
We lay schemes through
the lukewarm eyes
of our enemies'
pierced scalps
Shout About
NOTHING
The cloud of a derelict
night
shadows a maximum
overdrive situation

Fracture the lights
with a crisis-like
power chord
The bar chord speaks in shallow
whispers
dribbling insidious litany
like a titanic symphony
Back the bitter facts
with a golden fist
punching the
crumbling space shuttle
Just sit back and
watch as
the world dissolves under
the thumb of a
blundering bummer
fumbling summers
running in numbers
tumbling down hills
of a stunning understanding
We man the rally
and let the chained man
tally down the days
till they free him from
this place of
utter decay

So Out of Place
RIGHT NOW

In the closet
robbed of truth
situations deplete
me
leaping thru hoops
lined with acidic
knowledge/
a rageful delay
    a wasted decay
        my bravest foray
brace yourself for
The Fall
of 1,000 Nations
in the crossfire
       ....locked   &&loaded

Untitled Poem

Lights
Flashes
In the Night
We frolic down
lucid avenues
like a lewd
ambition
Crumbling
downward
Fumbling loudly

We hide in
fear
Scarred by the sheer
illusions
a lonely star casts
through delicate channels
of a
nudist's scandal
A dandelion doesn't care
and yet
it summons crisp
alleys of a nicked giraffe
They wonder
where
we went
when
the blundering sound
breaches
the wandering town
Dawning my crown
I found it
but I lost it
and now we're bound
to ourselves

Days of Brutality

I cater to my own
devious notions
my own
derelict devotions
Time is passing me
Time is lapping me

I'm lapping up the dirt and grime
from beneath the concrete living room
I walk on shallow waves
I dance at my mother's wake
Between you and I
I don't think it's ever gonna change
But who would want it to????
anyway///———not me!
        for I enjoy my own
          overcrowded solitude
From rows of bloody tulips
jabbing delicate tubes of
denial run wild into my
crumbling veins\\\
I follow the fairies around
I hovel and I'm
desperate
falling shimmering into
the rotten mush that grows
spic-n-spam
between my crisscrossing toes
I see the rivers lashing
I see the fires thrashing
I see the rolling death
But it doesn't stop
with shame and destruction
It doesn't stop with
blitzkrieg deduction
It doesn't stop
with bonefied lust
This madness to which I escape
embraces me with this
sheer desolate desertion
I desert my own mind
when the time is right
Throw caution to

the thunderous hailstorm
that comes in blundering
and bulldozing me pale and
broken
I sold myself to time
I sold myself to demonic design
I sold myself to
boys wielding billclubs
and knives
I've sold out and I just can't seem to remember
where I'd left my heart
       last night
I must retrace my steps
But the sheer thought of
going backwards
causes me to outwardly
project vile
So trust me when I say
it's a sight for sore eyes
when
the broken fat bitch sings

Wounded

The wound
spreads across the face of
a conveying merciful endeavor
The trigger-happy
meandering leper
scurries down the dilapidated
reddened sea
The wound releases
a river of glitter

Buried beneath
the wilting sea of truth
lies a maniacal
menacing brute
We run from the foolish stooge
like fleeing from the scene of
a clamoring stampede-like
triathalon
The wound offers nothing but
skewed delusions
served fresh in a garden of tears
The salt from the inner cavity
of a churning six-shooter
is loosed like a Molotov
Saiki
and scatters
with Gatling-gun velocity
Cover the wound before
we brandish a vernacular of
rattling linguistics
The wound burns
as we relish the flag of
a thief
yearning to turn back the
time

Untitled Poem

All I see when
I look out my window
are vain interactions and
jaded connections
and I try to disconnect myself
from these empty erections\\\

A Vague History of the Wheel

Wheels are kind of a fascinating item. They help us in so many ways—ways in which most people take for granted. Before the wheel, it was a block. A mere chunk of clay. Until one day a cavemen said, Wait a minute, what if the edges were round? Of course, everybody mocked him for this concept. A block with rounded edges? Please! Try to pound a chunk of meat with something like that. Are you out of your freakin mind?? But then the guy was like: It can help you carry things around. Please, the people said, all at once. That's preposterous. Just gimme a few hundred slaves and fifteen whip-cracking men to keep the slaves in line, and we can get from Egypt to Saudi Arabia in only a year's time. No problem! Granted, this was way before the slave-trading days in Egypt; this was back when men still lived in caves, drew stick figures on the walls, pounded their thick, hairy chests to get people's attentions, and spoke in that oompaloompa language that consists of grunts, groans, and squeals. I mean, dinosaurs were roaming the earth; what good could a goddamn wheel ever do?

Well, we certainly showed them….

The Bush Burns Brightest at Night

We all decided that
it would be in our best interests
to
disassociate

Dotted Lines

Join the dots. I'm scattered and lost. The dots spiderweb outward. I watch them materialize and then evaporate. I see them coming at me faster, exasperated diligent and tyrannical. The dots are magical. I'm shattering pictures frames. Watching deranged bumpers cars as they bounce and plow and jump. The dots are my friends. They keep me up at night, and they put me to sleep. If I join the dots—— Sometimes I feel disjointed. Fuck unity, it's a blundering delusion. I'm rude and snotty, but I can also be sweet and soft—but I won't! I'm ruined by institution. I'm losing the fight as the dots divide and turn blue. I watch the pain explode. The dots the rut the knots the fuck?? I'm stuck—stuck stuck in a black hole. I try to join the dots but they push back. They smash my good faith, they lash out at my ways, they trash my fuckin place! Fuck the dots, I love the dots; they love me they love me not. I'm running away but the dots come tumbling after me. I can't get away—I can't! If I joined the dots, my mind would implode and my heart would grow cold. But why join the dots when I can shatter pixels instead!

Nighttime Blunders

Life offers me
vibrant distractions
defiant infractions
empty, shallow endeavors
A whole wide world
scarfing down
powdered lies
I can see it in your
liquid eyes
The way you shamble down
blackened corridors

with backalley smiles
and dilapidated denial
frolicking past
damaged cobblestones
swaying viciously
My intuition is dismissive
a privilege to submit
I lean over busted
boardwalks
Disgusting showmanism
Throw caution down
frowning lanes
devastating framework
Shattering the maimed
manikin
through a series of
punctured names
Wondering
I plummet
through
my tortured ways

A Pain in My Diction

A tropical squandering
A devastating evangelical fortress
Footsteps in the night
Climbing treetops shone in the light
The echo of nonsense
The rueful do-diligence
Beautiful monsters
A spike filled with vintage sperm
Worming its way down

back alleys aligned with fur
We the soldiers
Officers of nowhere
Severe youthful beings
Truthful liars and thieves
We the villains
Anti-heroes distilling tapped wires
Flying the thoughtless
Trying on our uniforms
with motley significance
Fought with demons
We see the mutinous semen
Spotted with leprosy delight
We are the nightly woes
Slighted by the material foes

Exponential Interpretations

Friendship

Ever had a friend who just seems to get you? Just, Get You,,,, you know, like understands you in ways that no one else would. Not a boyfriend or a girlfriend, not a soulmate or a best friend, but just someone you can walk around with all night, shooting the shit, and it never gets old. He challenges you, you challenge him—you're not soulmates, so not every discussion is equal, not every point made is equivalent with one another, you don't see eye to eye on every single subject. So some might construe your discussing and debating as arguing and bickering; and so some might wonder, "Why do you hang out with someone who thinks so differently than you?" And in your mind you might say, *Because he challenges me; he pushes me.* In your mind you know exactly why, but on the outside, in the outer world, you just shrug and say, "Uh, I don't know," even though you do know, and you are also well aware that it just goes way over the heads of this culture's norm, which is simply: Surround Yourself with Likeminded People, Likeminded Thinkers, People Who Say YESSIR to Everything You Say, Thinkers Who Nod Their Heads and Don't Think   at all— those kinds of thinkers———the lack thereof breed,,,, you know the type.

And then you go and say something a little bit out of line, like one kernel of truth that doesn't seem to sit right with this friend of yours, and he, simply enough, brushes his hands together in a wiping-clean-the-slates gesture, just cleaning his life of you   For Good———not like everything that came before your outright remark didn't mean anything to him. Like,,,, What the Fuck

Did I Say That Was So Damn Bad? It was nothing personal; sorry I won't say YESSIR and nod my head to everything you say like everything is oh so kosher in our relationship and nothing can get in our way, as long as we stick together through thick and thin ... right?

Well, on many occasions, I learned I was very wrong for thinking that this person got me. (And when I say "got me" don't think I mean he agreed with every point I made, concurred with every remark I put forth, even got down on all fours and tried to analyze my vomit as it left my mouth in a nasty stew of projectile leftovers—cuz that is <u>not</u> what I mean. What I mean is: someone who doesn't turn the other cheek when I get too absurd and obscene, too intense and bitter, for the likes of them.)

Talk about insightful garbage until I make a joke about suicide, and then he goes, "You can't joke about suicide dude; not cool, not cool at all."
Talk about all the wonders of the broken rainbow as mice with helmets and swords and shields are being chased down by cats who don't have any armor on at all, chased right out of the darkest corners of desertion—don't bring a mouse to a cat fight, right?———but look at that, a fluffy, gray mouse is getting mounted right as I speak by a thin, blond cat with a patch of white fur right beneath his mouth that looks almost like a beard; he mounts and <u>rapes</u> hi——
"Don't say rape dude; not cool, not cool at all."

Goodbye, Good Friend

But on the contrary, I have had some friends who enjoy pushing buttons just as much as me. They push my buttons, I push theirs; we stamp our feet as hard as we can on each other's switchboard, kicking levers, twisting knobs, driving heel after heel into turntables of an insightful appetite————because the only thing we do happen to agree upon, he and I, is that in order to learn and grow as a person one must plow their heel into your toes as hard as they can any chance that they can. Just hurl a handful of nails into the road. Derail trains with a penny the size of the universe. Throw yourself off the side of a bridge that goes over the highway and then come straight down, feet-first, on the windshield of your next of kin. Kick and stomp and thrash and bash and plow and jam and beat and fuck and torment and hate and love too, of course, but only if it's not mutual, because anything done in unity is a sure-fire way to see yourself explode while looking straight in the mirror—just spontaneously combust: blow a top like a rocket and your head is launched ten feet twenty feet thirty feet into the air, whistling like a sprocket as it rounds the sky in an almost imperfect circle and crashes into an iceberg that had sprung out of nowhere—one moment it's a nice summer evening, and the next, your head splatters with blood and bone and bits and chunks of gooey brain matter and all that fun and delicious stuff   it racks against the side of an iceberg and your whole world collapses.   YESSIR!

Now, that's what friendship is all about—True Friendship, that is. Calling someone out on their own shit, and not letting them go about thinking their shit don't stink....

And acceptance of your friends for <u>all</u> the demons locked inside their closets. I'm thinking now, what with this culture being so damn judgmental, how does anyone stay friends with anyone anymore?? Dismiss him for the first skeleton that lunges out of the dark and latches onto you completely unexpectedly. I guess that's why we tell each other lies, keep the conversations shallow, remark on the weather; and when we veer off course from what's acceptable and normal, it's best to not insert your own opinions here and there. I get it, I really do. There are certain crowds that I don't feel entirely comfortable sharing every bit of crucial detail with, even just for the sake of keeping the peace, because 1. they would never understand how anyone in the right mind could think that way, and 2. the mob has spoken and I don't feel like becoming the subject of a townwide witchhunt tonight—or any night for that matter.
And that's where true friendship comes in handy. When you don't have to apologize for your own beliefs.

This culture, built by Facebook and the like, is all about surrounding ourselves with ones who think exactly the same as us. On Facebook we see the posts from Friends that we frequently LIKE, and we don't see the posts from Friends that we frequently ignore; and that renders us helpless inside a safe and sturdy bubble held up by people who share every single opinion as us (and I'm hesitant to call these likeminded people friends—for they are not, in no way, shape, or form—because <u>real</u> friends don't reinforce bullshit; they help dismantle it, guide us through it so we can see the faulty logic, masked behind butterflies, flowers, and bliss).

And that is why I'm so glad to have <u>real</u> friends; and time, as we all know, will always weed out the fakes ones….

Blind Submissions

I'm not going to blindly submit to anyone, male or female. I realized earlier today that that fact gets in the way of my being in a relationship. I force people to own their own shit, and doing so forces people to own their own shit, and the only shit most people do in fact own is the denial of their own shit, and even that they deny; and I refuse to blindly submit.

Divide- -Unite- -Crucify

Is rejection a form of
cynicism
or perhaps is
acceptance an
insidious practice
We live in such an
insipid culture
where the truth is
whitewashed
the answers we seek
sterilized by
mass-
consumptionism

The prior function of
human anatomy
   or should I say
   parasitic
   compositions
is to waste away
Our number-1 prerogative:
Follow the Leader
Join the In-Crowd
Dismiss the Out
Find Someone Better
to Idolize
another futile thoughtform
another useless ideation
Search for Meaning
in a Meaningless Paradise
disciples of the Third Reich
disciples of the ones who
fight kill & die
Descendants
defending
elemental
melodies
mentally
descending
menacing
lemmings
of a wanton assembly
Assemble and divide
brandishing this thing and that
seeing the world through
layers of distortion
through
tele
vision
Diminish the wisdom

of
our infinitely brilliant
predecessors
Fatalist Preachers
Nihilist Teachers
forfeiting a lordly burden to
the mindless breeders
breeding ideas that reek of
futility and
shame
Don't you forget we live in a
free country
harboring ideas designed for
a free world
a world leaking cretins and freaks
creeps geeks & systematic sheep
The shepherd has died
tonight
prematurely
Death to a deadhead
a less than human defendant
defending territory
of a battered catholic rambling
bringing nothing but sheepish
idiosyncrasies to a bleakish
nothingness
I see a televised
nightmare
realism seen through an insipid
screen
I watch as a screaming past
careens straight through the blackened sky
The future is dying by
moonlight
Steal the stars from the
fiery night

Blow up the sun
and watch as everyone
decides
Decide to do something
anything
vote pick choose
take sides
divide divide divide
no surrender
show no mercy
fight until you win
deliberately destructive
wage war
Wage war on the
fascist hatemongers
Shoot an anarchist in the
back
Tear up the American flag
Rebuild a burning nation
from the ground up
Discerning I learn to relearn
to relearn to relearn
to relearn to
turn the other cheek
on all the violence
and the in-fighting
and let the politicians
and the political activists
and the preachers and the protesters
and the picketers and the
witches and the Christians and the
hipsters and the Trumpster elitists
and the phony women and the
lonely men
of an unfolding culture
fight and kill each other

and maybe then
the undivided, undecided
king will rise
No sides
Fuck the left fuck the right
No sides
Only self-righteous assholes divide
No sides
Ride the tides until you die
No sides
Mount the tumultuous catalyst
Listen to the sounds of
hollow warfare
and sooner the anarchist is
crucified///

Untitled Poem

I will forgive you

for your ignorance

      if over time

you learn to forgive me

for my own ignorance///

Generation Z

This generation has no foundation. My generation had little foundation. We live in a world where everything is done second-handed. Sex is boring when it's not happening on a screen. There's no action; there is little passion. With everything at our fingertips, what's the point of living anymore? We don't need to live because directors and choreographers are spoon-feeding us life experiences. There's nothing that I see today that I can't reference to a book or a movie or a TV show, or even a song. In a world where we have everything at our disposal—i.e. the Internet—living becomes useless and redundant. I mean, I saw it happen last night on Netflix, so why bother making it happen today? Rockstars speak on YouTube, while I sit at home and twiddle my thumbs and jerk off to big-titted pornstars because life is easier, better, and more accessible when I get to watch it happen to someone else.

Taken by Delusions

With poetry

the two most common ways

to explore love

and passion and romance

is through

sexual descriptions and

heartbroken derivatives

So what does that say about

love? when

society's most sensitive

can't even seem to

capture it quite

right

Animosity

    Talk disagree dissect and delve

   Break societal norms create controversy

   Look for flaws and diverge in utter
      nonsense

   Debate bash argue wage war on
    a typical thought process

   Be obscure weird and overall
     thick-headed

   Listen analyze and prepare a
     rebuttal
    to the most common
     procedures
    of humanoid thinking

Destroy terminate and shut down
that of your fellow
parasites

Realign testify and lick the grime
from inside your mind's own
eyes

Be a germ a geek a twit or
just a rudimentary nutsack

Form strong opinions and then prepare
to have them terrorized
by evocative provocative or just plain
ironical cynical or maybe
tyrannical dictators
with too high of an opinion of

themselves
to be called
an android

Annoy the masses
and blast them till they
retaliate with some more tautological
wordplay
of the morally defective delay

Caring

She only cares so that I will care. I only care so that she will care. He doesn't care because nobody cares. She only cares about me when she benefits from it. I only care about her to the extent of how much I gain. He's closing the book on caring because NOBODY CARES. I see her in my rearview mirror; she's picking up trash on the side of the street, holding up a sign that says: LOOK AT ME, I'M PICKING UP TRASH ON THE SIDE OF THE STREET. I watch her work; she works with a sweet finesse. I watch her fade from my sight as the car flashes forward—and with a ***rump-rump*** I see him lying behind the car with blood and organs splayed out all around him. She doesn't care, I don't care. We see no reason to care.

Liberal Mythology

"A liberal institution ceases to be liberal the moment it is established."

— Friedrich Nietzsche

The Rebels Union:
what they call rebellion
I call conformity

Misconceived Courage:
what they call bravery
I call pandering

The Fifth Reich for Tolerance:
what they call tolerance
I call rejection

The Greatest Lie Ever Told:
what they call freedom
I call oppression

Emotional Reasoning:
what they call expression
I call censorship

The Last of the Freedom Fighters:
they force me to accept differences
they force me to reject arguments that go against
their own political agendas
I refuse to submit
to their mixed-up dilemmas
because frankly
I've got a mind of my own

The Good

It's a freeing realization when you understand that you don't haveta be a good person.

Let me explain: Growing up I was a dirtbag. I'm very open and honest about that. <u>I was a dirtbag</u>. Then I got sober and the people in the rooms said I had to change and be a good person. And I believed them, too. But they lied to me. Truth is, I don't haveta be a good person, I just haveta be me…. I'm sober now, can you believe it? and I've found that in sobriety I've become even more of a nihilist than I ever was when I was using drugs & alcohol. But I'm happy now, that's the difference. I thought I was a nihilist then; but really I just wanted to die. Today I'm happy—<u>truly</u> happy!——well, some of the time, anyway. Nihilism is liberating…. See, I don't haveta be a good person, I just haveta be me, that's all….

CaSe-SeNsItIvE

Computers don't care
about our case-sensitive
poetic agendas.
To them it's all the same
uppercase or lowercase;
it drives me absolutely insane
because I'm quite specific
about how each individual letter
appears down the page....

All-American Dinner

Boy asks:
"What's for dinner, mom?"
Mom says:
"Flowers."
Boys says: "flowers!
Again?"
Mom says: "I've got it
all prepared for you
on a silver spoon
just the way you like it."
"Thanks, mom,"
he says.
"You really know
what I like,
don't you, mom?"
She smiles and nods.
"I sure do."

Sometimes:

Shitty Places   +   Shitty People   =   Great Poetry

Blind Hatred

There are plenty of reasons
to hate
        Just before you do
make sure you find one

Blind hatred is the most
caustic design///

When the Dominos Fall

You can always count on this

> Every hero needs a villain. Every protagonist needs an antagonist. Every story needs a challenge. Every saint has a past. Every good guy has a bad side. Every utopia has a ghetto. Every hopeful message has a hopeless beginning.

Fuck Society!

We have been conditioned to think certain words behaviors attitudes and emotions are wrong. Repress repress repress, that's what our culture wants us to do—repress yourself, and that's the best, most effective way to fit in. And if you don't, people will shun you for it. Thinking aloud really does hurt, in a culture full of PC Nazis. Repression is the fastest way to be a part of the crowd. Hide your innermost thoughts and feelings and there's no way to go wrong. Me, I won't do that. Fuck society and it's mindless, oppressive culture. And now I'm sad because I don't belong. Fuck society for making me feel afraid. Fuck society for making me hate myself.

It's Party Time, Dude!

The problem with parties is you got X-amount of people packed like sardines into a tiny apartment, all with their own agendas, their own headcases, a unique brand of drama waiting to happen. The music is playing, sweat is pouring down your skin like slime, seeking refuge inside your socks your shoes and in between your toes…. It's boring and quite horrifying the way seemingly ordinary people get together to release their wretched side. When I was drinking I'd usually set up shop in the corner with a bottle of whiskey and drink myself into oblivion watching the cloud of bodies turn to drooling liquid before my very eyes, swarming like ants escaping a massive attack on their home…. It's dreadful and gross, to be just another number a rancid partygoer an attention-seeking prince or princess—one or the other will work just fine———just waiting in line behind hundreds of more attention-seeking princes and princesses, just weaving in & out and in & out;;;; and then my eyes start slipping rather quick, my body turning to mush, my loose limbs folding together like an irritated envelope after a long day of being stored and opened by whiny miscreants who don't even have the common decency to murmur a simple Thank You before they tuck you away…. It's just so posh and futile the way they come together just to become a single unit for the length of the night….

An utter disasterpiece of apathetic creatures, waiting in line just to take a big, heaping gulp of cyanide: just waiting to die, one by one, two by two, three by three—as though they are clueless lemmings waiting in line just to plummet off the side of the bridge into their own unfortunate but rather untimely and yet quite predictable demise…. It's just sad is what it is.

So sad…. But at least I'm telling you the honest truth—such a rare and unseen entity floating around the party like a ghost, just wanting to be seen and to be heard———this is <u>my</u> honest truth of what I see when the useless drones line up outside of a frat house ring the doorbell rack fists on wood; or when they wait neatly and tidily inside a kitchen for when the keg is pumped and poured, red plastic cups sloshing as drunken mockeries stumble and stagger around virtually retarded, slack-jawed and stupid. Just another number another nothing another stupefied joke lost to bad music and boring people who grin filthy grins of glazed and bloodshot eyes—lost to the plebian drudgery the boring nothingness the hopeless force of nature that festers here like fruit flies clinging to trash….

So glad those days are over now and now I can sit across from someone at the coffee shop having a real, meaningful conversation///

In the Loop

So glad
I'm not in the loop

                    of the noose

because frankly
I've just got better things
to do

Talking to God About Ethics

Man: What's the difference between right and wrong?

God: If it feels right, then it's probably wrong....

Fuck Art, Let's Dance!

When I write, I'm not trying to give you this fabulous, Avant-garde experience. If you want that, go to Rome. (But then, when in Rome, be an asshole, like I once said ... when? five minutes ago? ten?) What you'll get from me is raw emotion. I didn't spend my life observing life, like some writers do. I spent my life living and learning and loving and hating and fucking and throwing it all away and then rebuilding from the ground up. That's what I did!—what the hell have you ever done? Well, except for take a writing course and learn how to write and buy a pen and a pad of paper at the store. And now you're a writer, right? Well, as they say (or, I say?), when in Rome, *be an asshole!* While you're in school, I'll be drawing cocks on the Berlin Wall. I'd trade polished, formulaic sentences for raw emotions and real-life experiences any day. But then, what do I know? I'm not an artist, I'm a vandal. I'm a thief (isn't that what an artist is, anyway?). I'm a punk and a shit-stirrer. You got some shit, I'll stir it for you and top it off with a nasty wad of spit. Pretty, right? Fuck art! Write on walls with Sharpies!

Love Is the Monster Beneath My Bed

What's love for? you're asking me. It's just a simple algorithm that consists of rhythmic thrusts, a slew of yummy McCheeseburgers, and of course the lies that television sets pump into our minds and the images smiling degenerates with big, plump tits and shiny white teeth holding hands create on looming billboards up in the sky. See, love is not real, it's just a mass-produced drug that the jacked-up American corporations are getting rich off of….

So don't believe the lies created by two smiling degenerates up in the sky. Happiness is being sold by the dozen; it comes to us in a vile of mass-produced smiles that feed the downhill spiral of a crumbling nation at the whims of a sacrificial lie.

Hate the Closet Case

I hope you get to know me
<u>before</u>
you hate me. Unless
you're a liberal because
liberals don't need to know
        they just hate!

But don't tell that
to the liberal media because
then they will hate you for it.   Because
        don't you know!
liberals don't hate/

      —Just Saying—

Overboard

If someone falls
overboard

you can reach
your hand out
and pull them
back in

but if you jump
overboard to
rescue them

they'll pull you
down too

The Foundation

Forget your stripes
your colors and your banners
Forget your leftwing preaching
and your rightwing pandering
Forget your cultures
your clubs and your exclusions
We're all equal
We're all great
No matter how big you get
do not forget about the little man
cuz it's the little man that gives you
the power to hate

like the rest of us
We're all equal
We're all great
no matter what side one
decides to take
Forget your gangland warfare
Left or right you're all such fools
for letting the government fool you
like they have
Turn your backs on the ones who struggle
all because they voted
for a different MAN than you....

When I say jump

I don't have a cause
I don't stand for
        nothing
I just wanna live
my life
        but I will fight
        for that
        for the right
to live my fuckin life....

Will You Get Behind Me?

and fight with me
for the right to speak
and the right to be
to exist
and squander diligently
deliberately breaking societal norms

                        it's not a privilege
                        <u>it's a right</u>

capiche?

Will you stand defying
against the corporate breed
against conformity and the like
against the few that shame the good
into being
dastardly things

Fuck the future
today's all that counts

Fuck the past
I only see what's
before me
and what's before me is
a convention for the
mass conformists
waiting to tie me up in
bondage and chains

I care about nothing
I wanna blow up the state
I wanna bomb churches
and drown children in blood
Fuck this culture
and the slimy mutant breed
we need not fear
differences
because differences are what make us
human beings

I care not about
respect and decency
I care not about
politics and political discrepancies
Society tied a noose
and now they're waiting
for me to place my head in the loop
and that
        I will not do
Fuck this system and everyone
who expects me to be
less like me
and more like them

I don't vote
I don't waste my time at
protests and marches
I don't go to mob gatherings
and for that I owe no
apology

because the foolish masses are
lining up like lemmings
and one by one
  two by two
    three by three
      four by four
they're all taking a dive
But me

                I'd much rather
                stay alive

because it's the only way
for me to survive
in a pigheaded state

full of incessant philosophers
and self-righteous politicians
and delusional charities
built upon
the emotions of a
a nation in ruins

I don't have a cause
I don't stand for
      nothing
I just wanna live
my life
      but I will fight
      for that
      for the right
to live my fuckin life....

Will You Get Behind Me?

Live Free &—DIE HAPPY!

Life is boring
when we spend all of our time
in front of screens & spending money
on things we just dont need
      Most people tho
Im sure wud disagree
but fuck em cuz
Im happy living minimally
The only things Ive ever hoarded
Im happy to say
      are books
but Im also happy to say
when I moved I
          gave em all away///

For Sure

      I believe that I don't believe,

      but I can't be certain of it because
      certainties create dividing lines,
            create enemies
            create wars
            create nothing   etcetera.
      So I believe in nothing because it's
      the only way for certain to allow
      for everything….

Blacklisted

I don't believe in heritage
      a friend texted me and said he was going home for passover and i al-
         most said, in return: *no shit, i didn't know you were jewish;* and
         then i would have added, as an afterthought—which is something
         I do quite frequently, send out lingering afterthoughts—*not that*
         heritage is important to me or anything

I don't believe in heritage
because I create my own history
I make my own way in life
I can't live off of the triumphs of
yesterday's heroes
regret the follies of history's villain
my ancestors killing and raping and pillaging
like everyone was doing back then

       killing and raping and pillaging used to be the thing to do way back
           when; everyone was doing it—because they could.... have i ever
           told you how much i just don't fuckin care

Most people though
when they hear me say I don't
believe
they assume I'm bashing their own
set of beliefs
       hey, if you wanna live in your ancestors' shadows, celebrate the fetes
           of your forefathers, plead for forgiveness for the sins of men you
           never even knew, go right ahead. but me, i'm <u>making</u> history ...
           it's easy, you should try it sometime
       just don't expect me to submit and commit to these traditions that
           just seem so obsolete
       do what you want. just leave me the fuck out ... okay?

I don't believe in
sexual orientations
gender exclusive behavior
sexual preferences
       but by all means, i am not stating that you should not believe. these
           are my truths, and they should remain as my true delusions. i
           have the right to not believe

It's all just fabricated
nonsense anyway
a way to divide us up
You got lettuce tomatoes &
carrots
       but to me they're all just vegetables anyway; throw em in the bowl
           and shake em up and pour dressing on top and it's no longer let-
           tuce tomatoes & carrots because now you've got a salad

> we're all just human beings; we all have desires and fetishes and wants & needs—we all want to be different, unique, free to establish a brand-new faction, a practically useless band aid to cover the wounds that were never there to begin with. we all want to have an identity
> is a blanket statement to represent your personal lifestyle really the way to go? i don't think so

Classifications are just ways
to keep us fighting
ways to separate us
to keep us divided
we are all member of the same race
in the end:
>	the human race, That Is
Don't you forget it!

LOVE

I've loved and I've lost
I've come and I've gone
I've been there done that
round & round & round
>	It's sad isn't it? when the
>	whole wide world is obsessed
>	with love.

DeStRoY WhAt yOu lOvE
before it destroys you
>	overdone // overplayed
>	>	luv is so cliché

boring boring boring
I'm sick & I'm bored and I'm
screaming for something more....

Tell Me Something I Don't Already Know

Fuck Sadness

Fuck sadness/Get angry
sadness is a curse that leads to
extreme apathy
whereas anger motivates
when I'm sad I
isolate
when I'm angry
I dislocate the
sun from the sky
throw rocks at squawking missiles
buzzing
through
the rumbling dystopian solar plexus
destroy the stunning
wonderment
of elusive
thunder
set my head on my pillow
and evaporate as
my soul churns
and fades
bedevil the billboards
with menacing force
level the ozone
shatter the coy mutants

with nuclear voices
toy with broken glass
and watch as the inanimate
objects dissipate
and the horrorshow of laughter
disastrous madhatters
running amok through phantom lanes
barrel down in waves of terror
bury the flame
seize the day with razorblades
and electric pen knives
or bury my head in my bedsheets
and wait for the sun to
melt
ecstatic with everlasting tears
forever
cursing the wanton flame
for ever becoming
such a ruminating haze
such a day to fade
such a way to decay
just another way for my
relentless worries to erupt
and demolish
my ever-sensitive volition
and I'm stuck inside of
an endlessly brutal decision
Fuck sadness/Load the pain like
rueful ammunition
and watch as the menacing extensions
distend a hand to
the burning hole
inside your twisting soul
Fuck sadness/Blow up and
destroy|||

Pick

I'm losing a battle I never wanted to fight.
The axe comes down and I think, *What's with all this strife??*
Forced to choose, forced to hate.
Forced to decide my entire fate
in only a few seconds/
What would you have done in my shoes?
I suck under pressure.
Liberal or conservative, make up your damn mind!
Blue underwear or white underwear, I really don't care.
Stop this pulverizing pressure; I'm sick and I'm stubborn
and I refuse to pick a side that I despise/
I refuse to choose a path that is just not right....
I refuse to settle down and have kids.
Stick to the same job year after year.
Pick a preference of politics or be condemned for life.
Come and Hate with us!
Ostracize the opposition/
Come and terrorize!
Throw a cocktail for the name of
Bernie Sanders/
Pick a fight for the name of
Donald Trump/
Be a feminist and look down on everyone
who stands against
Hillary Clinton///
Stand tall for what you believe in.
Believe in me!
Believe in this and that and everything something anything.
Just have faith that it'll all work out in the end.
Choose a class to fight for and
it'll all work out....
<u>With us or against us</u>.
America or Iraq

Israel or Palestine
Man or Woman
Just because I have a dick does not mean
I stand for chauvinism;
does not mean I'm a chauvinistic prick;
does not mean I hate women///
You've got it all wrong....
Just because I refuse to pick a side does not mean
I'm gonna blow up churches on my free time.
So leave me alone and let me not decide in peace!

LISTEN.. to me, please!

I have a lot of ideas, a lot of really great ideas, but nobody cares about it anyway, they're much too happy living in their fascist fabricated realities. They call it Democracy, but we all know the truth about what it really is.
Me, I'm a fascist too, don't you forget it. The only way to get an entire misanthropic race onto the same page is by having only one page to get on to. I get it, I really do: fascism means Death & Destruction for the sorry few, Rules & Restrictions, and no more free-thinking, either—well, that's kind of the point, don't you think?
Well, I suppose it's all about putting the proper leader in charge—one who knows what the people need, one who's oppose to corruption & greed, and one who is, plain and simple, ME. I'd be the ideal leader for the people, don't you see? But nobody does care about it anyway; they're much too happy, as I have said, living in a dream.
Me, I had a dream too; I dreamt of truth. Or was that a nightmare, I don't know. Either way though, you should elect **Jeremy Void** as The government official, The supreme ruling force, The highest dictator of your entire free world. First order of business: Kill Everyone Who Stands Against My Way of Doing Things.

If only they would listen to me, for a change....

Pander Division

Yeah sure
If only you want to pander
to the lowest common denominator
We can surely cut
chop and shine
your artwork
sand out the genuine touch
you added so delicately when
your emotions got the better of you
smooth it down to a furbished finish
and mount it in
Times Square so that
the whole world can see it when
they sit on a stairway that simply goes
nowhere in the end
a stairway designated to sit on
like the bleachers of a basketball game
and watch as the blinking lights flash blink
and flicker
and there you go
it's a work of advertisement
selling you mouthfuls of that brand-new cereal
called Cyanide Crunch
Eat Up, Sonnyboy!

The Night Sky >>>

Do you know how long it's been   since I looked up at the night   sky. Why would I look up there when there are so many flashing lights down here? The night sky is dark and ominous. I look down the street for life == for life that will make me feel safe // for lights that will make me feel calm // for some ruthless distractions || because the night sky is diabolical and dark. Do you know how long it's been   since I   prayed—I mean, really <u>prayed</u>!!! But then, why would I pray for help & comfort & guidance   when I got everything I need   down here!!! The night sky is menacing & bleak. People run amok. Lights flashing blinking. People lights shouting spraying. Do you know   how long it's been since I   had faith   in something   other than   me. Why would I bother with faith when the world is only going to dis   sipate soon enough.… Do you know how long it's been   how long it's been since I cared   about some-thing about someone about somewhere about____. It's been too long since I cared and now I'm scared of what the night sky beholds|||

Mommy, I think I wanna be androgynous when I grow up!

Me: Sex is so boring!

Her: Then yer probly just not doing it right.

Me (thinking about that): Have you ever met anyone who doesn't like pizza?

Her (thinking about that): Um … maybe once. Or twice? I don't know. I mean, I'm sure I have at some point in my life.

Me: Then they're probly just not eating it right! don't you think?

It seems like these days I'm more attracted to the idea of being with a girl than actually, truly, being with a girl. When I pass a hot girl on the street, I think, *Yeah, I would totally fuck her!* but then, when I really, truly, think about what fucking her actually entails, I'm kind of put off by it, to tell you the truth. These days, sex seems like such a filthy act. When I was drinking I rolled around in filth; sex included—and there was plenty of that. But now it's like: **Yuck!** Why would anyone wanna partake in such an atrocious act, anyway? Beats me!

And, not to mention, it's just so boring and uninteresting.

It's just a ridiculous ritualistic act passed down throughout the ages that men and women both participate in. Subtle manipulation, passive/aggressive subterfuge, moving people around like they're Chess pieces and I'm the Player and it's all about **Sex** in the end. *Seeeexx!* sex, sex, sex—SEX! S-E-X———seeex!... What's even the point?

Traditionally, sex is sex. Spice it up by switching positions, roll-playing—you're the victim and I'm the rapist (been there done that)—trying out different kinks, whips & bondage, chains & leather, scratches and claw marks, screaming at the top of your lungs **I'M A LION** while straddling some drunk Punk rocker in a puddle of mud and slop, concealed in the shadow of the stark, green dumpster out back of the venue.... Yeah, been there done that too.

Men: spewing rotten clichés from their mouths. Women, who you'd think would be smart enough to not fall for such a load of oversold crap like they always do (so maybe they aren't that smart, after all): nodding and bowing and perking up at the unoriginal compliment, like: *I'm so happy you noticed!* even though the guy didn't notice anything except for the size and bounce of her luxurious breasts and the V-shaped crevice in between her legs and the way her *booty* sways when she makes her way across the bar—like zeroxed beauty—to mingle with all her friends, to order another drink (order as much as you want babe, so you can get all good an sloppy, or at least enough to fall for my cheesy one-liners that were made up by a sleazy old man with a shriveled-up sack and only half a brain located in the tip of his penis—order the world so that later I can order you to do swirls an splits an spins an twirls, all on my dick when we're back at my place), and of course to fall into the guy's manly embrace—a man who had locked her in his sights at the beginning of the night, as though seeing the world through infrapink goggles, with a lust-seeking missile set in place and ready to be fired outward—a man who would eventually (and inevitably) *boink* her in all of her naughtiest places, in all the most blasphemous positions, carrying on the dirtiest, filthiest, most decrepit tradition this world has ever seen.

And girls know this, too—they're not <u>that</u> stupid. A lot of guys would like to think that they are, because then they wouldn't feel as timid as if they knew they were not as smart as their targets. They want to believe that <u>they</u> are the ones in control of the situation, that <u>their</u> cheesy, overly used lines are the ones that sealed the deal for the night, that <u>they're</u> the only source of the manipulation going on here—because otherwise they'd feel used up and spent like a worthless slut who has only one purpose for the night, which is to fuck me hard, and to fuck me right///to produce pleasure for their greater, more powerful halves. So of course, it's always the guy in charge of the situation. Never the other way around. **Never!** ...   I'm drawing the line on that one.

Although, granted, times have changed and now girls have come out of the closet and admitted to the fact that they want it just as badly, if not more, and I'm sure that intimidates a lot of guys—it sure as hell intimidates me—because now they have to compete for the power and control of the situation and typically they'll always lose. I know I sure as hell lose—<u>always</u>///there's no question about it.

Sex is just a boring, redundant ritual, a losing battle that most try so hard to fight, a game we tell ourselves is luv or lust or somewhere in between or somewhere so far from that it's kind of hard to imagine anything without it—a tradition we pass down throughout the ages, a quest for the most superior lay, a plebian drudgery that the whole world participates in and doesn't think twice about it because they're told that this is normal, this is okay, this is fun, this feels great, this feels <u>awesome</u>, I'm cumming right now, I'm cumming I'm cumming I'm cumming—in case the moans didn't give it away—*ooooohhh* I just came on your leg, and now I think I'm gonna go to sleep, while the girl lies beside me, only partially satisfied by what we had just done———and did I mention it's just another *FUCK*ing game we play?...

Disgusting

Boring

Repetitive

Promoting this ever-so-common Gimme-Gimme-Gimme mentality

Re-enforcing that Me-First attitude

Think with your dick, not with your head, and then you'll be all set in the end….

Why even bother? It's such a futile, disgraceful endeavor that I'm so happy to evade for the time being, or at least until I fall in love———now That's where the <u>real</u> joy falls into place….

Pillage!

Empower yourself

Disempower everything else

A naked man showers in the spray of a hunchback whale

The ocean drifts rolls tumbles & unfolds and sometimes watching it move and swing and sway and splash, makes me wanna escape. Imagine if the ocean could just devour me. I could escape in its rowdy surge. The sea is not nice, it is not kind, it never apologizes, it just releases its predatory roar and lunges & destroys whatever gets in its way. People like looking at the ocean; they think it's quite beautiful. If only they knew just how sinister it really is. It's ugly and gruesome and preys on weaker beings. It's one of nature's biggest, most vicious predators. But if I could ride atop a hunchback whale and feel comfortable enough to bathe in its spray—now, that's complete freedom, I think/// It's that fearlessness, that state of not caring. Just walk through downtown New York City and become immersed and then devoured by the flow of the mob. If I could shower in the spray of a hunchback whale, I could go anywhere, do anything, and I'd be set—nobody could touch me. You can't get screwed, if you don't fear the results....

Identity Crisis

I think I'm non-binary. I don't like sports, and I don't like dolls. Oh no, I'm not a stereotype, but please, oh please, classify me as something, give me a label to ease my mind so I don't feel like such a freak after all. Satisfy my desire to be marked up like a toy for sale, color my face and give me a price. So I've decided that I'm non-binary, because your stereotypes don't contain me in any way. Some days I feel like I'd trade my dick for a pair of tits. Other days I want to trade my left arm for a pack of chips—does that make me a gimp on the inside?

卐

Blinded by hate

it's a broken fate

your worries dissipate

when you place the blame

Exclusive

Challenge the conventions, an extension of dimensions, a sophisticated dilemma. The cultural norm, the status quo, an oblivious bore, an insidious blow. Follow the rules be on time run with the pack make your shoes shine. Exterminate the deliberate demeanor of a society gone mad, shatter the fads, a witless, thoughtless, irrational endeavor—I'd much rather explore elusive misadventures than surrender myself to an exclusive predator.

PC

Don't call me a racist
because I refuse to
abide by the code of
Politically Correctness

Hey
I'm not the one responsible
for mass oppression

I'm not the one trying to
control what we hear and see
I'm not the one putting a ban on
words and images and symbols
I'm not the one telling you
what conduct is suitable for
the culture that we live in

So don't call me a fascist
because I refuse to enforce
an assbackwards virtue
being imposed upon you and me///

In the Big City

I had come to a big city
for the opportunity
They had promised me
more outlets
to help me get ahead/

But what they neglected to tell me
was
here in the big city
there was so much more competition
to hold me back\\\

Lifeless America
Flip the Channel I'm bored

Ever realized that
the people who say they hate
Drama
are usually the ones that
cause it the most?...

Me ...
 —I won't lie to you———
I love drama
love it want it need it it drives me
inspires me
I'm a writer
 after all
and without it
I might just dry up
I thrive on it
need it like
a hyperactive child needs
hysterical activity
like a photographer needs
models or scenery
like a painter needs
a paintbrush

action action action
Romance and Passion
I'll kick the TV in the face
so that the drama eases out
through the shattered screen
and embraces me
and together we'll make sweet sweet
Hate
through a loveless haze

action action action
Romance and Passion
Fuck your short attentions spans
      I've got one too
so let's get together and dance
atop the dead actor's graves
tappity-tapping as we go on
loving and hating
creating drama
every which way
with every pivot and stomp
throwing wrenches
into this passionless existence

Today nobody wants
to experience their lives
because somebody else did it for them
So What's the Point?? ... right

action action action
Romance and Passion
I live to annoy
yes just another dramatic decoy
In the end it's what
makes the world go around....

The Popular Opinion

I get it
The Popular Vote
= success
I get it
Being liked does not
mean you are an
artist
I get it
Lugging pretty shit
down decrepit roads
past dilapidated storefronts
through lanes of waste
and human decay
I get it
Paris Hilton the Kardashians
I get it
I really do

Revolting Sensitivity

Never

in a room I've never been
in a world I've never seen
in a life I've never experienced
pushing through a hole I've never dug

Liberty

Nothing makes any sense
The stories that people tell
The lies we believe
The games that we play
The subtleness that I just can't shake
The moment we decline
The instance we decide
The plunge that comes
at the end of the climb
We're fated to dissolve
destined to destruct
Totaled fucked abused and abstract

Surreal shapes materialize in the face of
tomorrow's dreadful decay
We see the truth in the eyes of
the mongo nuts and the frolicking cunts
The fascist elite weaving subtle deceit
We believe the lies and dissuade the truths
Sometimes it's just easier to submit to
a phony fabricated corny dilapidated tale
too good
too nice
too sweet
too bitter withering scales of lascivious
perpetual perversions persuaded to
believe the versions intertwined by excursions
A stunted cursive version of an
upended reality blurred by love
by lust
by sensations too murderous to be understood
too detrimental to be true
The stories we tell ourselves
The lies with which we dilute the realms
Fallen for another sacrificial distension
We extend our feverish hands
like peering into the plan that
a godless universe has in store for
this wanton demented land

Searching for the Present Ending of a Delirious Mirage

I miss your painted lies
your inebriated disguise
your one-liners and your
wine-soaked eyes

I fall through grotesque tunnels
as I search for
a fumbled past I blacked out
through tortured labyrinths

I wonder
Where the hell did it all
go wrong?
I lit the fuse of
a bombed-out future
and my cuticles are soaked
in streaks of blood as

I scratch out the mirror's eyes
I'm standing in the center of
a flaming highway
I'm free and I'm
spiraling
backwards
down blackened
alleys
as I

search for
a cracked solution

a smashed delusion
a shattered cement truck
rides the
tidal waves of time

and I'm plunging
straight through
what I thought
would never amount to nothing
but a future buzzing with
decay
is relinquishing a tear
in the timeline

of a banshee
screaming just to
DIE
but now I'm alive
and now the future is ripe
and now I fill my lungs with
tar
because that is where
the power lies

Lovelife

I need no one
Surgically disconnecting oneself
from the weakest link
can be disturbing & tricky
But it must be done
and I'll survive the fall
I've hauled my heart over broken glass

time & time again
I think I can outlive another
wasted & broken
heart
I will overcome the turmoil
of one thousand pin pricks
hot & cold body ointments
ups & down in a tortured soul
lefts & rights I lost my woes
This Way That Way
I've done it before
and I'll do it again
I got charisma and style
I think I can outlive & outlast
another splattered lovelife

Cause & Effect

To me
Cause & Effect
seems to be
a foreign concept
How one thing leads
to the next
I find to be
quite astonishing\\\

PANIC ‖ attack

What Happened?
What The Hell Had Happened
I Freaked Out
I Freaked Out I Panicked
I Was Going To The Library
I Was Going To The Store
I Was Going Home
I Don't Know Where
I Was Going
I Was Going Wherever You Directed Me
To Go
I'm In A State Of Distress
Say The Magic Words
And I Might Just
Pass
Out
Press My Buttons Twist My Levers
I'm Wearing A Pea Coat
Tonight
I'm Wearing A Leather Jacket
Today
I'm Naked And I'm
At School
In Math Class
Climbing The Schoolyard Fence
Gotta Get Home
FAST
I'm A Villain I'm A Freak
Wearing My Underwear On My Head
Wearing A **KICK ME** Sign On My Eyeballs
I Don't Belong
Anywhere
Everywhere I Go

It's All The Same
It's All The FUCKin Same
Everywhere I Go
Anywhere I Go
I Flipped Out
Ten Minutes Ago
Five
Four Three Two
ONE
I've Lost My Mind
My Head Is Too High
I'm In The Clouds
Spaced Out As
I Walk
Shrouded With
Emotions
Just Emotional Excuses
To Not Do
ANYTHING
I'm Jittery I'm Tight
I'm So Fuckin Bitter
I Can See My Own Reflection
Everywhere I Look
Everywhere I Turn
Everywhere I Look
You Stand There
Staring
I'm Scared Of
Your Haunting Glare
Losing It
I'm Losing My Freakin Mind
I'm Geeking Out
I'm Seeing Clouds
There Are Birds
Flapping Diabolical Wings
Of Razor Blades

Around My Battered Brain
Help Me
I'm Floating In Space
Help Me Please
I Can See The Nothingness
In Your Disinterested Face
You Don't Care
I Don't Care
No One Cares
Anymore
It's All the Same
I'm Going Insane
Crowded By Thoughts
By Vain Attempts To
Be Somebody Else
I'm A Mess
Says The Zookeeper
I'm A Mess I'm A Freak
I Just Want to Love
But I Find No Reprieve
No Release
No
I Have A Disease
I'm Relieved By Your Flesh
Free Me Believe Me Let Me Be
ME
I Just Wanna Be Me
I Just Wanna Be Me
I Just Wanna Be
ME
I Tell Myself
This Is What I Tell Myself
When
I'm Sitting There
Watching The Paint Dry
Staring Into The Sky

Staring Off Into Space
Staring Any Way That I Can
Except At The Mirror's
Benevolent Face
When I'm All Alone
I Tell Myself
I Wanna Be Me
I JUST TELL MYSELF
I WANNA BE ME
What Does That Even Mean
It's Just What I Say
When I Don't Sleep
When I Stay Up Late
GOTTA STAY AWAKE
Loaded On Caffeine
I Really Just Want
To Be Me
I'm A Mean Kid
Having Come
Straight From The Streets
Or So I Think
But Really I'm Just A
Rich Suburban Geek
Straight From
The Rich Suburban Streets
But I Tell Myself
All I Want
Is To Be ME
Anybody But Me
Will Do In The End
Just Lend Me A Helping Hand
This Is Just
Another Blatant Excuse
To Receive Your Attention
Is All
Just Another

Cry For Help
Lost In The Mail
But I've Been Robbed
I've Been Robbed
I DON'T KNOW WHAT I WANT
Don't Help me
Please Don't Help Me
I'll Help Myself
I'll Pull Myself
Out
Of The Quicksand
I'm Being Pulled Back In
Deeper
Deeper
Deeper & Deeper
Deeper & Deeper & Deeper
I'm Sinking Deeper
But Don't Help Me
Please Don't Help Me
Just IGNORE
Just IGNORE ME
Just IGNORE ME PLEASE
Pretty Please
With A Helpless Dash Of Sprinkles
Splashed On The Matter
Like Quicksand
Just Like Quicksand
You See
It's Because I Don't
Want You To See Me
Falling
To My Knees
Please
Look Away
PLEASE
Avert Your Eyes

I Won't Ask You Again
But Then
It's All Just A Lie
Anyway
They're All Just Lies
I Tell Myself
They're All Just Lies
I'm Telling You
YOU
You You You
About Me
ME
Me Me Me
I Hate Myself
I Wanna Be Somewhere Else
I Wanne Be Somebody Else
I Wanna Be Something Else
I Wanna Be Better
Or Worse
Anything's Better
Than THIS
Than This Predicament
I'm In
I Don't Fit In
ANYWHERE
I Love To Write
I Love To Dream
I Love To Hate
And I Love To Be Me
ME
Me Me Me
But That's About It
That's All That I Want
To Be
In The End
So I Wanna Climb Into

A Cave
At The End Of The Day
Lose Myself
To Nothingness
To Darkness
To A Void
Lost In Space
Floating As If I Got
Nowhere To Go
Nowhere To Be
Nothing To See
You See
That's Where I Wanna Be
Nowhere
With No Wants Or Needs
That Keep Me In Chains
It'll Be Bliss
Pure Bliss
Blissful And Acquisitive
Satisfaction
You'll See
Or You Won't
Because Won't That
Defeat The Purpose
You See
I'm A Villain I'm A Freak
I Hate The Way I Talk
I Hate The Way I Look
I Hate Myself More Than You
Could Ever Hate Me
Whatever That Means
You'll Hate Me
Guaranteed
You'll Hate Me
A LOT
Fuck You I'm A Disgrace

I Know I Am
I'm a Fuckin Disgrace
You Know
You Know I Am
A Disgrace
Wasted Again
On Indecisions
Gotta Get My Jollies Off
Gotta Get My Kicks
Anyway That I Can
Trying To Evade The Law
Cuz Then I'll REALLY
Be In Chains
But That's Just
No Way To Fuckin
Live
GODDAMNIT
It's Just
No Way To Exist
But Then
I Don't Live
I Don't Exist
I'm A Sheer
Nonentity
But
I Must Add
Before You Take Off
I Must Say
Who Cares If You Take Off
Because You Already Have
I Know
I Must Relay This
To You
Why
Because It Completes Me
To

I Must Say This
To You
PLEASE
Why Bother Going Out
Why Bother Going On
Why Bother Making Friends
Why Bother Being Anyone
I'm A Villain I'm A Freak
I Gotta Be Somebody Else
Anybody Else
Destroy Myself
My Image I Gotta
Smash It
Smash It Up
I Can Be
Anybody I Wanna Be
If Only
I Set My Mind To It
But My Mind Is
Broken
Sold On
Broken Theories
Captivated By
Broken Ideas
It's In My
Broken Nature
To Hate Being Broken
And Love It Too
Because
AS I HAVE SAID
I Am Broken
But Then
Don't You Know
That's
Just Not Me
Well Not Anymore

Anyway
So Why Don't You
Just Let Me Be
He Or She
But Just Not Me
No Way Am I
Going To Be
That
Again
Again & Again
Again & Again & Again
I Can't Escape The Facts
They Embrace Me When I'm
Down
& Out
I Can't Escape My Own Reflection
Everywhere I Look
Everywhere I Turn
Everywhere I Look
You Stand There
Staring
I'm Scared Of
Your Haunting Glare
You Just Won't Let Me Go
There Is No Hope
For A Freak Like Me
Do You See My Point
Cuz I Sure As Hell Don't
I Don't See Anything
Except For You
& You Just Won't Go
Away
You Hate Me
Don't You
Well You Are Gonna Hate Me
At The End Of The Day

At The End Of The Day
I Can't Seem To
Relate To Anyone
About Anything
I Know I Won't
I Know I Can't
So I Don't
Because
I Don't Fuckin Know
Anymore
So Fuck The World
I'm Staying Home Today
And Tonight
Too
Because Nobody
Can Hurt Me There
Except For
Well You Know
EXCEPT FOR
Me
It Burns

Killing Time

All I ever do these days is kill time, it seems.

        One of these days, I swear, time is going to retaliate.

                And I'd hate to be there when it does.

I'm Fine!

Something is wrong. But me, I'm all right, I'm doing fine—say it enough times and you'll eventually start to believe it. Yeah, but if I believed it, does that make it true? But yeah, I'm doing okay, I'll even prove it to you too. Just look into my eyes and call me a liar. You can't, can you? Just look into those bright red veins that are traversing the milky white balls—or more like the veins are pink, or maybe they're orange, or maybe even black, or more like lack thereof. I am staring at a wall, watching the Dominos fall/// Watch this: I'll dive head-first into the bricks. Just watch as my fist flies through. With the impact of the supersonic hit the bricks crumble and roll and tumble and crunch and thwack on the stony ground beneath my combat boots/// Watch this: watch me jump, I'm a bungee jumper, plunging into a giant gorge. I'm falling and flailing fast as lightning as I sail straight as a missile and the ground is rising quicker and quicker and I see it coming until the noose catches my fall, catches me dead, and now I'm suspended thirty-five hundred feet above the diminishing ozone layer and I'm swinging back and forth back and forth, but unfortunately, there's no one there that can see me swinging because I'm way too high to be seen, dying faster than I can blink. But I sure can see me; it isn't pretty in the least. Just look into my eyes and you'll see exactly what I mean.

I am not all right >>>

The Story of My Life

I don't know
That's
the story of
my life.
I find I'm in
a place

that I can't help
but hate
& I mean really
really
hate
That's
the story of
my life.
Two days ago
maybe three
I dipped into a
low point
a hopeless wallowing that
is sucking me dry
currently
I'm in a coffee shop
surrounded by
bodies &
voices
& I can't help
but ask
I can't help
but wonder
I can't help myself
from pondering
a lost & hopeless
diminishing thought
that goes something like:
Is it so much to ask
that I can have
a single meaningful conversation
with someone
with anyone
but all I see here
through a desperate haze
are shallow faces

& plastic stances
too vicious & stuck up
to care about what
I've got to say
or maybe I'm just
projecting my own desires
because I don't really care
about what you've
got to say
I'm projecting this need
through desperation I project
a desire to be understood
by all
in the process rejecting
the needs & desires
of all my fellow parasites
We're All So Carefree
& so frikken careless
a bunch of
narcissists needing the
acceptance of others
to feel whole
the acceptance of a race
of hatemongers
waiting in the back rooms
on the back streets
in the back of the
classrooms
looming tall on
dilapidated rooftops
just waiting
just waiting
just waiting for <u>you</u>
to come up to me
& see <u>me</u> for
who I really wanna be

but how you perceive me
& how I'm received
I find no relief
pandering to this blatant need
to be cherished
but not loved
as I perish amid
a locked derelict closet
I'm so lost & disturbed
hurt
deserted & I'm
rather perturbed
Now that's
the story of
my life.
Standing on the edge
of the knife///

Untitled Poem

I feel like I
deserve the best
only what I always get
is far too less/

On This Warm, Sunny Afternoon

I just want to sit outside and
listen to music
I just want to sit outside and be seen
listening to music
I just want to sit outside in tattered clothing
messy hair
sharp sunglasses and
listen to music
You can join me if you want
on this warm, sunny afternoon
and together we can sit outside and
listen to music/
cuz all I wanna do is sit outside and
listen to music
All day long
till the sun goes down
and I can shut down the tunes
and together us two can go
to the Punk rock show
that'll hit this town….

Haunted Reflection

The Mirror Breaks

Fuck everyone
Fuck this town
Fuck this place

The Mirror Shatters

Why the hell not
I mean it doesn't matter
anyway

The Mirror Crumbles

Eaten by dismay
Swallowed by despair
Disjointed & tumbling down

The Mirror Fractures

I flatten the noose
across my neck
and say goodbye to the laughter

The Mirror Glows

I can't take the hollow glare
my eyes cutting through me
my reddened eyes diluted

The Mirror Wallows

My sunken glare
My gaping grin
My pale complexion

The Mirror—— Fuck the mirror!

Dissected by my reflection
I cock my fist and let
my body wreck the frailty

of a forlorn boy searching
for a way out|||

A Traveling Companion

If I were to choose a traveling companion, I'd choose myself. I'm a loner, and I prefer to keep it that way. Otherwise I don't have too much to say in that regard. I'm tired today, and my brain seems to be on strike- - -for the time being. I try to bring it back, to revive it from the dead, but you know, my brain can be quite stubborn at times. If I travelled, I'd go anywhere but I'd go there alone. I'd lose myself to distance. Escape inside my own head. Forget where I'd previously resided, following a stream through my own mind. My head is where I go to unwind. It never seems to buffer, never seems to troubleshoot, although some days it can be quite stubborn and I'm forced to suffer through reality for a bit—that's just the gist of it///

On the Edge

The river devours
all sins
The rapids of
yesterday's storm
form the wakes of
tomorrow's mishaps
I break down at
sunlight
when dawn fights with
blackness
I rack my head like
an electro-sonic
mutation
I hate the way in which
I acted upon
instinctive outrage
I sit down at
the river's edge
My friends
strum the brink of their
guitars
Acoustic deliverance
Brutal memories
flank my epic
awakening
I sink into
the delicious vision
of tyranny
shown through the blur of
a worry like murder
I drink in the sin
The din of an epic rush
The river

rinses my indecisions
I walk on water
deterred by
the derelict drizzle
The river devours
all sins
blistered by
insidious whiskers
I sit here at
the edge of the river

The Last Void Standing

Just for once I would like to meet someone who talks like me, acts like me, and thinks like me

———just so I can destroy his life///

On the Offense

I love being
     offensive

but I hate when people
        take offense

Customer Service

It makes me wonder
how someone like you
could ever work in
customer service/

Live Fast Die Young

Live Fast Die Young,
I said
Live Fast Die Young,
I shouted
Live Fast Die Young,
I screamed
stomping my feet
on the ground
Live Fast Die Young,
I pouted
because I got the first half right
but the other half??
I just don't know what went wrong///

Pedestal People

You're no better than me
Keep riding your high horse
we'll see

I CAN'T

I CAN'T FOCUS

I CAN'T THINK

I CAN'T READ ANYTHING

I CAN'T I CAN'T I CAN'T

GIMME A HAND THRU
this labyrinth of the mind

BEFORE I DROP DEAD
& DIE!

Gratitude … ?

I am grateful for   … How do I finish that sentence? I could easily relay a list of clichés—things I <u>should</u> be grateful for—but it isn't that simple. <u>I'm healthy I can walk</u>. Sure there are a lotta thing I <u>oughta</u> be grateful for, but that's just it: I'm not! Fuck I mean I know there are people rolling around in wheelchairs right now—gimps for life and whatnot———people dying from horrible diseases. I know all this and yet … I'd still trade my life for theirs. This is an honest reflection, right? a lucid introspection, a crapshoot of a dissection. Honesty???? I don't know the first thing about being honest. I'd much quicker stand on my head than tell you the truth. The only thing I know about the truth is how to abuse it, manipulate it so that I <u>seem</u> like the good guy—that's <u>my</u> truth///the ultimate lie…. The greatest trick the Devil ever pulled was convincing the world he was good: the Devil: a master of deception—the Devil: a wordsmith an illusionist a ditchdigger who would trade you dirt for gold///

So, gratitude! What the fuck do I know about being <u>grateful</u>? I'm just trying to be honest here. Honest? right! I'm grateful I'm not you. I'm grateful I don't walk around in your shoes. Even though your shoes are much flashier than my own—my dirtencrusted Nikes. See, I'd rather walk around in beaten, torn, and smelly sneakers than gloat my shiny black dress shoes. Because you, you're a phony, a fraud. But hey, at least I <u>know</u> I'm a bad person!—me myself & I…. Come join our love triangle of Hate///a triangular yank, as you will. Yeah I'm bitter; yeah I'm meanspirited; and yeah I'm a dick. But at least I'm honest about it. Honest? right! See, I don't trust anyone who smiles too much because I smile too much and I smile too much because, well … wouldn't you wanna know?

So I'm grateful for a lotta things. I'm grateful that I never got to know you…. And Thank God for That!

Restless Body Syndrome

I think I got Restless Body Syndrome; I can't sit still I can't stand straight I can't lie idly—I can't quit shaking scratching panting wiggling rubbing shifting. I can't stop moving; my mind is restless, my body uncomfortable. I gotta DO Something sooooon, before I do everything I'm not supposed to do, everything frowned upon—shock and awe, pause and tangle, dangle the losing cause in front of me, hold the moving facet still and secure before I smash the assets of a lastly passive theatrical tantrum. Duly noted I feel unruly uprooted and unorthodox. Distill the boring minutes of a disorderly burden I can't sit still any more than I can forward my chills through a million and one channels that shadow my growing impatience like an anxious wax museum set on top of a hill overlooking a pen of angry dogs…. I think I'm gonna go toss and turn now until I hit my head on the wall and pass out.

Untitled Poem

I can't walk down the street
without someone complimenting
my poetry
I look at the faceless man in the mirror
He winks at me and I simply
hate the sight\\\

More

Why take 1
    when I can take 2

        Why take 2
           when I can take 3

                Why take 3
                    when I can take it all

Self-Destructive Tendencies

First things first:
I'd like to make
a major apology
to the ones that
have ever loved me
taking on a burden

to tough to
        carry
those that cherished me
thought I was something better
smarter
sweeter
a bad boy with
        a silver liver
but my heart was covered in
slits & burns
        so you better be
            ware!

Love is something
I could never see myself
feeling
ever again
I try to shield myself
from all that
delicious hell
        just so delicate &
            stale

To me
that block of slick black ice
which I could never foresee
is all the romance
that I need
Ride it all that
you want
You'll never die amid the
riotous tides
Take my hand why woncha
We'll glide down the sidewalk
skidding to a delightful
yet devious

collision
A Crash-Course to Insipid
Indecisions
I'll pull you close
kiss your brain
lick your nerves

Love is the devil's
burden
It makes me demented
Drugs & Booze
are cool ways to
spend the time
      too
but love makes me
crueler than
you'd ever assume
      I always seem to lose

It brought me to
the lowest levels of
existence
a deformed non-reality
I surfed the hollow wakes
skated the veiny alleyways
the heartless droves
bore the gutless evidence
of a destructive testament
I buried my head in
your cold hands
swam in your blood
till my heart
gave out

Love me once
I'll smack you

Love me twice
I'll stab you
Love me three times
I might just love you back

I will never
ever
go back there
not now or ever
Love makes me mad with
obsession
setting out on another
futile endeavor
I'll shatter the glass
slash the tires
bash the future with
a radioactive jackhammer
I'm lost and broken
destroyed by this caustic affliction
Unreliable
Irresponsible
Negligent & Careless
Rash & Immature
I'm slipping down another
twisted
mudslide

I'm deranged and
confused
Help me before I
get lost in this horrid delusion
I can be rather
elusive
if you only rub the
proper nerves
Punch My Buttons

Twist My Levers
Love always eviscerates
my moral extensions
I'm way too strong
to ever fall for it
        (((for you))) ………
ever again
It's just no use///

Won't somebody
love me
just so I can find another reason to
get out of bed
another worry
another cure
another burden
another useless theory
a demonic presence I'll quickly
learn to
regret

That said
I must apologize
to soften the racing injustices
that barrel through my
explosive head
It's a mental maelstrom
a thoughtful tsunami
When we come face to face
you & I
we will get lost in
another restless
hatred
My eyes like beads
Your eyes like
needles

puncturing me down the
center
My core aches with
utter remorse
Save yourself
from me

Don't light that fuse
I won't refuse
Don't burn that bridge
I won't give you an excuse

Let's walk the other way
before we get
tangled....
Cut our losses
before we become
undone with rage
It's just no use
to feel so thoroughly destroyed

Let's dissolve in each other's
void

Untitled Poem

WHAT AM I
    doing here?

MY MIND
    is shattered

by

        PROGRESSION

Transcend

Isolation

Darkness

I'm changing
I'm transforming

Isolation

Darkness

She's changing
She's transforming

Isolation

Darkness

The world
outside my window
no longer feels so
dim

Isolation

Darkness

My eyes are open
My mind's at ease
For once I feel the comfort
of another body
and for once I let
her in

Isolation

Darkness

This feeling
These sensations
total bliss
Now I know
what the big fuss
is all about

Isolation

Darkness

I'm learning to fly
all over again
I'm learning to love
like a baby hen

Isolation

Darkness

I can drop my defenses now
I'm learning to feel

Withdrawn

You never really realize
how bad it really is
until you're presented with
something so much better

But still I always
abandon the latter for the former
because I'm simply drawn to
disorder

Untitled Poem

Rejected
Dejected
Neglected
Misdirected
I hate you
So save your
rhetorical ledgers
for someone who cares
History has taught me
time&time again
to be wary
of all that you're offering
So this is the last call
the last call for you
to get lost

Sip Hit or Fuck

in with the out-crowd
it's a fascinating joke
out with the in-crowd
it's a bitter sociological hoax
I'm running with my kind
no kind for me
would rather die
than dance
unless she asks me
in which case
I'd laugh
and howl and
hoot and sneer
I'd much rather watch
the mockery
from afar
lost in a relentless
brainstorm
lost
in tomorrow's
zombie rising
people praying on
——not brains
but lame dance music
today
join the crowd
be a drone
a fool
just another sip hit or fuck
another vodka martini
another bumping rhythm
another thumping beat
another hot chick

and another handsome stud
to take home and
FUCK
but no not me
cuz I'm nothing
but
another wasted bum
I'm bored
sitting in the corner
drinking a coffee
till I fall asleep
Wake Up!
or you'll be just another
sip hit or fuck
I mean
I've had my fun
many eons ago
I've had my thrills
and now I'm going
home

Giving Up

I don't wanna be a poet anymore
I don't wanna be a writer or an artist
or a philosopher
I just want to spend the rest of my life
in the shallow end
like the rest

What's the Big Deal?

Pick on me once

It's not a big deal

Pick on me twice

It's not a big deal!

Pick on me three times

It's not a big deal!!!

Pick on me four times

It's Not a Big Deal!!!

Pick on me five times

IT'S NOT A BIG DEAL!!!

Pick on me six times

It's not a big deal

    It's Not a Big Deal

        IT'S A BIG FUCKIN DEAL!!!

Stimuli

I seem to have
an energy deficiency
constantly needing
artificial supplements to
proactively counteract
where I lack in
internal stimuli

L.O.S.E.R.

once again I felt the cold, sharp, brutal sting of rejection

I was once rejected

      <u>because</u>

           I was afraid of being

rejected

Dumb luck
    being stuck in this
    useless
    human body
    for all of
        eternity/
has it that

        I'm an easy target
to reject
            I'm an easy target
   to neglect

It's rather easy for me to be
     <u>abused</u>

Girls know it too
Guys use me like a tool

Avoided
   Ignored
      Disrespected and
         disparaged
I take part in this
losing battle
           a battle to
           take back control
knowing all too well that my fate
has got a plan of its own
      consisting of
me being socially mauled slated & demurred
time & time again

        Knocked around like a
ping
    pong
        ball

back & forth I rack the wall
<<< the paddle >>>
   <<< the wall >>>
      <<< the paddle >>>

So now I'm feeling rather
              dis
                      couraged
surmising a blasted tsunami of
hope-shattering doubts
        shrouded with
        hollow taunts and
        shallow remarks

Terminally lurking

        deep
        deep

in the shadows of
a dystopian society
brimming with
        waste and
        decay
like a rotted apple
decomposing from the inside
          !! OUT !!

Dive headfirst into

        the throng of
            flashing lights

Run smashing crashing through

        the mass of
            sparkling glitter

the ever-so-delighted passersby
once again delivered
through a fog of
thoughtless
       endeavors
              another wanton
              misadventure
I set out on at the peak of the
       evening
       in decline

They laugh and they
chatter
       They laugh
       and they chatter

laughing at the
              <u>freak</u> >>>
that is **me**
       not another
       lucid ideation
           <u>not again will I</u>
           <u>dream dreams that were</u>
           <u>never meant to be</u>
           <u>dreamt</u>
               <u>not again will I</u>
               <u>bend over backwards for</u>
               <u>somebody I'd</u>
               <u>only just met</u>
or somebody I'd known for years
who <u>still</u>
doesn't see
       what I'm worth

        Me,
with my yellow, damaged teeth
and red-splotched pale skin
but with eyes that radiate like
crisp
      radiant
          laser
              beams

bright & blue as emeralds
but blank as
a white slip of
printer paper
         waiting rather patiently
         to be
               defaced
once & for all >>>|||

And I won't look back
again & again
            <u>not again will I</u>
            <u>gaze into the past</u>
            <u>surrender the present to</u>
            <u>a dissatisfied yearning for</u>
            <u>something that can never be</u>
                <u>changed</u>
       <u>will</u> never be the same
           again

and thank god for that!

And then I actively erase
    the intimidating void
by running lines of whiteout
        over my
            withdrawn face\\\

But in the end the cold, sharp, brutal sting
    of rejection
sinks ***deeeep*** into
        my skin
like it always did—<u>always</u>
        and forever
I lie in the empty, wasted lot
waiting for somebody to——

But I know they never will
        <u>not again will I</u>
        <u>fall victim to</u>
<u>dreams</u>

because in my world
I'll never find my
    reprieve

Soundly I lie awake

Don't think
    I can't think
        I don't wanna think

Thoughts of regret
    Thoughts of self-loathing
        Thoughts of disappointment

fill my mind
    when I'm all alone
        Thoughts of remorse

burning me to the bone

I can't stand my reflection
    I hate my reflection
        My reflection stings

Don't sleep
    I can't sleep
        I don't wanna sleep

When I close my eyes
pained memories fill my mind
When I close my eyes
all I can think about is
    dying
        driven by
                    thoughts of
                    suicide

I mean

don't you?
    think about dying
all the time
        when you close your eyes   at night

Goodnight
    Sleep tight
        Don't let the bed bugs   **BITE**

because they bite

because they're biting me

because they do bite
and they're biting me

in all the wrong places
   ... deep ...
   ... deep ...
      so deeply
      &
      sincerely
they bite me till

I fall asleep....

It's only a
disturbing dream
Soundly I lie awake
waiting for that
precious prick
of a thousand swarming needles
ripping into my skin
   I wait for it
     I live for it
       I lust for it
         the pinch the pull

so grotesque
&
devious

like orgasmic bolts of

lightning/
    striking
    delightful
    cataclysmic
    spectacular
    mind-numbingly
      <u>dull</u>
all the senses are active now

Like Galactic Creepy Crawlers
acting
like a catalyst
for disaster
like a supersonic surge of
unpalatable actors
working against
the Will of God

Who the hell
are you working for??
        anyway

Blasted now

I'm falling
        through turbulent hoops
I'm falling
        into flaming laundry shoots
falling
        I'm falling through

a mental maelstrom

a devious thought process

a derelict brain
        My anguish
        My pain

comes to life
    at the edge of the knife
    when the nighttime peaks
    as the dawning of a brand-new day
    stolen by an insidious thief
    breaks in half
        shatters like glass/

Now ripped apart
my past reaches its twisting head
through
the clutches of time
such an ungrateful beast
like kicking a dissatisfied clock
    in the face
& breaking all of its teeth
        in the process

Just another product
of
what some would call
a diseased mind
      spewing faulty logic
all across the land

and then

my   lights   go   out >>>

                              **What a glorious way
to spend the night!**

Untitled Poem

Just for once
I wish I
could just
take my own
advice

To love me

I know what hurts
and I know how to hurt
I don't want to hurt
Nor do I wanna make you hurt
But the tears of being burned
always appear in the eyes of those I hurt
Every day it hurts
to know that I'm the cause
of your being hurt
I'm sorry that it hurts
to love me
when it only hurts
to love me
cuz it always hurts
to love me
and I see that it hurts
to love me
But I can't stop hurting
the ones who love me
and it hurts me to know
that the ones who love me
and who I love in return
will always walk away feeling so hurt

Thought Police

I know what you're thinking
It's a talent
I can read people
so I know what
you're thinking

You're thinking everything that
I'm thinking
and then some
and I hate you for
thinking that

What I Get Back

They say you get back
what you put out
but all I can put out is
cynicism and negativity
I'm depressed
sick of the mental regression
a fragile digression
I'm loaded up on
agile explosives
Gun powder love
is all I got to spread
Anger instead of affection
Defuse my hatred
Dilute my infatuation with
otherworldly infractions

A deafening tantrum
awaits

Stupid

i am goin to do somethin stupid, its just how i get my kix

Illegal

I can't break the rules >>> **I can't!** But sometimes I do. You see, I have this utter compulsion to create disorder, but then afterwards I'm immediately driven to mediate the situation, to gently stroke the waves of confusion and disarray until they settle,,,, to caress the misanthropic desert where sand storms roil and terrorize the great plains on which the cacti perch, till the tumultuous, stirring wind fades away to allow a serene, soothing breeze to take its place hereafter. Until the raw, brutal, devastating turmoil settles and we can now go home feeling safe—safer than we were, that is. See, I'm not sorry to offend but, I'm happy to make an amends. So believe me when I say: I'm feeling rather conflicted right now, quite indifferent, totally ambivalent, and a tad-bit disheveled—I'll be the first one to flip over the sailing ship, and the first one to dive on in and rescue all my flailing crewmates from their impending deaths, and then later I'll claim that my rash decision-making was merely incidental and I promise you that it'll never   happen   again. Only, I'm lying—<u>completely</u>!—for it'll **_always_** happen again—again&again&again/// I mean: fuck it, right?? rules are meant to be broken! and laws are meant to be ignored!... Because there ain't no crime if there ain't no law…. So fuck the cops! roll em around in dirt, kick em in the teeth, beat them till they're black and blue and bloody—but just please don't inform them of these deceitful thoughts I'm having because I can't afford to face the repercussions of such an act.

I don't know how to be

I don't know how to be
I exist
only
in an inflating thought
I'm thoughtfully devoid
I can't exist
The now is ebbing
fast
the future is looming
the past is dimming
quickly
The world is brimming
with commotion
noisy and explosive
I sit in a bubble
following an erratic train
through layers
of braided consciousness
decaying
stuck
forfeiting a life that was never
born
I'm alone
on this timeline
Alone on
this tumultuous stalemate
I'm a dullard
broken
holding onto
something
that never quite developed
Enveloped by sin
embracing the

chaos
ventriloquist living
Trilling about
in a hole that I can't
get out of
Bracing with all my strength
something that has recently
perished
I don't know how to be
I'm hugging the days
of degenerate scum
The history of a loosely standing
quickly demanding
bashfully sporadic
practically nonexistent rebellion
of a kid
with too much loaded devotion
Yesterday is gone
I'm grasping for the wanton
activity
I'm dismissing today's
ammunition
I'm shielding my eyes
my face
my fated travesty
from tomorrow's
mysterious titanic blast
I don't know how to be
Only in the past am I
a living being
I don't know how to be

Structure

All my life everyone said I needed more structure; they said that's what I needed in my life.... Well, fuck structure! They tried to set me up with classes: I got high. They tried to schedule me appointments: I got drunk. I flunked outta their precious schools. They said go to school; they told me to go to school; they demanded that I go to school   school....   School will offer you more structure, they said.... Well, fuck structure! I didn't need systems; I needed derailments. I didn't need to focus; I needed to eradicate systems. They said if only I had more structure then I might stay out of trouble; I might do better. They gave me deadlines to adhere to : : : schedules order & control || control CoNtRoL CONTROL == totalitarian control....   I'm right you're wrong! they told me. They TOLD me! They tried to drill it in to my head. I'm right you're wrong || I'm right you're wrong || I'm right you're wrong\\\ im wrong im wrong im wrong! Then let me be wrong, goddammit.... Just let me be wrong, For Fuck's Sake||| It's my life == I Reserve the Right to Be Wrong. IT'S MY LIFE, not yours. It's My Life, NOT YOURS. It's my life, NoT YoUrS- - -so let me be wrong. Just let me be wrong, for krissake! I never needed structure; structure was always what pushed me over the edge. I needed Freedom and Chaos and Beauty and Disorder and Undiluted Romance & Passion. It was [is] what I strived [strive] for == it was [is] my life's soul driving force. It was [is] the thing that made [makes] life worth it || made [makes] it just a little bit more bearable. I thrived [thrive] on the absence of control///the lack of structure.... If you wanna instill a sense of control, then do it to your own life. Create your own goddamn systems. Because I've got systems of my own == which help guide me through your societal prisons///the ones you've made to keep people like me in chains. I'm systematically unpredictable || a pressing force of indestructible, untouchable, incorruptible mania that spreads its wings and flies away/// Because with the lack of systematic control, I feel like I Can Be Me for a change. So let me spread my wings and fly : : : maybe someday you'll be able to fly alongside.............

In This State

In this state
my patience thins
my filter diminishes
So don't call me
a prick
an asshole
a worthless twit
Because it's not me
it's you
and in this state
of oblivion
I can finally see
the truth
and in this state
of delirium
I can finally say
Fuck You!!!

Time!

Time is my mortal enemy. It's not even real, it's a man-made construct. And yet I stab it and shoot it and kick it in its ticking head. I may have won the battle, but time will always win the war.

My Love & Deceit

What we have in common
mostly
            ME
So I wonder
with all these incessant
self-obsessions
is loving for me
really in remission
Please I just wanna feel
something really real
but feelings are just
intangible dealings
I reach out
look into the core
of my blackened heart
play my part
know where to start
My soul just feels so callused
& scarred
Hardened by years of charred living
But then I convince myself of
all these hopeless yearnings
cuz nothing beats it:
My love & deceit///

To Hearts Unknown

blitzed&belligerent
      I think I'm
      Checking Her Out

Disintegration
It's a futile
tug
Of War
Will you catch me
when I fall
into you
like snow
When I crash through
the walls you so gently
deploy
I'm mutated I'm delusional
It's a ploy
My Love
    <u>for you</u>

Crumbling
like the
meandering dream
I reach out
My Love
    <u>for you</u>

I will be more
some   day
one day maybe
I will explore you
Adored by the mirror's glow
I deplore my own skin

So sick of this burning
nature of mine
this undesirable irony
I have to fight
every time you come around

This inexorable lust
This hatred I feel
This blatant nature
This damaged dereliction
I'm destined
to be no one
maybe someone
You'll just let anybody
come near you
  won't you

Only My Love
you fear
Treated Like a Mere
disease
like a lost pup
needing
wanting
a home but you
will never know the
sheer passion
I feel
& for that
I'm sad to say
in another world
 on another planet
  in another broken
fantasy

I watch & dream
that one day
My Love
will become real

        Just Me & You

Sorry

                              I'm Sorry For A Lotta Things
                              But I'm Not Sorry For Being Me

My Apologies

I'm not sorry to offend, but I'm happy to make an amends.

Untitled Poem

For the crime of
not paying any
attention ____
May god be your
witness/
Sir
I know not what
I do....

Hysterical Resolutions

The Sky Tells No Whys

Down cavernous tunnels
we walk
Across shallow waters
we fall
Into mountainous zones
we fumble
Through dower roads
we tumble
Inside of powerful coves
we ventures
Up skeevy trails
we cower
Down lonely archways
we follow
Into swerving dungeons
we wallow
Across crying meadows
we drift
Around thriving alcoves
we tread
The dead of night
swimming in shattered seas

we revel in the madness
brought on by
the tears of a crying sigh
Denial in the daytime lie
A wafting crater succumbs
What has he done
Through the battered sun
we fly

On My Mind

I've got a lot on my mind….
But I won't tell you what///

I mean
with a name like **Jeremy Void**
what the hell do you think
I'm thinking about?

Wretched Neon

I'm lying
        in a bank
by the sea

I'm finding destiny
        in an undecided
dereliction

I'm Broken
   I'm disturbed
I'm destroyed
      and I'm hurt

My fates are crying
My worldviews are dying
My life
   spiderwebbing through
a dissipation
   of cruel tales
that slip right through
the tips of my fingers

falling
   Catch me before
   I connect
with the concrete ocean
   on the brink
of nonexistence

I slip through the cracks
At war with
   the monkey on my back
I cashed in the chip
   on my shoulder

burning a hole in
   my soul
like
     a smoldering hot
poker
   I'm swollen with
dismay
   fading

      away

Taken by solitude
a crude destruction

Like an unbreakable mirror
I come Face
              to
                      Face
with my distorted
              shadow

bloated
        &coy
I live to annoy
    the youth of a faceless
plague
                      draped in
shattering glass
Listen as I

                      pray

My words are getting staler
Listen to me why don't you
Listen as I

                      shout

at the burning bush
Radiant
        it echoes   verses

of two crumbling birds

They try to fly away
          but a lone
skipping stone
          jumps up
and kills em both

And I watch as
          the feathers disperse
spiderwebbing beneath
          the laughing moon
Bright and disturbed
                they trickle downward
like
          a blooming flower

The dawn of a forgotten night
          ripples   and
plunges

                and I sit
                beneath
the rising sky

as a million beautiful stars
          blink out
and the sun burns
          a hole in

the universe///

A Sick Mind——

Now
take my darkest poetry into
consideration
for just a minute
——the stuff that talks about me
——about me being an insidious teenager
——about me being a twisted, ill-minded adult
——with a desire to tell you lies
——with a desire to lose my own mind
——on all things hedonistic
——and magical and disgusting
————things that only surmount to the blackening of
————my own eyes with a pasty, glistening charcoal-like
————substance
————that holds them in its grasp
——————just like a cradle
——————holds
——————a baby
a day shy of becoming
too old to be alive
——with a desire to break down walls
——to kick the consumer in the balls
——to break his face and turn his eyes
————into ice cubes
—that I'll smoke like crack
——————having a blast as I watch
——their pupils disintegrate
——beneath the flaming torch
right before
I touch it to my own eye——
       You Know I Once Heard That
       If You Touch the Ember of
       Your Smoldering Cigarette Butt

    to the Pasty Whites of
    Your Eyeball It Will Erupt
    Like Dynamite
    cool, right?
    ——I've always wanted to test that theory
    ——who wants to be my Guinea pig
    ————we'll have some fun won't we

But I'm not demented
I wish harm on no one
In fact I'm a very happy person
I'm quite cheerful quite honest
I'm a fast-talker who will wrap you in vines
of hopeless deterrents so fast
——that you'll probably just wanna die
as a result
——and it'd be my pleasure to
——supply you with all the proper tools to accomplish
such a fete
————think of it as a pair of jumper cables
————jumpstarting your career in
suicide
You know what happens when you commit suicide right
you die—lights out and you can forget about
<u>everything</u>—that's the best part I think....

But I'm not a sick person
I'm not sitting on a park bench
with a limp neck thinking about how much
life sucks as I scribble down words of destruction
on page after page
——mental deterioration is an equally valid way
——to spend your time too
———by the way....

I will be marveling at the young boy
not more than 5 years old
pushing the even-younger girl
back and forth on the swings
——it's probably his sister
————I wonder if the boy knows about
————what she and I did last summer
————I hope not
————he could very well have a fit
—————a tantrum screaming and yelling for
his mommy to come
and save him
like she did the last time
—and the time before that
————I wonder too if the boy knows about
————what she and I did last winter
—————his mommy and I
went on a killing spree
our weapons of choice: a toilet brush
and the smell of expired perfume
——————————that's what!

I have a sick mind
is all
I'm not a sick person
I just happen to
find these things hilarious
You see
the world is a rather broken paradise
——that I think is absolutely fabulous
———and I wanna roll around naked in
————all of life's
—————grit
The earth is always
spinning and it'll never stop
———well I hope it does someday

———in the process flinging the masses
———straight for
——————————————the sun!
————now wouldn't that be fun
which makes it quite hard to not
crack your head open
every time a mailbox comes
whizzing past your car
a hundred expired perfume squirts
per second
————and your skull will fracture
—————the wooden panels
—just in a day's work

I'm not hanging my head and thinking about
—dying
all the time
——but rather
I'm laughing and
thinking about dying—
        all the time
It's the only way for me to live
——and plus I'd never miss a chance
———to fuck with the masses
——————it's the only way
——————for me to get by
and by that I mean
diving down a beautiful, winding mudslide
littered with dead fetuses

because otherwise I'd truly be
dying
        all the time

I didn't claw my way
out of my mother's womb

―――――truth is
――she forced me out
――I had no choice in the matter
just so I could curl up and die/
I pulled myself out so that
I could instead derive pleasure
and comfort
        from displeasure and discomfort
like   say

curling up and dying   for one….
       ―just in a day's work

Phantoms

I don't feel right
about this
anymore
Lock the door
Turn off the lights
Keep the noises down
Stow away in the seams
of a dream meant for two

On the Road

The stolen car moves
glides
slides thru the dusty fog
as I ride down the road
on my way home
to a bed I'll never know
to a world I have forgotten
to a life I have strived against
to a lie of 1,000 faces/
Midnight the fog
drifts & fades
to & fro
the road twists & turns
& I find myself
like a vague thought
lost in a vain transition
I find that I'm wondering why
what
who when & where
I ever went wrong
& for that I'm losing steam
cruising down a broken lane
hatred glimmering deep down within
like internal acne creeping out of me
& I might die soon
but when I do, be sure
to hold me in your heart
like cancer——

It's all that I'm worth....

Pop'd

There is a slew of bubbles
floating outside my window
and I want nothing more than
to pop each one of them....

tainted tapestry

beauty
molested
infested with
confusion
fuse the feather
with dirt-encrusted leather
wandering down
slanted alleys
spinning the bullet
shaving the mullet
i can't feel my
gullet
i stamp the puddle
watch the water
stumble
fumbling with the night
quite a
devious sight
the derelict carries a child
the junky wears a smile
the ballerina
smashes the tiles

all the while i sit back and
act out of defiance
i'm too shy to be riled
listening to the knife as it
brings me straight to cloud 9
the gunshot sounds
all over the town
i'm bound to astound
the feather sits on
the steaming kettle
disheveled and mean
i send the injured birdy
straight up into the sky
as life eviscerates the times///

Bed Time

I could go to sleep forever
and then I'll wake up

and I'll never sleep again\\\

The Sky Speaks

I try to do the right thing
        //if I can afford it

I try to do the wrong thing
        //if there's no one there to report it

I try to be me
        //if there are no negative repercussions

I try to stay free
        //as long as I can do it my way,,,,

Deep-Fried Love

Midnight
the music plays
we walk the streets
going nowhere
going somewhere
we might be going there
but in the end we go
everywhere we want to go.
It's in our unruly nature
to follow the red brick road
that traverses through
the darkest corners of hell....
We go up we go down
we follow the flaming soldiers around
as they fight each other to the death///

Throw gas in the water
Melt the whales to charcoal
Pave that path to hell
as we surrender lay down our guns
and watch as a nation burns down around us.
We'll fight till the last man survives
and then we'll fight some more
as we thrive on mayhem we thrive
period——we thrive on death
and in death only survivors perish
and in death only the slayers of hearts
can grasp the madness
that grabs our love and surrenders
us to death/// In Death we die....

Useless

This is the state I lapsed into
when I knew everything was right
but I felt like everything was wrong
and the fog of another loaded wet dream
settled over me with a renewed vigor
and my knees folded
as I prayed to the poisonous toad
to help me get over this mental bog
I fall into when the time becomes slotted
with pin pricks and itches
My depressive warden is enforcing
oppressive hypocrisy
down my spinal cord
I'm singing in the rain as the raindrops
cut razor slashes in my
eyes

I'm balling on hysterics
rampant with tremoring deliriums
My mind races when you pinch me
in the right spot
My soul
dwindles when you
look at me
under the right
light
I'm fighting the night
watching the stars all
in the sky
die when I claw at
the surface of the moon
The sun shines through
but in my tormented gloom
I thoroughly disuse the whys
of a lost & wasted generation
I'm frantic and benign
The droning morning, ripe with rising light
The festering afternoon, bright with fright
and sad enough to run scampering
down wanton deserts too stale to saturate
properly
The descending night sky blossoms
and blooms
devouring the ill perfume through
its cataclysmic snout
I feel misused
mistreated by diseased leeches
fumbling for relief
jerking for release
holding the pistol of a discordant
orchestra
close to my chest
the trigger rests beneath my

underdeveloped tongue
of spiteful raw energetic systematic
magnificently magnetic
catastrophes
You sold me on your
masterpiece
I laugh at the wasted feces
of a lazy feline predator
searching for deliverance amid
a terror-induced circumference
The lonely men shed tears to the tune of
moaning whores riding a manpig's glorious
pecker in high-definition
on the face of a screen
It's a window to the soul
a mirror to the world of dreams
an hourglass counting backwards down
a pedantic mocking buzzing
as times slowly churns
and churns
to a complete and total standstill
as the wasted few
try to dissuade their useless minds
a brutally challenged tool at that
from ever interacting with
a dilapidated public
pissing their names in the snow
while the plows wipe clean the slates
and our fate swells with misanthropy
and our confusion grows into a fading
monotony of X-rated tyrannical
monopolies where we monopolize
our minds
and disenfranchise
the thought police
contract drones to aid us in

any unemployable, futile infraction
that brackets tears
and rackets fear
and cracks open beers
and we whack open brain cells
on a shell of useless, uninteresting theories
of an elusive, dreary
sacrificial parody
that shines light on the dark places
of our lives
So that we can see and navigate our way
through
the shadows of our minds
My eyes bleed when the light tears through
My heart feeds when the sky veers ruefully
down lanes lined with razor blades
and shotgun shells
and dirty needles
and blown up condoms
and dead fetuses with eye protruding
from their underdeveloped skulls
and finally
my mind needs nourishment so badly that
the diverging mass public
can never measure up
Sometimes I feel like I'm
measuring the weight of my
own dick and the length of my
own pinky finger
and the depth of my
own underdeveloped
soul
Store It in an Envelope for Safekeeping
and When I Die
Please Fold It into
a Paper Airplane and Send It

Sky High so that maybe
just maybe
I can make it to heaven
and my soul will forever have
another losing battle to
pit itself against
It's my dying wish to never
surrender///
Just mail me to the sun
and watch as my core turns to embers
Why bother?
It's just another worthless endeavor
to set out upon

Pedantic Ransom

Ma
nip
ul
late
me
before I
er
rad
dicate
a loaded vacuumed
alibi
I bribed the
cor
prate
fangwhores
I lie like an
alli

gator
Driven
to behave
par
taking
in sly
inter
ractions
minus the
malad
justed
I talk to bendy
spinal
cords
I can't afford
to
wor
ship
your lord!
I'm a bratty kid
a man
amid
a mental
war

Evacuate!

I'm getting some really weird vibes today. EVACUATE! Evacuate! evacuate! before it's too late, before it's too late, before it's too late, and there's just no escaping the tumultuous tug of lust and desire and everything else that'll set your brain on fire, turn your mind upside-down, run screaming stark naked through flaming churches while babies have ground-shaking tantrums all around you. EVACUATE! Evacuate! evacuate! before it's too late, and it is. Too late. For this. So you better run and hide if you know what's good forya…. Run & Hide! run & hide! RUN AND HIDE……. Fuck me I'm suffocating beneath the life-threatening pressure—all these voluptuous, deceitful fumes that are applying their own brand of devious terror along the ridges of my tortured and decaying heart, ripping me apart from the inside out with toxic, insidious notions of self-righteous, self-destructive, self-loathing concepts that seek to destroy me in every way possible; I'm riding the tidal of waves of manic explosions…. Just let me off let me off let me off—LET ME OFF THIS FUCKIN COASTER AS I SPURN THROUGH THE AIR LIKE AN AIRBORNE STONE AIMED AND ZEROED IN ON YOUR SKULL!!! crash break and scatter … this was not what I signed up for … not the plan I had agreed upon in my prior dreams of glory, what a horrific story that turned out to be … the floor drops out from beneath me and I'm crumbling outta control in a downward-spiral-like storm. Because it is. Too late. For this. For me. For this for me for this for me for this for me…. Fuck me I'm done for.. Again.. and Again.. and Again.. Overtaken by impulse! Again!!!

Untitled Poem
with Anonymous

My sunglasses melted

but they didn't put out the sun

I'm lying on my back in the

rows of tulips that haven't bloomed even though it's May

I feel a nefarious itch tearing through my brain

And all I can say is I feel alive and dead all at the same time

I listen to the rhyming blue birds as they quake through the devouring sky

And again even though it all amounts to nothing in the end, I praise the first sunny
        day I've seen in New England in a long time

So I say to you:
        Goodbye///

Bible Stories

I stand in a crowd
of loosely swaying bodies
The band plays loudly
maybe annoyingly so
but I'm here
        now
            and there's just
no going back

I'm simply flustered with
exhaustion
  limply stomached
  two seeds
of adrenaline-soaked flowers
that are blooming crevices
through
  my disorderly
    soul
I'm in the midst of
indecisions
   Part of me
wants to
  go home
while the other part
   more logically driven
knows
  I've got no home
to go to
   when the sky shatters like
A Drastic Surge of
Sheer Power
   I'm blasted through
time warps

Take me to
the past
  hold my hand
  as we demand
some <u>real</u> action
     to be stamped out
like a fierce, fiery garden
where

   Adam bit into
a devilish apple

and Eve peeled off
>		her own face
a horrific mask
to cover up
    her shotgun-wielding
Siamese
twin
>			hidden behind
layer
after layer
      of a grotesquely woven yarn
to conceal
her <u>real</u> agenda

I know it's a <u>real</u>
dilemma
      how

the singer prances around
a burning bush
        as hot as
        the sun
which God had
planted as
      a <u>real</u>
decoy

>			a sinister ploy to both destroy and annoy a coy-looking universe loaded with naked little boys running around in a furry of burning toys///

It was all
only in
      a day's work

But don't call me a jerk
or I might just
        go berserk
all over your Kentucky-fried
face
              Don't say that I'm

lame because
            only I hold the truth
It comes locked inside of a
loosely woven
dance session
              Today's Lesson:
                  How to do "Ring
                  Around the Rosy"
                  and do it right ...
for krissake

because my standards and
expectations
        even exceed that of
the *Über Manch*
            with his
flamboyant cape
that flaps and rakes
like actual wings

              He <u>thinks</u> he can
              fly
                  but

it's only the
brown acid
        whispering devious lies
inside of
his shriveled-up and dying

brain
     promises that keep him
rather insane!

He's plummeting in
haphazard spirals
         Up Up & Away
he goes

      plunging

      through

      fiery

      hoops

The *Über Manch*
the Super Man
the Lewdest
     Deviant
he collides with
crass
        pavement
CRASH BASH SMASH

But that's quite okay
     because he's got
another eight more lives
     to go
So Let's Go >>>

Conversation

I want to talk to you until your head explodes.

Royally Fucked

Assume nothing. Unless, of course, a cop pulls you over and demands that you assume the position. Arms out. Hands flat against the roof of the cruiser. Legs spread shoulder-length apart. Butt in the air. Cop standing behind you, feet planted firm on the ground, holding his dick—I mean his pistol—I mean his gun—I mean his dick >>> Yes, <u>his dick</u>! Talk about getting fucked by the law.... They tell you to assume nothing—because you just never know, right?——— well, unless you got ol' Johnny Law barreling down on your ass. Hit the brake. Veer to the side. Put the car in park. Wait. Only speak when he addresses you. Answer all his questions honestly, talk softly, exchange the necessary pleasantries that this situation calls for, always say please and thank you and yes sir, breathe normally, act normally, be normal, don't let on to the fact that you're having a manic episode, that you're a skitzoid in heat, a horny deviant on the prowl, that you're driving with a suspended brain, an expelled heart, you lost your soul in a game of poker—— Don't let him know or he'll force you to assume the position, discharge his big, black, firm stick and hit you over the head with it until you die. Assume nothing and never surrender, you're worth more than a battered corpse.

When in Doubt

When in doubt
buy a pen
steal a pad
of paper
stand on your head
count to ten
when the midget screams
shout out the most obscene
verses of absurdism and tweens
doing upside-down sneezes
on tissues made of overgrown pubes
tell someone it's your birthday
have them buy you a cake
then as a parting gift
do your diligent duty
as a paranoid human being
by punching the man in
the nads
the woman in
the pads
give the brats a cake full of
razors and cherries
that are set on repeat to
EXPLODE
IMPLODE
or DETERIORATE through
candy-coated eyeballs
like an ice cube placed neatly in a sling
swirled and fired across three lanes
of staggering traffic
and then the cars on the right
suddenly do
an insanely bold U-turn

that pushes all the other cars
particularly the ones on the left
off of the grassy mole that seesaws
rapidly and out of control
like an ocean having smoked
way too much crack
but behold the epileptic whale
that panders to a broken audience
of only one
sea monkey
that cracks its knuckles
lacks a shovel
and snaps its wagging tale
which in effect
flings every flipping car out of
the slowly ripping ozone layer

When in doubt
show the bastards that you know how
to dance like a cow

Ode to Chaos

There's nothing like
spiderwebbing opportunity
when anything is
possible
Life—at your fingertips
The future
dissipating
Branches breaking
My fate evaporating
I watch the full moon

spraying translucent gloom
over the lucid meadows

The hawk doesn't mind
if it meets its demise
It just goes on winding and
threading
its way through the
vacant sky like
        an airborne torpedo

We sit in a safe place
    afraid
of what
will happen to us
next
But we must embrace
this seldom force
before we dissipate///

I chuck a stone
It goes up curves and comes down
and
            crashes through
the misty fog
I stand in the

fiery field of lost
dreams
      spanning
            ancient
overcast across the land

I walk on the water
when the moon is right
Through the labyrinth

of triangular
light
                    I crest the
decrepit shadow
Going Nowhere in the end
The perched owl yammers
I stand

amid the nothingness

feeling oh so blessed
that I know nothing
and that I've just got nowhere left
to go >>>>>>

Untitled Poem

Broken-eyed stare
Stressful layers
Brown-bottled geeks
Wandering thieves
Lowlife laundering
Desolate ponderings
Fellow negativity
Hopeless longevity
Running through holes
Refusal and soul
Boring lectures
Painted ledgers
Disgustingly nothing
Crass crude & funny
Worldly treasures
Twist the immediate levers

Watching it turn
Feeling the burn
Worries deeply about
So headless and cloudy
Lines so sad so sad
Shadows nightly fads
Warriors of destiny
Malevolent festivities
Branded by love
Tainted by lust
The TV screen shatters
A lewd and disturbing disaster
Fight the nightly woes
Praying to find home
The results of atmosphere
Showboating worthless fears
Fun-loving and creative
Crying dilapidated
Mongoloid pride
Eyes so foreign and wide
Tears shake the plane
Tremors surface again

Anti-Hero

My hero is a
zero gravity
blurred reality
The girl sneaks through
the beam of the city's
gloom
She hides
concealed by starlight

Something's wrong
She walks jittery
down back alley dungeons
concealed by the tilt of
her hood
My hero latches onto
the spirit of
lacerated satchels
I channel my inner heat
bring about deceit
My hero is a leach
a scumbag
a bag lady carting rattling cans
down roads paved in
decay
My hero is a king
The girl searches
the looming towers
of a city in heat
jutting up through the dawn
of a city so fond of
deception
My hero is the leper
behind every failed endeavor
My hero is me
and I will forever mount
the hills of contempt
behind the ebbing dream
My hero will persevere
The girl watches as
he appears

Stupid Questions

Troubled
I'm miserable
Killing time with
nonsensical syllables
It's dribble
if you ask me
If you ask me anything
I might just kiss you
belittle you
twist you up
and tell you a riddle
if you ask me to
If you ask me
I will not answer
I'll have a tantrum
learn tantric love
or sex
One or the other I'll
do it backwards
A squirrel doesn't care
if you ask me
If you ask me that
I'll call you a pansy
trade you my underwear
and color your face dandy
But don't you dare ask me
because if you ask me
if you ask me
if you ask me anything
I'll tell you I'm just trying to
kill time a little
or maybe just raise it
like a ticking zombie

set it off like a time bomb
and then I'll ask you
if you ask me
If you ask me
I'll just say
I've got nothing to share
nothing to give
nothing to offer in
a world where the only answers
to give
are those to be hidden
So don't you ask me
stupid questions
if you don't want me
to mask the truth
with diluted sequesters
that are nonsensical
by definition

Reprieve

I think I'm just gonna go to sleep
Truth is I need reprieve
from all the blinking lights....

the siren's song

you hold me
    in

melting
       dripping
       dissipating
           limbs

like lava holds   a child

fading
       into

       your   soul

becoming embraced
          by   your every whim

this is my   self
   destruction
       listlessly
                             indecisive

falling
       crying
                                 i'm undecided on

suicide

<u>run</u>   for cover
       your life || my life

dried up &
    broken

hold me till
      i   fade away
immersed
      in
          your
              tears

honey i will die for
        your sins

to the death
      we ride deep
      deep
      deep into the night
our shadows are like
        nuisances
diluted
      we drip like melting
      soldiers

kill the lights
we're taken by
    the lonely fright   of

                the night

Incompletion

Why do I
feel so jaded and
cold
so many relentless faces
obstructions
destructions
malfunctioning malice
I'm so flip flip flipped
dripping with indecisions
the misery slipping through
my fingertips
like melting sand
cresting the frozen palace
I see the stars of a bare-knuckled
forest
My life open I pray that
I can put the pieces back
together again
before I
explode
just please don't let me
go >>>

Livestock

Hate Thy Neighbor // Love Thy Stranger

Independence Day

Fireworks blast off
It's the Fourth
of July
and fireworks sail
the dark, mysterious skies
of eternity
Every day of the year
people scurry out of their houses
to jobs/
punching clocks stacking papers
repeating boring phrases
such as
PAPER OR PLASTIC?
WOULD YOU LIKE FRIES WITH THAT?
DO YOU NEED HELP BRINGING THE BAGS
OUT TO THE CAR?
Every day people shuffle around
in monkey suits playing games
playing putrid fuckin games
of life, trying to pretend
playing make-believe
waiting—waiting waiting
for sacred salvation/

Tonight flickering flashing lights
sail the heavens and people watch
as their future unfolds
here
now
wasted lives…. boring mundane
wasted life, people dying mundane deaths
It's the Fourth of July and
firework tear up
the dark sky….

Wordplay

Priority
Prerogative
Monogamy
Photography
Mummify
Liquefy
Insidious
Insipid
Institution
Elusive
Municipal
Principal
Establishment
Fabricated
Situated
Masturbation
Sensational
Irrational
Bastardized
Pasteurize
Faster than the sky
Minus 45
Plunging
Plummeting
Thundering
Blundering
Stomach ache
Hateful
Irate
Discography
Crass graffiti
Plastered
Blasted

Sacrilege
Shattered temple
Master of calligraphy
Distilled
Shit show
Blistered
Bitchy
Rich & tasty
Bloody butthole face

my shadow

—— in real life im a fairly happy person , generally quite pleasant , but when i write i can be overly introspective , brutally reflective . my conscious is rather bitter & i <u>need</u> to dig deeper . deeper . i need to pry — or i might jus die — cuz i jus cant rely on my shallow forefront any longer than i can rely on a threelegged chair w/a cracked & busted leg thats supposed to effectively hold me up for a total of 3 or 4 or 5 minutes , right ? like <u>that</u> wud happen , anyway . i might be skinny but im not stupid . so why dont you jus take yr car & try & race a dashing train plowing down the gleaming copper tracks then try & cut a sudden left & slug it over the tracks before the train hits you & takes you for a ride >>>||| —— just   like   that !   —— lose control of yr whole rig like losing control of yr own mind; let the train string you along the tracks like a puppet being yanked this way & that , as if god himself is reaching his shiny , golden hand down thru the ozone layer , plucking you up , & delivering you to a place of peace & happiness ,,,,   jus   like   that ! like <u>that</u> wud happen, anyway . like a slap of thunder & a sudden zap & a quick strike , nunchuckfast , of lighting jaggedly crashing into yr skull , but not to pump you full of knowledge & insight but to blast you dead , a karate chop straight to yr throbbing head , electricity splicing you down the center & sending you flying 10 feet 20 feet 30 feet high & another 40 feet wide ——

                                            why does my shadow hate me ??

—— its like i walk around w/led in my shoes , dead weight holding me steady & in place . i try to run away from my shadow clinging on to me like a leech sucking me dry from my neck to my feet — oh my ! everywhere i go my shadow comes following me there , carrying a knife a razorblade a hammer or a gun , jus waiting to slice into me , to stab me , to hit me , or maybe even to cock & fire at me w/a series of radioactive pebbles gunning right into my left eyeball , plowing straight into my face , my nose exploding beneath the fierce blows one after another as it tears me apart from the inside out ——

                                        why does my shadow hate me ??

—— my defenses ready , my guard standing large & in charge , i peer one suspicious eye around every corner , down every alley , around every turn . i dont take my chances cuz my shadow always follows me around . everywhere i go it seems at times . becuz everywhere i go its always there jus waiting for me to come rounding the bend , projected onto walls , onto sidewalks , stuck to me like gum stuck to the bottom of my shoes ——

                                        why does my shadow hate me ??

— — but anyway ::::
                today life is great , it really is . but if only my shadow saw it that way , too — the same way that i saw it ….
if only that was the case i might be a better stronger & wiser human being . but instead im a suffering little cretin who constantly has to battle his own shadow in an everlasting effort to stay whole . jus running scared all the time . becuz everywhere i go its always there jus waiting for me to come rounding the bend (<u>always</u>) , scar tissue creeping thru the rabid , ghostly figure that is me , so demented & utterly twisted — so fuckin irate its almost like my insides are being analyzed & put on display , and **boom** ! here i lay angry & irritated & ive jus gotta get away from my godawful shadow once & for all!   —— lost & aggravated in a world being torn apart by knowitall preachers im running & im running & im running but i jus cant seem to evade my fuckin shadow in any way — & ive jus gotta get away before its too late — & it <u>is</u> too late way too late so late its like i jus dont fuckin know what to do about my fuckin shadow anymore. but i will survive in the end , becuz thats what i always do – i cant imagine an even worse fate than that ——

why does my shadow hate me ??

... im running out of ideas ...
... im running out time ...
somebody help me

PLEASE

Deface Me Like Cubicles Made of Stone

What day is it?
Did I lose my face again?
My soul wrapped in havoc
I weave together
these devious infractions
like I'm not even here
and I can't seem to
get it right
I just can't seem to
live my life
when I've got these torturous burdens
of diluted fairy tales
prancing tantrums
of delirious plastic and stuff
running rampantly
around my racking head
So will you pray with me?
pray for damnation
pray that these
turbulent storms
come cramming
vicious, spastic lightning bolts

splicing holes in
my tormented mind
jamming the will to be socialized
through mass suicide
into my rebellious veins
even though I know my will is
ablaze with
the need to stand apart
from the unified buccaneers
beckoning me down
phantom lanes

The Queen Bee
buzzing spaciously
without a care in the world
fading and free
it careens through the tree line
deliberately vicious
with a sting as forceful as
a one hundred-watt
electrical surge
I watch it drift and whine
as I sit in the crowded forest
shrouded by mountainous trees
looming like mutants
flowing as the droning wind
pushes through
the flurry of
scratching branches and
flittering leaves

Right Here
Right Now
I know I've
lost my face again
It's a freeing realization

It's a startling sensation
an insidious inebriation
that allows me to be
one with the monstrosity
known as life
and all of life's splendors
and so now I explore
the glorious festivities
that leave me ravenous and bright
hit with a newfound Excitement
mixed with Rage
and a hint of
Playful Vivacity
like a child
having never been born….

I'm wild and
free
and curiously
animated
The Queen Bee
perches on my head///

Untitled Poem

The hill unfolds
to open up the mind
I try and unwind
but it seems
the whole world has gone blind >>>>>>

A Poetic Threesome
with Melody Fair and Emily Lopez

Running down broken lanes

Roses dipped in subway trains

And you were swaying

Roiling decapitation through sweltering flames

Drunk me inquires: What is your name?

The last time I looked under my coffee table there were three coins, a plastic bag, thread, and something that was moving

An insightful delusion I'm losing steam

Thought I saw pink till I saw your face sooooo closely that it looked like me

Me! A big round moon!

A meager tweaker I was meant to be running loosely woven spirals of systematic gloom

Lame looks like zip zilch

Nothing to see here, so long, so long, a mosquito lands on me and spits

Eager to join us in a poetic threesome that reeks of bliss a magical disasterpiece that'll live on forever though swollen eyes of lust   in the first degree

The Ghost Robber

Knock knock. I open the door. It's a ghost, standing out there with a transparent sawed-off shotgun. It stands on my front porch for an awkward and tense five seconds. Then it says, "Gimme all your money!" I tell it I'm broke. The ghost raises the gun, cocks it, and says, "I'm not gonna say it again, gimme your fuckin money!" I say, "No." A deafening **pop!** and my blood is splattered all across the wall. As the ghost rummages through my pockets I say, "Step away from the dead body!" The ghost's head whirls and it swings the shotgun to point it at me, standing behind it, holding my own sawed-off shotgun to its head. I say, "What, you thought you were the only ghost around here?"

Did It My Way

Do it your way. Do it my way. I try to do things my own way. I try but I don't always achieve. Sometimes my way gets me into trouble. Sometimes I can be impulsive: speak too quick, act too fast, shoot from the hip, put down put up put out. I don't know, I make mistakes, I guess. Someone today said if you act with intention then it's not a mistake. I always act with intention, but sometimes my reasons are erratic. Sometimes I put my shoes on the wrong feet, my pants on backwards. My mind races and for me to stop and think—to slow down the manic pacing of my frantic brain—too much time would pass and my decisions would then be obsolete. Weigh out the pros & cons—I can't decide which is up or down, right or wrong. Everything is equivalent. For me all actions end the same: trouble. Which comes in all shapes & sizes. A slap of the cuffs,   etc. I'm getting evicted. But fuck it these kinds of consequences are inevitable—or at least they are for me. I know at times I can be racist sexist homophobic, you name it…. I can hate like the rest of them! But I'm okay with that. It's just part of the human condition. What's really important is that I'm aware—I'm aware that if I did it my way you'll hate me all the same\\\

Girls

When a girl looks at me with what I interpret to be intrigue, my first thought is to say hi, my second thought is to run away, and my third thought is to jump up as high as I can, grab the moon out of the sky, pull it straight down, and hand it to her. Say: "Here, I got you something" ... and then I'll run for my fucking life, faster than I've ever run before.

Pulp Fiction

Two men meet in a bar. One is sober, the other is not. They sit on the curb outside and bond over good music. The drunk one turns to the sober one and says: "I gotta tell you something. It's kinda personal. Never told anyone this before, so don't judge me." The sober one says, "No worries. What's on your mind?" "Well," the drunk one says. "I find that I'm slightly attracted to that parking meter." "Which parking meter?" says the sober one. "That one! There." The drunk one points at the parking meter straight ahead. "Okay," says the sober one. "Okay. So what do you wanna do about it?" "Well I'd like to give it a blowjob." The sober one says, "That sounds like a great idea! I'll join you." They both stand up and walk over to the parking meter. When they reach it they drop to their knees and begin sucking and licking and caressing the metal pole. You can tell the parking meter is enjoying it, too, because the needle is slowly rising, as if someone were filling it with change. It goes up up up and up. When it reaches its peak, the meter starts rattling. The sober one lifts his head, turns to the drunk one, and says, "Is that normal?" The drunk one stops and says: "I don't know. Never done this before." He continues sucking and licking and caressing. The meter stops rattling for a moment, and all of a sudden a clanging and clattering sound rises from inside the shaft——— ———and then, the meter explodes—just _**explodes!**_—and coins start gushing from the slot, one after another; just spiderwebbing outward like the grand finale at a fireworks show. The sober one watches the drunk one take in a mouthful of change. The drunk one falls to the ground clutching his throat and choking. He's sputtering and coughing and gagging. In an instant he stops cold, and the sober one knows that he's dead. The end.

AK47

Sometimes I just wanna escape
        the fire

Order

Packed in cubicles
clicking keyboards
fake smiles phony grins
walking the line
dress shoes clacking
pencils scratching
the faint sound of printers
spitting out page after page
The boss comes down
smiles & nods
bows & points
says Good boy, you've been doing fine.
How about a raise?
Your ears perk up
your head rises
your smile shines brighter
this is what you live for
more money in the bank
The wife will surely be happy
about this
<u>THIS</u>
this safe and steady life
easy pickings no hassles
just cruising with no waves made

just smile & nod
bow & eat shit
shovel it & eat it
safe and sound
ordered living
easy money just do what you're told———

——it will all work out for you
in the end ——————

until the ruler snaps
until the pencil cracks
until the cubicle collapses
and you're standing in madness
You realize you haven't been doing shit
just wasting away
boring drawl
losing it
you're losing it
losing it
the pendulum tips & sways
and you're hurled into chaos
a new way
The magazine clacks as you cock
it into the butt of the gun
cocked & loaded
losing it slow and steady
you're losing it

You're lost
you drift away on

7 Words

splattered, burst, platter, torn, bent, laced, knuckles

I pick up the fractured platter and smattered it to look a disaster and then splatter it across the slanting mantel sill but I just ended up feeling oddly torn and yet bent normally but with these fictitious, distorted laces scraping my knuckles; I dusted my uncle with sheer bursts of a disfigured pedigree. Sometimes I live in the past; other times I mount the future and kick the present in its diminishing ass, but then when my crass descendants burst through the glass picture frame I find that I'm splattered pedantically across mirrors galore.

Antipathy

Are they looking at me
or at the stark face
in the mirror's edge
Drifting eyeballs
Lids that flicker
A tipsy cowgirl's
forlorn introspection
boring proof of disease
She guzzles the tainted ale
ment
and stumbles
to her jaded knees
Me
I dash and stab
the world with
my petty injustices
judging you from a skewed and slanted
distorted plateau

a distant musing
ruling out all foul play with
a dwindling perspective of
a pesky indecision
I pet the mule on the nose
decipher a wanton cruelty
It really does go
a long long way to
doodle crude ironies down the
fascist's brooding pose
I see him in the pictures
lurking ridiculously amid a
berserk and wild lot of timid hyenas
So I bring the snottyness
into question
descend upon
my derelict suggestion
the unfolding demeanor of
a questioning coyote
like a soiled towel
put into practical use
I milk the loaded vowels
like tortured cattle
battling for composure
while surrendering my exposure
to the misanthropes of
a roped-in nation
We hang on but it shows no such
satisfied misdirection
Lucky to set out upon
an ill-advised misadventure
I'll horde the sun
and hock the moon
utilize the necessary tools
one would need
to be defeated by

the fools at the top
But I warn you deeply
my restless fidgeting
is at best an inhibiting symptom
of living with this active misgiving
of a broken cowboy
amid
a throwback void
We roll the fat
like dough so coy

A Clusterfuck——

I think that's the only term that describes it/

                                                                        Yes,,,,   a clusterfuck….

The Mirror of Youth

You can find the truth buried in the back of a mirror, traipsing through a funhouse with a 12-gauge sawed-off shotgun strapped to your back. Destroy the fuckers, one pump and a ***crack!*** at a time.
It's all fun and games, till someone gets hurt. Lose my face to sinister things, deeds that come straight from Hell itself. I walk through the mudslide
unstoppable
unbreakable
so faceless and epic
nothing will put me to shame today,,,,   no act of passion, of hate—an endless search through relentless deserts where mirrors are forbidden.

I search for me.............   I search for her.......   I search for him.... I search for a distraction, a lost transaction, a needy world full of evil action, a disaster on a platter. In a matter of heartbeats I'll be there, so lost and alone, sold on symbolic madness. In a matter of clicking fingers jittery & cold I walk through waterslides pouring blood and guts down spiraling tracks where trains crash and fight one another———a battle to the death.
A lonely war in my head.
I feel rather victorious when the skinny little boy cries.... He hates the way his body feels when the fat lady sits on his back—snap to yesterday when he was tall and strong and mean, and the world was his he was only 93///
That's the story of my oh so gory existence in a horny world where boring men and women sit around a 40-foot apple tree that reaches outer space it's so massive and lean. It sits alone in the white forest and ponders things no one will ever understand—no man or woman or boy or girl or anorexic cow it's alone in a world where the human race is retarded and the only thing that stands between it and freedom is a laughing mirror that gawks and spits obscenities through its gorgeous snout.... What a lousy bore this universe seems to add up to when you walk on your hands through a forest of eggshells, and what a stupid plan you had when you thought you'd succeed, just chuck jagged rocks at passing cars and watch as your future fades away.. Just become one with yourself, become two with your enemy, become three with whoever wants you, and finally, become four when you masturbate cuz only then can you watch yourself make a gooey mess outta your pants but at least you don't haveta do it alone, cuz any action done in solitude is almost like it had never happened to begin with. And nothing I do seems to have any impact on anyone and that is why, my friend, I find I'm sold on customs and traditions and everything that happens to me
cracks like the abandoned mirror
that shows me my past
my future
and everything in between
but God forbid it show me
the present
because that is something
I just don't wanna see....

i hurt

there was a day when i hurt
other people
simple becuz
they deserved the treatment
i was dishing
outward like
broken glass shattering
deeper
into
the mind of a shipwrecked mutant
i delved thru bloody letters
unfeathered my derelict
like a revolving shadow
i walked on broken nails
holding in my hands
a pale & distorted symantec
deterioration of leather-bound
churches in the sun
wait for me on the other side
of a jagged desert
the size of jupiters towering oceans
devour me like an ozone
invaded by roaming pirates
i disintegrate
i disseminate
i masturbate while surfing
a disturbing mountain
thru pounds of cokedout
humanoid freaks
i hurt
that was the nature of my problem
i desert the flaming torch
probly deserve more

torture me as you beckon the
lollipop lesboids from the land of the coy
birds
they cure me
of the
hurting but
im lurking on the
bigtitted blonds front yard
she stands on the porch
i set the roof aflame
w/arrows that venture outward
like blossoming disasters
the rapture is among us
& it hurts when i fall
becuz
i hurt

Inspired

In a brick maze
My head expanding
My gut expounding
The walls are deliberate
ly pounding
I've gotta get
outta here
before the brick walls
dissolve into ashes
I'm falling through steel halls
lined with dead orphans
I'm throwing up in
a projectile disfunction
Losing sleep ain't no good

when you've got an
absorbent heart
You watch the crowd
through an icy fog that's
shrinking
    shrinking
        shrinking
with every ejaculated thought
bumrushed through
doors that bleed
infants clawing at the red-
stained glass
It's derelict and disturbing
I'm on another plane
playing a game of
broken Charades
I sit here in the back
of the flaming classroom
cringing each time the dominatrix
of an insidious dream
runs her exploding nails
down the gray board
with a waxy sorta meow
like that of a cat
being hit with a hammer

Now
I'm mad
I want to destroy
I want to chuck bricks
through imploding churches
I want to spraypaint my name
on the crying child's face
I want to leave boot prints the size
of an Elephant
on the doors of every
pub in town

I want windows to break
when I come marching through
I want people to say my name
when another twin tower falls
That was Jeremy's doing
they'd say
as I sit in a cave somewhere
pressing buttons and
pulling strings
watching the fall of
another civilized empire
come crashing down

This is the day for surreal
deliberation
the day to feed the ants
and starve the giants
This is the day
the last day
the only day
    for that matter
to give the bastards
hell....

Of Unknown Origins

My thoughts are racing; I'm in a place of unknown origins—a place I must familiarize myself with if I wanna keep my sanity in check. The first full day in this strange city, a city I have only seen out through a car window, a city whose inhabitants seem rather curious to me, like the absence of knowledge and familiarity will induce internal bleeding, my organs leaking, my bones being torn apart with a sharp, reverberating **snap,** the bone marrow seeping out through the open gaps, like my sanity is in question, like I'm a diseased freak, like I must see and be and watch and understand and maybe, just maybe, become one with them, someday—but probably not!

All this futility, as though I'm crawling backwards through a swollen and throbbing void—a void that encompasses my whole life, my entire existence (**Jeremy Void, at your service**)—a sucking and slurping hole in space that pulls me closer as though suspended by a frozen bungee, just holding me there it won't let go....

My first full day in——
         Where am I, anyway?

Must I speak the name of this fantastic, brand-new world aloud, or else the sweltering silence will swallow the sound up whole; just swallow it with a mega, chomping snap of its vicious dicers—***crack!!!***   crack   crack   crack!———I'm outta control; out to lunch was once used to describe me. I'm skipping dinner and going straight to dessert. Swallow the whole cake and desert the plate. Then gurgle a menacing burp and pat my stomach as it snorts and wallows in tortured anguish///   And then   I'll   never   eat

again ____

Unless, of course, you serve me an epic lunch that I can take out with me on a date, take it straight to dinner, but instead set the whole dinner menu aflame, and in the glimmering, flickering red glow of the flame that's devouring the entire table even as I speak, you might chance a peek in my direction and see, if you're lucky enough, and if you share the proper perspective///———you may possibly catch a glimpse of my grinning, depleted soul as I wink a snotty wink at you, just smile and nod, and take in a heaping bite of that shiny chocolate cake set on the table before me, which I'll probably in turn just vomit up anyway, in an additional twenty minutes from now, out in the Rite Aid parking lot.

So, where was I? Scattered as ever; sleeplessly surrendering myself to a sort of delirium that sets in when I'm nervous, and lost, and so very cold and alone and hopeless at this very moment, having wandered into a place of unknown origins, where unfamiliar people sit around talking and laughing and joking and laughing and sharing brilliant words of wisdom, and yet telling disgusting, derelict stories of the terminally defective; and just then I think to myself:

I think I've been here before....

i hear her now

I'm standing on the roof of my neighbor's Jaguar. How I got here and what I'm doing exactly, let's just say the details are unclear.
Up the hill and around the corner I see a menacing four-wheeler come careening into sight, rumbling like a fighter jet, and dive-bombing.
I hit the clutch and crank the wheel and my head whirls as I catch a faint glimmer of my diminishing shadow whither into dust.
I hear her now: every word of her relentless yammer striking to destroy.
I hear her now—I listen to her image sizzle in the wind like grilled bullets.
I'm standing on the roof of my neighbor's Sedan.
I'm standing on the roof of my neighbor's Humvee.
My neighbor bought a tank and I'm standing on its roof.
I'm standing on my neighbor's roof, looming over a messy sea of debauched scenery, thick steam wafting through the shattered images I paint when I hear the sound of her voice, projected through channels of sheer hatred.
How I got here and what I'm doing exactly, the details fade into focus. I can see much more clearly now.
I hear her now—her voice tinges the insides of my eardrums like bile singing the back of one's throat.
Up here on the roof I watch through misty eyes the sun fade into black—it blinks out like a candle defused.
I watch the moon shine in the blackness like a glowing void.
I watch the stars, glittering with a multitude of colors, and littering the immense, black beyond that blankness my entire futile existence. I'm frightened by the immensity of it.

I hear her now, as clear as the shadows cast down by the glare of the sinister mirror. I listen to her voice, and I cringe in dismay. She sounds like a tortured goddess, her voice slicing through the swirling clouds of yesterday's storm like a plunging comet—it showers me with guilt & disgust; it shows me the darkness that festers deep down inside of me which I'd rather keep locked up inside of a solid, indestructible safe to which not even I possess the key.

I hear her now. The TV is on. The radio plays nothing but static.

I hear her now. I killed my neighbor—shot him in the head, due to a tremendous, rippling tantrum that overtook me completely—just so I could stand out here without the risk of interruption—just so I can listen to the sound of her voice in complete solitude, taking in all the tearing and biting and ripping and shattering that follows thereafter.

I hear her now. An explosion casts blackness in the sky, and now all I can hear is the sound of her voice yammering inside my head.

5 Words

logical, steamed, moved, believed, considerate

I believed that the steaming boat was moving considerately down a logically driven sea of beaming Neanderthals with hatchets and shotguns, what a slotted mystery my logically deceased grandma believed my mind to be. I steamed my way through grade school, traded smoke for sand, and downgraded the marching band made up by electronic panthers. It was a day without logic, a day I believed to produce a steaming sonic boom that reverberated through my inner ear canals and the drums thudded and pounded their own brand-new sensation. If the sun explodes in my lifetime, the only thing I hope for is that I outlive some of my surrounding peers so that the last thought that passes through my head is: THAT WAS FUCKIN AAAWWS—— And then vaporized/// It's a logical travesty, too considerate to show any malice whatsoever, as the last living Mexican bungee-jumps from the surface of the big, gleaming moon which appeared in the dark night sky like a steamed eggshell, spiraling delicate spiderweb-like designs as it moves in full rotation around my implosive mind. I soak in the rays of the ocean, cry for the ozone to melt or erupt and just simply decay but then I deny this festering, fading dismay as I pass the blame which is only a poor system of belief….

Prayers of the Lonely

Lost in midnight's glare, a lone wolf howls at the solid, glowing moon, because he's got no one but himself to cherish existence with. What a fright it is to hear the beckoning owl of a stolen dream hoots hoots hoots through the riveting fence that intercepts the wolf's connection with freedom. They beckon him closer to the madness, to his own destruction, dark & derelict. He follows the welcoming calls and ignores the many yielding chants of cloaked witches who try to steer him somewhere else, the swirling cauldron of dead children splashing and thrashing—and the owl's stark hooting cuts through the dead of the night. The lone wolf's bleak howling brings forth a sickening depletion that seems to complete him. His feet rise from the wood chips of fallen hopes and stolen dreams; and he looks down as the dwindling ground fades away like a vaporizing black hole; and then he looks up, at the blistering full moon. The witches chant & the owl hoots hoots hoots, and the wolf is all alone, a deathly brooding seizing him from head to toe; and he drifts away on the thinnest wisp of gray smoke like a dastardly wet dream—and he's alone, lost forever foreboding….

A Race to the Top

Like Candy Land
in a forest of
candy canes
a tall, windy staircase
remains unscathed///
It's a race to the top:
Gingerbread Men
& women too
fight to the death
as they climb to the tippity-top
of the rickety rocking banister
that popped out of nothing///
One day it was a wasted & dead
plane; the next levels rose straight upward
up up up- -to the top
It wound a traversing tapestry of ginger
& frosting & gummy bears
& Mrs. Frosty thought to herself:
How do we exploit this new finding?
Musing over it, the sinister cunt she was/
Her nefarious reverie spun a web
of greed & glory & greedy glory///
She masterminded the stakes
& divided the clan into 51 states
of rich & tasty candy
& so then the Gingerbread men
& Women too
wielding gleaming swords of chocolate
& vanilla spears
& shimmering scythes made of caramel
& shields of cookie dough
lined up at the bottom///
When the hammer dropped in

mounds of creamy ice cream
& the peanut flew from inside
the mouth of the sweet & gooey volcano
the men & women of this fantastic world
hurled themselves at the staircase
... one after another ...

The Darkness, Afraid of Humanity

Nothingness

Emptiness

Plummeting

down
        down
                down
We free the mind through
delirious channels soaked
in the adrenal glands of a demented
man on his last hour
his last minute
his last second the past comes in
rearing a deformed,
defective head like rabies
We frolic in a world left deserted
by banshees on the run
from
a unified mass acceptance
quickly deriving they hide from a dying
tirade by defying the light of a throbbing
electrolyte-band
I embrace   the   emptiness

The ways of the old country
have got me stuck channel surfing
riding these static wakes
grinding
the denial of a homely
misdemeanor
I throttle a rapidly decreasing
world set to erupt destruct and
implode
when the skinny naked man
sipping a pint of heroin
through his delirious eyeball
whispers
disturbing
verses
of an
assbackwards   universe
set to decay delay and
distill
creating a rapidly fading
vapid façade
What a brilliant response
to an undulating
state of imprisoned hatred
repress   repress   repress
and surrender yourself
to
a decaying ponce of a man on the brink
of a twisted portrayal
I pounce on the dismay
like batman
on his villains
like a dare devil
without the disheveling of a
hellion breed
I seek dismissal

of the lonely creed
through searching I find my
swollen destiny
It swells with emptiness

Nothingness

Emptiness

Plummeting

down
        down
                down
We walk to the end of the line
just to defuse the light
and show off the night....

Haikus of the Future
personal goals & ambivalences

Money. Rich. Girls.
I want to be famous then
Book signings with help

Axe murderer man
Bank robbing ninja pirate
Flanked by hot girls

Dead of HIV
Turned into a zombie leach
Brains for nutrients

That which shall not be named

It's broken I broke it. I knocked something over I can't find what I'm looking for. A swollen brain is injecting into me menacing tremors and a bright & vibrant pain that induces all sorts of trembling discomforts I go to sleep on the moon. I hate the way the clouds look at me so fluffy and clean. I hate the way the mirror shapes my future my figure my delirious projections.... It's broken I broke it. I knocked back the keg like a goose-stepping drag queen. I read around the lines above the lines beneath the lines; but ultimately I hate the shape of my eyes and my own receding hairline—it's not receding fast enough. Although my gingivitis makes up for my full head of hair.
I can't remember my natural hair color, though. Beneath layer after layer of paint and carcinogens I break the broken glass into windows. I go to sleep on the sun I hate the way the flames engulf me as though I'm a high&mighty faggot sitting on a pedestal of bliss and fire. The clouds defuse the holy itch with fluffy supremacy===   Fluffy Power! the power of fluff? I start fights with shadows as my muscles grow into looming resentments that burn windows into my eyes I break broken glass into tables. Drop the brick and it goes **smash!** I start from scratch never smoke crack when you're pregnant ... with a 2-ton cement truck. Never shoot dope when you've got a head full of hope a belly full of hate and a lust for sensational madness that drapes you in a wretched veil full of undulating desires that wrap you up in a noose of Your Own Making.
Which brings you right back to your glory days when you were hazed by a succession of giant, junkless, rifle-wielding grunts who hate you for being too skinny for being too fat for being just right in regards to height and latitude they simply hate you because they hate you;

and boy does that take me back >>>>>>

Esoteric Demonstrations

Perfection

Perfection is a disease—but not in the sense that we become perfect when infected. But rather, we seek it like vampires after blood. It's a disease of the mind body & spirit; it reaps havoc on those who do not have it. But defective is a blessing. Acceptance of Your Follies is one of the greatest gifts anyone can ever get. When you look in the mirror and see a beautiful, disproportionate, oblong figure smiling back at you, now <u>that's</u> something to strive for.

conditioner

i cannot stop   being me
people have tried
to alter me
     they have tried
        to straighten me   out
but all their attempts   to make me
more like   them
     has only caused me
       to
reject them

even more
       & more   i continue to
       misdirect their
       redirections
becuz i simply object to
their phantom oppression
condition me
make me submit make me tick make me stand in line &
                         sit
put a lid on all your   relentless conditioning
i'm not a drone you can just   reprogram
to your liking
becuz I will not discern
obey or
relearn
i will not follow
       a code of conduct
that is in
direct opposition w/
       my own   fuckedup   ways
my own brand of
hysterics
    frenzied
       tangled &
          confused
menacing wrangled &   diluted
i cannot stop   being me
i will not stop
don't make me stop   being   **me!!!**
i will never ever stop >>>

Untitled Poem

They probly think
the kid don't drink
so then he must be
a frikken dope fiend

EgO

Give an animal an ego—now you have mankind. We are at the top of the food chain, the king of the hill—no one gives us the right to oppress, we take it. If you want an apple, pick it off the tree. If you want a country, better hope you have enough muscle and wit to overthrow it. We created technology, which makes life so much easier for us—because We Are the Best. We've overthrown the world and now we can sit in luxury and not move a muscle or think a thought again. We have nothing left to fear—we did it all! But what happens when technology becomes the new Alfa-race.

DISempowerment

        I'm not about empowerment

        I am about DISempowerment

AWKWARD Not Asocial

A Passive Protest: Creating adversity without being overly aggressive or blatantly offensive (i.e. dressing in a way that draws attention to oneself))). The cop sees a guy with a bright pink Mohawk that reaches nearly three feet tall, wearing a black T-shirt with big, bright-pink lettering running across the front which spells out: **A**LL **C**OPS **A**RE **B**ASTARDS! You don't really haveta do much more other than wait.
See what I mean?

I don't really talk to a whole lot of people, in the grand scheme of things. I mostly keep to myself. I'm a little bit asocial and I write long, intricate rants (or aphorisms) on Facebook because I have to talk to <u>some</u>body and the computer won't judge me—only the users will, this is a guarantee, but at least I don't have to look them in the eye when they do.
But the truth of the matter is, I'm not really asocial, I just don't know how to start conversations with people in a "civilized" manner. I just spew obscenities that get you to look at me. *Got your attention now, don't I?* But in today's modern-day world, that's only good when you wanna make enemies, not friends, with the people around you—<u>there's</u> something I thrive at, to tell you the truth———but then I guess, when it comes down to it, I'd Much Rather Be Hated Than Ignored, because at least then you'll recognize me as an entity with an impact. Whether it be a negative impact is entirely irrelevant. An Impact is An Impact! I guess I do stand out, though—or at least that's what they tell me—but I don't stand above because I never speak up and in your mind I'm just a silent geek dressed in all black from head to toe, standing against an albino sky. But I don't stand above, I don't stick out in your mind—just in a crowd, but not in your mind———because that is the ultimate goal: to be recognized as somebody with an impact, with a voice; but not just as somebody who can be, on occasion, pleasing to the eyes, with a handsome but gritty complexion and a sleek and wiry fatigue. Images are lost in the mind; I'm pushing aside brain cells and shouting and flailing until you register me in your memories as somebody deep and thoughtful and twistedly brilliant who can weave together words like a sewing machine, punching weaving & threading the needle and leading it so fluidly through the fabric…. Because voices get stored for-

ever and are rehashed again and again, whenever the words fit the present situation. I'm a writer, not a model, so listen to me speak, pay close attention to me as I discharge words and play with alliteration and form—but just don't watch me soar because I'm worth so much more; only my words never get spoken out loud and my truly unique voice will never be heard above the hiss of the crowd.

                                                           See what I mean?

Why not dream??

The future—dreams—unknown delusions—radical procedures—indecisive maneuvers. I chase dreams all the time. My new addictions is: I chase dreams. I chase them everywhere, all over town, and the greatest thing about chasing dreams is that you'll never be satisfied, and without satisfaction it's like I'm permanently gratified. I know that everything leads to nothing, and when everything leads to nothing, why not dream about something? It's the difference between reality and ideas. The difference between somewhat sane and completely schizophrenic. When I hear voices I know the difference. But that doesn't mean I don't get lost in their thoughts. Someone the other day said: Nihilists can't be dreamers. Then, mocking: I'm a nihilist and I dream about nothing. All that that tells me is that he is clearly not a nihilist who has a tendency to dream. I mean, when everything leads to nothing, why not dream about something? as long as I recognize that dreams never materialize the way that they're dreamt—or at least they never do for me ... so why not dream about something? It only offers me a way to wade through all the nothing without getting lost in all the crap....

Radical Deception

I hate the system
        but I need the system

I hate people situations interactions
frantic ass jockies passive plastic explosives
firebombed alleys and toilet bowl cherry bangers
crack heads winos freaks and rhinos
                I hate em all
but I need em all
just to get by

Call me an anarchist
I hate big business and government
but I rely on the government
for handouts and welfare checks

Call me a nihilist
I hate religions all religions dogmatic horse shit
                I hate atheism too,
by the way
                    ya drastic drag racers
                    when will you learn
                    that hatred for the other
                    is no way to discern
but when I'm broke down
hell-bound pent-up and wasted
lastly unforgiven for my matrix of
blasted sins blasphemous deceptions
        I fall to my knees and
                pray!
Don't knock it till you've tried it

I know no one cares no one listens
no one knows no god
no government official
no thrumming dismissal
no black belt disciple
or perhaps a maximum disheveled copper
lobbing beatings like horseshoes
I know no one is out there
        but me
                and you——
no, just me
                      Hope is so useless anyway
                      I know the world is gonna end
                      bloody
                      very very soon
                      —and I mean **soooooon!**———
                      and when it does
                      I'll stand amid the flames
                      dancing and laughing and clapping
                      munching on popcorn as I watch
                      the apocalypse commence
                      and everybody die in a burst of flurry
                      burying our entire existence
                      in the ground like a bone
so what the fuck is the point??

I don't know,
so why not let Big Brother feed you??
It's all meaningless anyway

Use Big Brother
but Don't Let Big Brother Use You
should be the anthem of us
anarchistic kids
of us nihilistic miscreants
the explosive boys and the flaming girls

the bright-eyed derelicts and the
shy but devious the sly but insidious
the insipidly benign terrorists
of a country
        of a world
                of an existence
on the verge of going down
in a burst of flames and explosions

I hate the people I see
but they're always so good to me
when I need something to eat

I hate the system but
the system supplies me with
the stuff I need to survive

I guess I'm mixed up
and a bit hypocritical too
But fuck it! I'm a nihilist
I think I'm entitled....

Untitled Poem

Another day
to forget about the struggle
Another way
for the corporations to make a bundle

Controversy

I need to clear something up: You see, there is a reason I don't write a lot of confrontational poetry anymore. I used to be more Fuck You than I Understand What You're Going Through; but since then I've changed—A LOT. Basically, no one can do to me what I have already done to myself. I'm the one who burned the bridge, not you. I could just as easily say it was the opposition who'd done it to me, but I'm the one with the Zippo in my pocket. I'm my own worst enemy. If someone wants to hate me for the way I dress, let em. They're the asshole, and I don't need to dwell on their hatred for me or else they win. Call me a hippy if you want, but I try to spread love everywhere I go; but I also recognize that things aren't so cut & dry that I can just say: YOU ARE LOVED!!! Love is not something that we deserve; we are not entitled to it. Sometimes the world (i.e. my own mind, for the world that I live in is only a manifestation of how I feel about myself) can be a very dark and scary place///peace & love are ideal, but realistically, violence & hate rule supreme. I try to spread love, but if you hate me, I won't hold it against you. Sometimes I really hate myself, so why can't you hate me too? I don't deserve respect, either. When I start thinking that way, I get very angry and accusatory because you're not giving me what I think I'm entitled to in the first place; and if you only knew just how bitter I was, maybe then you'd treat me with the respect & decency that I deserve. Right? Wrong! What the fuck have I done to earn it?? other than deem you an asshole—and is that any way to treat someone I respect? No it's not! because I don't respect you in the first place. Which brings me right back to: Why should you respect me if I won't do the same for you? Now, back to my original point:::: People are people, and sometimes we disagree, and it's not my job to please everybody who comes my way—nor is it theirs—and if I start getting all upset toward them for disrespecting me, then I've really gotta rethink my own values. My favorite poet said: *"If you want a revolution / learn to change your own internal chemistry / and do it quietly / if you can."*[1] He got shot to death because people were outraged by the poetry that he wrote.

---

[1] From "Tombstone as a Lonely Charm" by d. a. levy.

I am! I was not!

I make my own fate. The people in my lineage don't dictate the way I feel about things today. I'm **Jeremy Void,** defined by my own current behaviors. I don't let the mistakes of my forefathers affect my relationships with the world at large. I don't let the triumphs of my ancestors define the man I've decided to be in the present moment. I'm the ruler of my own destiny. I strive to be the best me that I can be, and when I look in the mirror, sometimes I don't like the man staring back at me. But that's all right because right now, at this very moment, and all the moments that follow hereafter, I will rise above it all >>>

Forced Ejaculation

Do what you please
Don't get caught up with
symbols like words for seeing
Release the beast and run
wild & free
Disinhibit the inner monkey
Rise above the bondage of
labels and classes
band aids and factions
teams and tribes
Dismiss the need to belong
to a herd of followers
Don't let symbols dictate
your sense of self
Forget your self
and peel off your skin
Lose your self to
an undiluted nirvana

Shed your layers
down to your veins
Show off your internal organs
and let your blood run
in chaotic symmetry
Don't obey symbols like
truths or wisdom
Ignorance is a blessing
We need to cherish our
disbeliefs
Let our knowledge perish
so that our blood can run
free & unstoppable
Liberate the mind and the body
will follow

Opinionated Friends

"You offended me and now I hate you!"

"So, just one minor disagreement changes your <u>entire</u> opinion about me? Is that what you're saying?? Then you must have had a very low opinion about me in the first place."

"Ummm...."

To Heaven & Beyond

If there <u>was</u>
in fact
a Heaven, I don't think
I'd be happy there either/
not any more than
I am now	anyway
	But not
for that cliché reason
I'm always hearing others
yammering on about
which is simply
I'd be surrounded by
boring old tea-toddlers while
reclining lazily on the other side
of those great big
pearly gates
up in the clouds
far
far
away
	from me/
	from here/
	from there/
	from anywhere I've ever
ventured
in all my life

Just think about it
half the time I'm not happy
anywhere I go
because
I just can't see an end in sight
It's the greatest mystery

I've tried so hard to uncover
so lost & blind
trekking a cold & lonely road
as I follow it straight
down
        to Hell >>>>>>

So tell me
how would Heaven
be any different?
for a person as sick as
me/
Because in Heaven at least I'll <u>know</u>
I'm on an eternal plight
        Going Nowhere seems
to be the recurring
state of things

Guess I'm
just a damned Punk
        anyway

So I'm sorry but
but but
I just can't see the light….

Nostradamus

This is what I predict for the future: 1. A civil war, Left vs. Right. Those who refuse to pick a side will be exiled and forced to live in squalor on the Outskirts of Civilization. 2. The Left will win, obviously. 3. America will go from marshal law to a totalitarian government in a matter of years. The fascist dictator of the New Government will be none other than Steven Durrak, the CEO and chief-editor of a popular fashion magazine called *The Nomad*. 4. The Middle People, that's what they call those who don't pick a side to fight on, will rise up against *The Nomad* and demand their rights be returned. 5. The Left and Right will then join forces and fight the Middle People, thus declaring new sides. 6. The Middle People will become enslaved by the Political Party, that's what the united Left and Right will be called. 7. *The Nomad* fucks everybody up the asses in the end.

hooRAH

Get lost in the football match on TV. In England football means looting and rioting and running with the boys, your gang—or, I mean, your firm—and when your home team kicks the ball with striking speed and brings victory to your home town it gives you reason enough to charge into the losing team's territory and boast and beat and kick and shout , , , because our fuckin team—OUR fuckin team—Our Fuckin Team—brought home the cup and your team fuckin sucks. Rub it in their faces with swift Doc Martins to the sides of their heads. In Boston when the Red Sox won the championship a citywide riot that brought death and embarrassment to the once lovely city spread like herpes across the land, just infecting the commoners, and they trashed the place—Fuck Yeah they did——— [celebrate pride in your city by transforming it into dirt and dust with swollen bodies from the riot guns and the heavy duty stun bags that project like, uh, real-live bullets, lying dead in the streets like human waste———literally like human waste].

But today there's a new competitive sport that has all of the twisted hearts of broken America beating and throbbing with endorphins and hate—it's called politics....   politics..   PoLiTiCs—Fuck Yeah it is. It's got white middleclass men and women marching like Gestapo through the streets; it's got black America rivaling with tormented chips on their shoulders like little devils squawking in their ears. Like an interactive game of Pokemon on my phone, the masses are lined up like dolphins getting stuck in fishing nets—it wasn't meant for them, and yet they still swirl and weave through so easily like thread moves through fabric———and the fishermen, the filthy politicians, the corporate giants with their falsely radical RAR badges that they wear on their cocks, they don't care—Fuck Yeah they don't. Like Sardines, Like Sheep, Like Dogs marching to their fate of kicked and beaten death, the inevitable big bad men are contracting dishonest men who believe that they are honest, hiring charitable people who say *But Not in My Backyard—Get out, Out, OUT!!!* It's an ironic truth, an absurd reality, a dream I had last week which I can't seem to grasp, from which I can't seem to awaken—a repeat stuck forever in one transformative state———everything fuckin changes, nothing stays the same, and if I don't get my way, I might just blow a gasket, kick the opposing team in the gut, because they're faggots they wouldn't understand, cunt nigger bitch A-hole twat-munching fuck faces who should get the fuck off my land. They don't know shit: have a fit, wave my fist, scream and stomp and say Holy Shit, this country is holding on by the thinnest thread already; it's a losing battle and my team lost the World Cup and now I'm gonna be a soar sport about it and piss and moan until someone hears my groaning cries until someone hears my groaning cries until someone hears my groaning cries until there's enough of us winy miscreants to fill an entire football field with relentless pestilence that zips and zangs through the buzzing swarm and rises up up up like an epic battle call that will kill and maim any-one who stands afar from the masses, the spoken mob: such a righteous façade—the few that demand some <u>real</u> action to be made, complaining that it was the fault of the Electoral College all along///these people who hounded me to vote when I said it was all such a futile act—what a laugh <u>that</u> is, ya foolish cunts!
Now, let's ostracize the opposition. But it's just a sport, a competition, the biggest mockery that had ever swept over this erratic country….

And four years go by and we're at it again: Rinse, Lather, & Repeat///

I say Power to the People, but Not to the Phony Politicians Who Perpetuate the Lie.

313

Formalities

Everybody thinks
they know a thing or two
Me I did poorly in school
I received no formal education
I know nothing
But at least I'm doing something
because that's so much more
than you've ever done

Terminal Cases

Most people are satisfied
to just take a number and
stand in line
as long as they get to be a part of
something so much bigger than them
A Mob of Worshippers is all
that it is

—so satisfied in fact
that the numbers start to define them
and the line stops being a line
and changes into a vacant
mundane
lifeless
series of
rules and regiments

These people
they don't even discuss
and dream about
what it would be like
to be something else
to be someone else
to be somewhere else

but instead their conversations are
How do we serve
this machine that is
killings us one by one by one

Fight for the system die for the system
live for the system
become a part of the herd
      <u>today</u>
before it becomes too late

Me I'd rather fight my own causes
I'd rather die on my own terms
I'd rather live for a singular purpose
which is to be a terminally unique cretin
of creativity
hell-bent on exploration
and conceptualization
and individualism

People might be satisfied
to just take a number and
stand in line
but I'm not gonna be the one
to peel the expired ticket
from out of their
cold and numb and withered grasps

as they lie there hard and stiff
like a zeroxed corpse who had
only one goal when he/she
was alive

which was to die
just like everybody else

Performance Art

It's a strange dilemma, wrestling with the point of performance art. I like to entertain; I like to stand onstage and entertain; I like to stand up there and make you laugh make you mad make you cry make you FEEL something. I'm a very selfish person; I like the sound of my own voice; I like when you like me—it means we have something in common: ME. So, what's my goal when I stand onstage—is it to make you happy? I'm sure that you think so! I hate when I see child actors; I hate their parents; I hate their upbringings and their rotten parents—the point of acting is to MOVE a crowd; children should only be allowed to MOVE themselves. Sometimes I question my own motives in regards to performance art: am I there to MOVE you? I'm sure that you believe it to be true! I'm a very selfish person and I like to tell you all about me—if that makes you happy, then I'm glad that I could be there to make you smile? I too am smiling, behind my haunting glare....

When

When the world burns
down to ashes
I'll stand in the pews
and start laughing
God is a fragile horse
Satan is a fraudulent flatuation
I am infatuated with
insubordination
Born to die in a basket
I was dropped off on the porch
of a lucipherian whorehouse
determined to suck the grease from the floor
of a hoarding minority
hell-bent on destroying
the boarded-up houses
that sway swiftly in the White House's
backyard
The dwarves the Hobbits & the Goblins
hide inside the busted windows
of a world on the brink of freakdom
When the world burns
down to ashes
you can bet hell that
I'll be the one supplying the gasses
Because only villains will suffer
the result of foreign goldmines
overflowing with salt and grime
Only anti-heroes will benefit from
the squalor of an apathetic childhood
Offsprings of the riotous ones
And finally
only heroes will die in
burning railroad cars

as the Nobodys ride past
having highjacked the entire train
hell-bent on leaving this country
and trading minerals for wine
when they make it overseas
When the world burns
down to ashes
I'll kiss the anarchist's asses
and bury the hatchet deep
into the past
When life amounts to nothing
I'll say I knew it all along
that life was just like a box of
cherry bombs
ready to drop and obstruct
the Justice Police
and the corrupted janitors
scrubbing clean the White House's bathrooms
will explode the moment Jesus
Christ turns the toilet water to
gasoline
So when the world burns
down to ashes
I'll be standing on the frontline
watching the fascist bastards
curl up and die
Smoke the fumes
Wear the ashes as perfume
Defuse the worldly corruption
and confuse the construction
Dilute the production
and conspire to destruct
When the world burns
down to ashes
I might just throw up
a wasted bucket of
forgotten tears

Incorrect Thoughts

In a culture where
pandering has become
commendable
an advocate of animosity is
detestable
a degenerate might be
heroic
being honest
is less than human
selfishness
self-preservation
self-obsession
and self-centeredness
as long as one's motives
are hidden behind
grandiosity
I might just call a friend
when the ones who openly say
I HATE
the ones who claim
to be less than honest
to be degenerate scumbags
refusing to repress
but tending to oppress
just simply standing against
well these people are cowards
and they don't deserve my respect
anyway
because the sheer act of
doing so
would only give them the power to
point out all the ways in which
I myself am
incorrect

Punk Rock in the Modern World

Nobody listens to Punk anymore.

And even those who do listen to Punk don't listen to Punk.

So I guess if you can't beat them
<u>kill them</u>!

Or at least hate them, that works too.

Dilapidated Derelict & Devoid

Writers thrive on a dissatisfied delusion. Sometimes it's easier to dream and preach and project, than it is to bring about change and help the human race prosper. I hold all these notions that will better the human race in my hands, but if the human race was better, I'd no longer have a drive to write. I'd have nothing to fight for anymore. Nothing to pit myself against. A reality of terminal bliss is the epitome of torture in the lost word of the writer. I know what I've got to do, but I don't do it because success is detrimental to my drive to write.

what for

when i die i want my life to mean something

when i live i want my death to mean something

Malfunction

Looking for trouble in all the wrong places—no wonder life is such a bore. There's no fun to be had in a world without trouble; thank God for laws for their deeming dividing lines to determine what's right and what's wrong and I always decide too sharply and start to veer left but in a split-second decision yank the wheel right, hard, and peel through grass and swamps and carve a tremendous path through street signs as I try to get back in line. Don't call me a vandal a disorderly scandal a panel of whacked-out antics for I wasn't the one who drew a precise map of morality and forced all to jump into the round hole and if you don't fit we will jam you in but deny responsibility for your misshapen psyche as the years go by and twenty years later they're tossing you into jail for making a simple mistake you tripped over your laces and tumbled and rolled and knocked over nine cops standing in a perfect triangular formation of futile despair and inflicted injustices and misleading deductions and destructively judgmental beady-eyed stares. It wasn't my fault for leaving my shoes untied, for the ramrod slamming and massively dogmatic enforcements of a brash code of conduct the corruption the swindled friction leading to a horrifying pounding trying to get me to fit in to a culture where vultures run amok and shed vicious diseases and yet I'm the freak me, it damaged my eyes and my fingers are twisted and my mind is almost lobotomized by the pressure of horny lepers who hate the extraordinary and try to reorient the disorderly and I'm lopsided and free. But fuck it I'm free.

LIKE this!

the way i see it, You don't haveta like everything, Nor do you haveta pretend to. it's okay to hate, Dislike, Or bash, As long as you feel self-righteous enough to justify your actions. you don't have to approve of every shit ever taken, As after all, Interest & intrigue are just a form of delusion, Anyway. you don't haveta love every man or woman who tries to sell you rubbish by the gallon; You can always crap on their parade and be proud of it, Too. like i always say, *It might not be for everyone but hopefully it's for someone.* but then, The only thing i know for certain is that the human race is a band of deserters, Haters, And crashers, So let's knock em down, Smash em up, Bash em like fascist pigs, Like self-righteous radicals, Like holy men on a holy mission to devalue that of others. sure, We can always say: *You did great!* But what i'm really thinking is: *Wipe that goddamn smile off your face!* because my shit is bigger, Wider, And fatter; My dick is thinner, Tinier, And sadder. you want to know the truth about the art world? *it's all shit!* but like i always say, *It might not be for everyone but hopefully it's for someone.* and if it's not for you, Then you can go suck a fat one, Because i hate you too.... we're all great; We all suck; And the fact of the matter is: *I'm the best!* the end.

Sign on the Dotted Line

> "We rule and you don't / We thrill and you won't / We laugh and you cry / We live and you die."
>
> — "We Rule and You Don't" by the Adolescents

When I was a kid I tried to fit in with mainstream society. I tried taking a dip in the stream of bodies all around me, the masses mindlessly riding the wakes to wherever it ends up taking them. But me, I was naked when I went in—I was about to go skinny-dipping in their precious little river—whereas everyone else wore designer bathing suits and they laughed and mocked me for being, uh … ME! For being somebody <u>other than them</u>, for being a **freak**. Yeah I was a freak all right—a freak who learned rather quickly that there was so much more to gain from beating my head against a brick wall than joining mainstream society because they were only heading for a downhill fall, about to take a violent plunge, as if they haven't already.

I wanted more than that—<u>so much more</u>! I did not want to be doomed to rot inside of a tiny cubicle for the rest of my life. I did not want to join Their Army—an army of suited drones, the only originality spawning from the décor of their $100 ties///how original is that?? Just leap headfirst into a roiling, devouring, and quite nefarious black hole known to the masses as CORPORATE AMERICA—be a number—just waste away in front of a screen, eating cheeseburgers at Micky Ds, and getting real fat and lazy and even better at standing in line—*it really does pay, too, you know*—taking orders and following them to a T.... I saw right through all that phony crap when I was just a little kid.

The town I grew up in? [Newton, MA—go fuck yourself! you phony urban wasteland >>>] These people, they were heading straight for a waterfall themselves, only they were unaware of the desolate existence they had signed themselves up for—quite willingly, too (vomit x 2 = a fat paycheck to keep the wifey at home rich & happy—yay!). Just sign on the dotted line and you'll be fine, you'll be completely all right; just sign away your entire life (hey, it's what the cools kids are doing so why not, right?))). Get a job get a bride get a big white house in the suburbs, complete with a white picket fence that wraps all the way around your entire front yard which glows like the sun, big and shiny and green, and with a garden, too, that is brimming with plump and colorful fruit. Keeping Up with the Joneses, is all you'll have to do if you wanna maintain that lifestyle——————and then you'll die, *boo hoo!*///you will die a nobody, you will die with nothing—you might not be alone in death, technically, but your cheating wife hates you, your unpaid mortgages are burning deep holes in your pockets, the barrel of a shotgun has sounded like a grand ol' idea for the longest time (for as long as you can remember, anyway), as your boss barks a series of orders and demands down your constricting throat in the most condescending way imaginable; and I bet your tongue bleeds when you think about all the nasty four-letter words you wanna use when he's around, all the mean little nouns you wanna throw at him, all the vicious little verbs you wanna hurl at his face, all the adjectives that could be stacked together to build

a hideout in the woods ... am I right? Yeah, you sure have it all, everything you could have ever wanted; you've got your hands on just about everything you'd ever need///fit for a king, fashioned for a man on the verge of having a nervous breakdown. (Bet a shotgun sounds fairly good right about now, doesn't it?) A house in the suburbs, a broken family, a boss who hates you....
And you think that I'm the freak??   Must I even go on??

Me, I'm heading straight for a black hole too, but at least I know that that is my fate. At least I'm not hiding from my destiny, running from the truth with a bucket of paint to pretty up my grotesque-looking face—and I mean it, it's pretty fuckin **grotesque!**

I saw right through the perfectly clean and painted fences and the lawns that are neatly trimmed to perfection, grass so green I can see myself flipping you off on the blades ...   ***vomit!***

— — — —

So you look down at me, call me a freak, say I'm not a Productive Member of Society—get a job get a life; you're barking up the wrong fuckin tree. You're right, I'm not a tax-payer, I'm not a home-owner, I'm not an ass-kisser, and I'm definitely not a push-over. But I bet I've helped out more people than you've ever helped with your lousy tax-paying.
So you can take your pointer finger and point it somewhere else—point it up your asshole, like where your ungrateful owner places his prick whenever he so pleases.

And I know I sound like a hypocrite by saying this; but guess what, I am a hypocrite, get used to it! You have been pushing me for long enough with your bogus, misplaced judgments, and now I'm taking a stance and pushing back with my own brand of righteous and rather enraged passing of the blame.

But it doesn't matter anyway: we're all to blame, nobody is exempt—not even me!———but at least I know that I'm sick, at least I'm out there living my life, trying to do something else, trying to make a name for myself—but I'm nobody's slave. Yeah, I might be an introspective little twit who forces others to look in the mirror for just a minute as they watch this pitiful wreck of a human being disintegrate before their very eyes—but I'm nobody's slave. Yeah, I might be an ungrateful little prick whose heart has been dipped into a pit of hatred when I was just a little kid—but I'm nobody's slave.

So why would I wanna take a dip in the mainstream, anyway? Just sign on the dotted line and become a slave. Who would want those kind of wages, right? Not me!!!

… so Count Me the Fuck Out!

The Devil's in the Details

We are condemned to knowing—too much, or too little. The universe of chivalrous rivalries meets the worldly philanthropist who acts only beyond the existential buzz of a new world culture to promote simplicity among a world where complicated and complicit walk hand-&-hand down roads of ruins. We are blessed to be able to access all the world's assets but do we not accept the fading truth when it rears down on us guns blazing,,,, the pregnant truth the layman and the mule the alleycats and the attack dogs and the muse of sacrilege raining down like fearsome hail we are blessed creatures for we are condemned to know too much and fancy too little throwing the rules of a diddling culture out of the Neanderthal's belly we meander down crowded lanes hoping that this day—Today—the only day to celebrate—to rejoice in a fate so forlorn we frolic like hyenas with busted vocal cords—the day that we foresee is to be deemed another wasted holiday. We are condemned to laughter, hindered and shattered by complacent madhatters; we carry the light in our heads, the darkness between our toes, and our woes are being taken care of by protégés of hatred. The greatest trick the Devil ever pulled was to convince the world he does not exist, and through the shallow wakes of time I see a little devil in the best of us, so hollow we take no time to exercise our rights in a diminishing pool of lost glories and the truth always evaporates on our tongues. I met the Devil, he revels in godly mutations, and we reject the wisdom of a mind so bent out of shape that the talisman of the holy is no longer glorious but reeks of shame; we carry the light but can't comprehend such a decrepit shade of beauty that the truth just fades away….

Disorder NOW!

Fuck politics
I'm a nihilist

Sometimes
    I'm a fascist
Other times
    I'm an anarchist

But when the moon is full
      I'm a practicing Catholic

Personification

Personified??

What do you mean?
    personified

We're all just
    personified

We're all just

personifiedfreaks

personifiedcreatures
        cretins
              meek&
practically   extinct

We are not animalistic

We're not we're not we're not ____
because   we are

          animals

who've only been granted
      free will

So stop personifying me

I shit sleep & eat

                    and think too

                                of course

The Big Picture

When I try to wrestle
with the big picture
I get overwhelmed

>We are all so fucked
>no matter which way
>you look at it____

Maybe the big picture is just
perhaps too big for my
finite brain to handle

>We are all so fucked
>no matter which way
>you look at it____

Untitled Poem

The goal is perfection
and it's that single desire
that drives me to
keep creating.

Perfection is always
just out of reach
and the closer I get
the farther I seem to be from success....

Categories

There is something that is bothering me. It's when someone crams me into their own categories and expects me to act accordingly, then gets upset when I contradict the classifications they had smacked beneath my nameplate. I don't claim to be anything other than me—whatever that means—because I can never seem to decide which road to go down. Sure, I may have called myself a nihilist. Sure, I may have called myself an absurdist, too. An existentialist a Catholic a Jew a fascist an anarchist a lover a hater straight gay bi left-wing or right-wing riding the flamingos broken wings through layer after layer of deep-seeded ambivalence.

So I said I'm a nihilist. Let's take that for example. What is a nihilist? See, this is where all your preconceived notions come into play and you find it much safer to cram me into a uniform—because now you can safely predict my next course of action///you can now understand me ::: I am a concept, I am an idea, I am a mirror   a mirror   a mirror that better helps you on your way to a more defined conceptualization of yourself…. So what does a nihilist look like? Tell me, please. Gimme a number, a set of restrictions, a code! To me nihilism means nothing. To me it's a joke. To you it means something; it's a serious branding———to you it has to mean something because you couldn't fully grasp how one could possibly, truly, believe in nothing so you classify me with everything you've learned on the subject. So now you've got me running around in my birthday suit: I'm butt-naked and my cock is swinging down below me like a pendulum and my butt cheeks are tingling in the wind and the cold air is causing my nutsack to shrivel——

                                          So I put on a pair of pants.

Nihilists don't wear pants, they tell me. *Why not?* I reply. *Because I was taught that believing in nothing means that there is nothing and when there is nothing you will be cold*———but I don't want to be cold, I'm choosing not to be cold, I have the right to wear clothes—for all intents & purposes, that is….

                                          See what I mean?

You see, I never claim to be anything for too long. The way I represent myself in the now, might evolve devolve or possibly revolve over time. Although I'm not trying to absolve myself of all the guilt & shame that I might feel for changing lanes and perhaps going the other way for a day or two or three, or however long I need for me to feel complete   ly wasted and change courses again. I reserve the right to change my mind on all issues, to go back on all of my previously envisioned convictions—but then, what convictions??—because I feel it's a necessary part of human growth & development to change my views constantly—<u>and</u> because I'm a nihilist and nihilists have no limits.

So, Just Don't Let One Single, Isolated Poem, among a very prolific repertoire of poems rants & stories, Dictate Your Overall Opinion of Said Poet. Let it represent the poet's emotional state when he wrote said poem.
Because boxes are meant for packages and packages are meant to be sent away and things that get sent away are never seen by those who can relate and the message is lost translated & sterilized by layer after layer of packing material like bubble wrap and bubble wrap is meant to be … uhhh, I don't know …… **POP'd!** maybe?...

So don't assume you know me! Don't put me in a box. I am not a useless category a malfunctioning allegory a charismatic prince tucked away in holy matrimony an elaborate ceremony meant to rid my of all my alimonies—I'm not a simple category,,,,   so don't put me in a box!...

The Jaded Soldier

A prisoner's first day in he sees someone get shanked, he quivers with fear. But after a few more stabbings occur the same prisoner can step jadedly over dead bodies like it's nothing. All my life I have never seen anything that either grossed me out or shocked me. Maybe I was just born jaded—or perhaps after absorbing, perceiving, and interpreting a sick, fucked-up, insidious reality, a jaded boy was born who grew up to be a nihilistic form of his younger, more derelict self—or perhaps I've just seen a different side of the world, brought on by mental deterioration and rejected thought forms and dejected internal genocides where the <u>norm</u> is no longer a thing to strive for, but a force to be reckoned with, to be shot down and destroyed. The far side of the moon?—yeah, right! Try the far side of the earth, the far side of human consciousness, the farthest side of abnormalities brimming with disdain and injurious blemishes that reek of absolute nothingness///and jaded I remain—a plastic doll with a useless heart and a soul revoked.… A person in the army watches his best friend get gunned down by a barrage of bullets, but after three or more best friends get shot down in the most tragic of ways, he forgets where he drew the line of sensitivity, where he felt an honest connection, where he relied on emotional reasoning and empathy like a love-struck teenager///only now he relies solely on insensitivity as both a defense mechanism and a weapon to keep him ready for battle. The jaded soldier has no one he can call his own, no friend or family member that he can count on, no wife or girlfriend he can rely on being there when his stint is up and he takes his leave of absence to all points nowhere just to regain composure before he gets shipped away again—next stop: the moon. He finds no connections no true interactions no comradery nothing but a rifle and a magazine and a clip—call him antisocial if you must, but don't be fooled by his asocial tendencies, for he'd trade his life of plastic and false interactions for a community that simply gets and understands him, any day.… The jaded soldier is the most insidious weapon the army can collect; the jaded soldier fights and kills and rallies and overthrows with no foreseen remorse or misgivings that can shatter his existence like what murders us via empathy and sensitivity.… The jaded soldier watches people from afar || and the only emotion he is capable of rousing in such a time of longing is a bitter hatred like bile; and the byproduct of such a feeling of forlorn is becoming the greatest threat to the opposition that this army has ever collected.…

Prayer & Meditation

I see no hope in prayer; I find no comfort in meditation. I meditate—when I read. I pray—when I write. But the formal act of falling to my knees, to me, is an unnecessary discomfort. On good days I identify myself as a Nihilist. When I'm manic, an Absurdist. On bad days I might call myself a Christian, a Jew, a Buddhist following a path of Zen which goes nowhere in the end—anywhere, <u>everywhere</u>, wherever———there are ups and downs and that's all that there is///the nihilist of all religions….

To get to the point, though, believing in nothing makes me feel like a king, a deity, larger than life; whereas believing in something makes me feel so small, alone, lost in a throwaway culture with no hope for a person like me—utterly hopeless, ironically so…. But maybe that's the point: to feel like nothing, to devalue myself and my existence, to rid myself of that nefarious beast called an EGO, acknowledging that I am not IT and I will never be IT. But I know I'm not IT. There is no IT, that's what I'm saying. But the absence of a holy IT makes me <u>feel</u> like I am in fact IT, loaded with self-confidence, however phony and shallow it might be….

Ask Yourself:

Do you want to talk and discuss?

Or do you want to oppose and oppress?

Ask Yourself:

Do you want a civil war?

Or do you want a revolution?

The Meaning the Purpose & the Deity

It's out there I am here. It's out there I am here. I know not what that means because I am only a mere human being. It's out there I am here. God is God I do not understand. God is God how could I possibly understand the thing that created me? I mean it did create me right? Like an amoeba can understand a walking, talking human being I try to fathom just what that means…. God is God I am me. I will not project meaning on things I just can't see. I will not create purpose in things that lack purpose. A deity what does that even me? A shapeless being that sees and hears <u>every</u>thing?? Explain to me how something like that might think. It's out there I am here. God is God I am me!

… <u>end of story</u> …

Like Clockwork

The problem is a system where we are forced to choose a side through severe acts of subterfuge. Through peer pressure and subtle acts of hatred, the government is winding up the masses like a fucking clock—**tick tick tock**—churning the wheel around and around and around round round, so that we're nice and tight and exactly where they want us.

Black Sheep

One of the hardest challenges I've ever had to overcome, which is still weighing down on me even today, is finding My Own Identity within a world where everyone is pulling me Their Own Way, trying to get me to think like them, to support their causes. Do I rebel, or do I submit? Which choices come from My Own Volition, and which choices are only as a result of wanting to impress or to reject that of Other People's Whims. It's like I'm being dismembered, limb by limb, driven by indecisions, and within these infringements I find it rather difficult to find My Own Identity.

My whole life I've been a sheep : : : but a black sheep. I reacted to Your Impositions; I fought them tooth-&-nail, because I was stubborn and righteous and defiant and would do just about anything it took for me to not be dictated by Your Will. I was a black sheep: I acted in accordance to what you didn't want me to be. I refused to conform, and to submit to standards set in place by people I hated. I refused to be like you, and I would have done <u>any</u>thing to avoid becoming susceptible to Their Ruling///a sheep who falls in line, talks on time, arrives on time, and leaves on time—a victim of conformity____

which was the farthest thing from me
because
I was a black sheep

But then time vaporized these foolish notions that I had — which were to defy the mainstream and the norm. I was an adult now, and I saw no reason to let others dictate My Own Actions, whether I'm going with or against the masses. A black sheep is still a sheep—just a sheep who walks against the flow and pushes currents of controversy through the airways as people gawk at this dis-colored specimen, and wonder why, when they say right, it goes left, and when they say left, it goes right…. So I have come to realize in my later years that making rash decisions based upon Someone Else's Demands, whether it be with or against, renders me helpless to the system—victimized by the same machine that I detest reject resent & protest. It means the system has control over me—or moreover, I'm giving up <u>my</u> control to the system, which just wants to mold soldiers and drones out of clay and let their recently developed figurines sit there vulnerable and thoughtless and easy to be reshaped whenever their makers deem it necessary.

No longer will I be a black sheep! because today I'm seeking My Own Way and My Own Identity to be claimed.

21st Century Artists

Some people are artists;
some people say they are artists;
and the rest are plagiarists.

Kid with the Replaceable Head

> "Now he can pick em at will from his heads on the shelf."
> — "Kid with the Replaceable Head" by Richard Hell & the Voidoids

I think I live multiple lives. Not a double-life, per say, because that's not what I mean. What I mean is: I'm lost between a multiverse of personalities that change depending on what my current mood calls for—depending on what my current surroundings provoke. Depending, of course, on who you ask about me. It all depends!!! One might say I'm belligerent and wild—a loose leaf, so to speak. I might not be drunk anymore but I'm still as zany as ever. Another might say: Who, Jeremy? That guy's so calm and calculating, even-keeled, cool like how the ocean might feel against your face on a hot summer day—he just seems so loving and happy all the time, like he has an appetite for living, while simultaneously maintaining that calm, Zen-like appeal, always promoting positivity everywhere he goes. But then, of course, there's the guy in the back of the room, avoiding the inevitable interview that he can't run from but he tries to hide, anyway—he says: Yeah I know Jeremy Void. What a hateful prick that fucker is. Only looking out for number-one, that Jeremy. Always scheming, always fleeing, just fucking with people mind's in an endless shuffle to stay high and come out on top. But, he adds, seeming as sincere as can be, that's his best quality I think. A girl once said that I fear rejection. I'm always vetting my surrounding fellows and then attempting to blend.

    Well we'll see about that….
    Surely we will >>>

So I know that, after reading this, you might be asking yourself whose opinion is the most accurate ::: one two three or four?...

The answer::::
||All of the Above||

As I once said, <u>I am not a cartoon character</u>. Got that: I'M NOT A FUCKIN CARTOON CHARACTER! so don't think that one moment is enough evidence to accurately assess my persona. (In fact, don't try to assess understand or assume at all, cuz I guarantee that you'll just be disappointed surprised or possibly even taken off guard, straight jarred, by your lack of factual information about me and who I am///so don't even try!) You see, my personality is constantly changing—it's always in flux, from day to day, from crowd to crowd, and especially from mood to mood; it never settles, constantly taking me down white-water rapids that smash and crash and flip and flow and bounce and thrash through my jaggedly beating heart, like emotional whiplash. But tomorrow it gets even better; it always does…. My moods always dictate my reactions;;;; but here's the kicker: the people in my near vicinity—well not the passersby I suppose, because they don't mean shit to me when I'm out with the boys—they drive my character traits to behave in ways I could never get them to behave on my own. Hang out with manic, wild, fast-paced people and you'll see exactly what I mean // hang out with chill, even-keeled, stoner types, and boy will you….
So is it really wrong to live a double-life? I mean, I know there's all this hype that speaks out against it. [But me, I'm a kid with a replaceable head, don't you get it.] Nobody acts the same exact way around everybody, now do they?

Be honest, they say/
    Be genuine
        Stay true to yourself

Stay true to yourself?? I have many truths. Unfortunately, they can't all coexist….

Dead Rockstars

Rockstars don't die, they live like kings, and then turn into gods. But I'll tell you, they should die. They should have died years ago. But I'm not saying this because they're addicted to drugs. But no, they should die because they're rockstar and no man should ever be treated like a god. Drug-addiction should just be the <u>cause</u> of their deaths. I want to say they should be crucified. But remember what happened to Jesus? Again, no man should ever be mistaken for a god. They should just get shot, stomped on, stabbed, thrown in front of a bus. That's just what I would do if I was a rockstar: I would kill other rockstars because I'm a rockstar and I can do what I want. Then you can crucify me not for the sins of the masses, but for my own sins. And then people will be thinking: *He died for our sins! We've got a clean slate! Now we can do what we want!* Every ten years or so let's crucify another rockstar and we'll be back to zero sins. **Hoorah!**

The Inferno

Do what makes you happy and
fuck those who
disapprove
When you shut out pain
you shut out everything
else
Sure, there's always
the risk of being fucked used manipulated &
DeStRoYed
but when you start to avoid
such a risk
you end up
pushing away something

that could perhaps
bring you joy
There's always the risk of
crashing & burning
I could get hit by a bus
tomorrow
So does that mean stay at home
all day long?
to avoid such an
awful outcome
Running away at the
first sign of trouble
means
turning your back on the chance of
something that could turn out
great
There are no happy endings
no sad results
Life goes on forever
and the only end is always
death
So why say no to
the inferno
that life has in store
when instead you can take a chance
and dive into the
flames
head-on

"I am smart"

I was thinking about how only stupid people call themselves smart. When everything is relative, and one's standard of intelligence is fairly low, then it would be rather easy to say: "I am smart."
When I say "You are smart," I am measuring your ability to understand and conceptualize theories and concepts against my own ability to do so. When I say "I am smart," I'm doing the same thing, only in reference to myself; I'm measuring my own ability to think deeply and intuitively against my own ability to think deeply and intuitively. Which might lead me to the assumption that I am a truly smart human being, a deep and wise thinker, the kind of genius that can blow any other genius artist or naysayer out of the water with striking quickness in regards to thinking and philosophizing and understanding concepts that would cause the average human brain to implode upon contact with said ideas.

Would you agree that, if I said I'm the smarter man I've ever met, I'm absolutely correct in my rather shallow and possibly naïve presumption of myself? I would! In fact, if you said it about yourself, I might just say: "You know what, that is one of the most accurate assessments I have ever heard one say about one's own self." It can't be disproven, it can't be argued—because I, me, this man typing this rant this very second, am an absolute genius/
in comparison to myself.   Makes sense, right?

Socrates said: "The only true wisdom is in knowing you know nothing."
          This is true, but it's not exactly what I'm getting at here. You see, I know I know nothing; I know that every miniscule notion, every diseased nugget of truth, every insincere fact that I carry around with me, in this bloated, but ever-so-shrinking, noggin of mine, is a crapshoot just waiting to be disproven. Break it to me gently, or punch me in the face with a blunt comeback that is sure to leave me seeing stars before the night is through—it don't matter, just hit me with the truth, lay down the honest-to-God facts, and I'll drop to my knees so quickly you wouldn't even see me do it, and then proceed to touching my lips to the concrete ocean on which we stand or float or both, kissing the ground on which you walk———Praise <u>You</u>! You are so much smarter

339

than me, you know so much more than me, you are a god with wisdom and a delightful conversationalist—perhaps you <u>are</u> me…. We are kindred spirits, you & I. Two peas in a blender. We mix like LSD when it absorbs into your brain and takes you for a ride through a world of complete wonderment and total astonishment. Because in order for you to prove me wrong, you must have an argument that beats my own argument/
according to me….

An argument about which, weighed against my own, I can rightfully say: "Wow, you've got a damn good point!" Let me buy you a coffee, a drink, a line of cocaine, a crack pipe but the crack ain't free, although with a very sharp and precise safety pin you may very well be able to scratch out a thinning layer of truth from inside.
<u>I am not smart</u>. <u>I know nothing</u>. Compared to the greats I am like an amoeba soaking up the wisdom of <u>true</u> geniuses, swimming in a pool of **words** and **information** that I couldn't possibly grasp in the same way the writers had. Granted, I do fancy myself as a bit of a philosopher—for this is one of my own philosophies, one of my own conjured-up theories, like all my concepts before and all my concepts hereafter———although truth be told, I am a <u>terrible</u> philosopher/

———or am I?

I do think my philosophies are rather sound and unbeatable, though, because my philosophies come from a place of my own thinking and of course I can't think any better or stronger than the amount I can already think and that leaves me stuck with a set of unbeatable, half-assed theories that I think are absolutely marvelous. Do you catch my drift?
Because I wouldn't\\\

He Said

When everything is recorded
documented
and posted on the web,
he said;
when it's all easy access
it's so easy to decide
I want no part
in the promotion of
negativity
I don't want to hurt I wanna
give and help
the human race prosper
I want to be
proactive
not counterproductive
So we, he added, as
human beings
in the modern times
have been conditioned
to be pro
and not promote the cons
just shut down
and shut out everything
that sends the wrong
impression
block the presses and give life
to a censored delusion
in a broken society
filled to the brink
with negativity
deeming the politically correct
union
a brave deduction

when putting others down
going against the flow
being mean-hearted and
just saying NO
to the norm and the boring
fascist preachers
who promote the forcing of
change
through ostracization
shunning the few who choose
to do it another way

I shrugged at
his bold assessment
of where the
human race is heading
afraid to agree
for fear of what they'll deem
me
to be
in only a few seconds
<u>I'm not a freak</u>!

Artists—

we lead a quiet existence // we leave a vibrant legacy....

Optimistic Nihilism

I am an optimistic nihilist/
Fuck Off

I find joy in struggling
I find hope in suffering
I see light in the dark
and I see no reason to mope
because when nothing truly matters
all that there's left to do is
grow///

The world that you worship
is caustic
and I transcend through
the dungeon's flare
rising to the top of
the glimmering mountain
of a nightmarish reality
beaten by Christians and Jews
shaped by politicians and business men
destroyed by the unbreakable grasp
of five billion men and women
who simply refuse to let go....

So I am an optimistic nihilist
and I see no reason to mope
because when you've got nothing left to cherish
the only thing there is left to do is
grow///

I am an optimistic nihilist/
Fuck Off

Unjustified & Irrational

I don't make excuses for the things that I do. I own every action that I make. I do not justify, and I do not rationalize, and if you find me justifying, or rationalizing, I will fess up to it immediately.

Yes, I am making excuses right now.
Yes, there is something wrong with me.
Yes, I am a hypocrite. I am a fascist. I am a terrible fuckin person.
Yes, I am sick in the head….
        So Sick

Now, it's your turn >>>>>>

Divide & Conquer

Left-wing || Right-wing
Really I need both wings
to fly\\\

Barred from the Garden of Eden

I will not conform
to your policies
      to your limits
           to your procedures

I refuse to obey
the restrictions
you've deemed suitable
for this day&age
I will push buttons
create controversy
make you uncomfortable
I will redefine laws
reshape values
demolish the virtues
put in place by
the corruption of
   the masses

      Fuck your social order
       It wasn't me
      who decided to
       take a piss on
       self-expression

I will demonstrate free speech
rendering the PC code
completely obsolete
I don't hate anyone
for their color of skin
for their sexual preference
for their gender identifications
for their millennial upbringings

      Race does not matter
   Who you choose to fuck does not matter
  What you choose to call yourself does not matter
        to me
    <u>as long it doesn't matter to you</u>
     <u>what I choose to call you</u>
    <u>how I choose to think of you</u>

<u>who I associate you with</u>
<u>in my own</u>
<u>mind</u>

Because its none of your damn business
what I choose to
do
on my own free time
So just don't expect me to change
      for you

I will establish a new kind of
mass public
who is unafraid to think
speak or feel
on any which subject
because this country was founded on the right
to criticize our government
even during periods of
war and other national emergencies
and that is a right
I refuse to surrender to
people who wanna ban
words
censor thoughts
keeping America flaccid
smashing the free presses
instilling social justice by
exiling the opposing view
decided by
a discerning few
the elite
the social warriors of America
the self-righteous hatemongers who preach
love through hate
peace through violence

protesting everything that sends
the wrong impression
and makes the sensitive ones
sad
well too bad———
                            Not everyone on this earth is here to please you
                                    Sometimes people simply disagree
                                              say mean things
                                           act out of selfishness
                                                     and pride
                                              and you just gotta
                                                  get over it!
                                           Because that's what I do
                                          when I'm treated like shit

I will stay true
I will stay free
I will fight for the truth
I will fight for the freedom
to speak and think and feel
because that is the most important right
we were granted when God
created Adam & Eve
Eve didn't haveta bite
        into the apple

Heaven

Beyond the Legend

Me: What's the point of life?

Them: To go to heaven, silly!

Me: Okay, so what happens in heaven, then?

Them: You get to go there for all eternity. Duh!

Me: Oh, great.

And then I walk away thinking: *God, you bastard!*

A Germ

All these new poets are always so political it seems. Mostly liberal propaganda seems to be the thing amongst them. The Intellectual Elite they're called. I mean, you don't exactly see very many rednecks huddled beneath their confederate flags writing hate rants, bigoted musings about how good a donkey's asshole feels when you're riding it like a brand-new rust bucket. It feels nice and tight, that's what!
So, as a result you got these liberal extremists writing poems about love, saying if you don't love your fellow man (and woman, too)—accept them for their differences and tolerate them for their defects—we will hate you till you die. If to you hate is as common as theft is to a thief—as normal as kiddie porn is to a pedophile, the sick, perverted cretins that they are———If that's you, then we will conspire to kill you, condemn you, kick you in the neck and watch as you bleed to death.   Feminism   Black Power   Muslims United   Vegan Elitism   Straightedge-Core   Bicyclists Oppressed by the Driving Race   The Driv-

ing Race Oppressed by the Pedestrian Outrage   The Pedestrians of a Nation Held to Blame by Everyone Who Festers in a World of Bigoted Hate   The Self-Righteous   The High & Mighty   The Nose-in-the-Air, Not-in-My-Backyard, Snarky, Judgmental, Finger-Pointing Human Being===   That includes me, it includes you, it includes him, and finally, it includes her too : : : it incorporates all of us sick fucks, every last one of us—we're all just phony radicals in the end, searching for a place for ourselves in a tired world///

But back to my original point::::   All these hateful left-wing extremists are chiding you into joining them on the downhill fall of the Democratic Party, locked in a self-destructive, self-sacrificial, self-delusional—the Intellectual Elite///in an a-religious, non-spiritual, totally tyrannical plunging spiral straight through Hell and back as they burn this entire fuckin country to the ground. And all these hipsters and hippies and shit-stirrers and misguided millennial brats will not stop at nothing until they're dancing butt-naked, high on pot, stoned on knowledge, wasted on self-righteous, uh, bullshit, atop the graves of dead veterans and atop the biggest pile of waste and decay and crispy, charred ashes that came from a sweltering hot flame as the whole entire country sizzled and burned and faded away into nothing///and then—then———and then they dance around the smoking pile of this nation's remains singing out loud and for everyone to hear: *Ring around the rosie / A pocket full of posies / Ashes ashes, we all fall down///*   **One more time, and all together now:** *Ring around the rosie / A pocket full of posies / Ashes ashes, we all fall down*———a job well-done….

Victory Is Mine
<<< bitches >>>

… just spreading propaganda like they do.
(And to think, they say that <u>I'm</u> the one spreading propaganda, ME. What a crock of shit!)))

But you see, I guess that's where I differ. <u>How</u> I differ. Through writing I am attempting to plant a seed in your head. An Idea. The Germ of a Thought. And it's up to you, the reader, to nourish it, to water it and watch it grow into something bigger == an evolved theory/// See, I'm not trying to tell you how to think, what to think, or even, who to think about (and if I was, you wouldn't know a thing about it because I have mastered the art of subtlety—or so I say).

I don't want to give you the answers
        nor do I have any answers to give/
I don't want to fill your head
with futile knowledge   (Now, put that in your pipe
        and smoke it)))
        for I'd much rather show you
                how to do it yourself....

Just plant an idea in your head. A Miniscule Notion. A Broken Fact Mended Back Together by the Act of Thinking Things Through, for a change. That's my goal; in fact, it's my only goal———other than the million other goals I try to accomplish when writing///

— — — —

See, all these poets today are trying to tell you exactly what to think. Me, I'm just trying to give you something to think about. Or maybe I'm just so totally full of shit.

        —|| THINK ABOUT IT ||—

Unity

THEY SAY
DIVIDE AND
CONQUER
I SAY
UNITE AND
STAND STRONG
BECAUSE
IF THE KIDS ARE
DIVIDED
THEY WILL NEVER BE
UNITED
AND IF THEY NEVER
EVER
DECIDE TO
COME TOGETHER
THEN WE'RE AT THE WHIMS OF
A DEMOCRATIC
MASSACRE/

in a way

I've always been a perfectionist, in a way, only to me perfection meant destroyed, meant defective, meant decrepit, and I sought this goal of creating a destructive soul, of creating a hole in my heart in my core in my head, of living to displease and find displeasure amid a dystopian universe. I've always been a perfectionist, in a way; I lived to perfectly disobey and I would ride the stolen jeep down lanes of hatred and waste and decay and of course there was self-abuse, too. It was the only way. So yes, I've always been a perfectionist, in a way…. Only to me perfection meant destruction and destruction meant creation and creation meant causing a ruckus in any way possible….

Bad

Just because I have a "bad" attitude does not mean I'm a bad person. I mean, think about it: People with "good" attitudes become advertisement consultants who steal your money. People with "good" attitudes become overpaid business men who lay people off. People with "good" attitudes join the army and kill for the name of religion, politics, or just simply because the voices in the back of their heads tell them to. People with "good" attitudes judge and condemn and join churches that judge and condemn. Just because I have a "bad" attitude does not mean I'm a bad person. I tell you what I'm thinking about, as oppose to lying to you so that I can use and fuck and destroy you.

TV Junkies

I left it blank for a reason. If I wanted a solution, I'd fill in the void with normal tendencies, like watching television until my eyes bleed. If I wanted an illusion, I'd join the masses in mainlining that television set, feed the regular programming into a bright and vibrant and glittery syringe that beams commercials into my brain as I drive the spike into my veins and float away into a fantastic, plastic non-reality. If I wanted a disillusion, I'd chuck that television set out the window and watch it go *smash!* as it hits the sidewalk >>>||| the perfect scheme to free myself from envy and greed and falsely idolized, rich Hollywood creeps. And then, when it's all said & done, we can set it on fire and dance around the burning box like a band of manic Indians celebrating their new-found freedom.

Hip-Hip-Hooray!

SOBRIETY!—A Deviant's Drug of Choice

I've always said I'm just as weird without the use of drugs & alcohol. But I'm thinking now that I'm even weirder These Days because drugs & alcohol only served to make me normal. I would always say, too, that most people learn how to cope with their emotions growing up, whereas I'm just learning how to cope with my emotions Now. I guess I could say the latter is true; but the truth of the matter is, Look at the State of the World That We Live in—drink drink drink, take take take, & consume…. It's everywhere you look: people indulging diverging and digressing. I mean, maybe a few of us—the "lucky" ones—have learned how to cope with their emotions growing up, but what I've always seen is that the first day we're hatched they shove pills down our gullets if we seem just a little bit abnormal to them…. We can't control you so here's a pill!... How does that sound? You'll never have to feel different again, and we'll never have to worry that our child student or patient is a deviant. Everybody wins!

Free Speech

You wanna talk about oppression?
Look in the mirror,
you'll find your answers there.
Focused on the repression and not
the individual expression,
you reject everything that puts the spotlight
on your own dilemma.
You run this vile nation
with your propaganda and your banners
of the relentless self-righteous pandering.
Put a ban on the airwaves,
making the Clear Channel happy,
the FCC frantic,

the masses just lapping it up/
No More Hate Speeches
No More Hate Parades
No More HATE
No More Anger, just loving & fucking
fuck fuck fuck, take take take
ban ban ban fly your banners high.
Make the world just like you….
No more thought no more thinking
no more creativity///
Kill the individual with deliberate unity.
Unified and so full of shit,
it's a dignified mockery that is washing over
this dying country—
not like the plague,
but like a holocaust your destruction of free speech
is setting this country aflame….

The Best Way to Win the Game

The best way to win the game—change the rules

The best way to win—start anew

The best way—admit defeat and allow yourself to lose

The—there's nothing like the present, light the fuse of tomorrow, watch yes-
    terday's flame turn blue turn red turn green turn the levers churn the
    severed brain and watch as the whole world becomes amused

The best way to win the game—stop drop & roll the ammunition around and
    around till you lose your brain and go completely insane

The best way to win—do it your own way

The best way—_____

The—don't ask me! figure it out for yourself; throw a wrench in progress,
       throw a wrench in time, throw a wrench in establishment, throw a
       wrench in mine

Filthy Abrasions

At the center of things, there is nothing. No matter how much you search for meaning, in the end you'll always arrive at nothing. I'm not trying to be a downer; I'm not trying to bring you down. But in fact, acceptance of this nothing should lift you up. It's a very liberating concept. You can go wherever you want, you can do whatever you want, you can be whatever you want. Because there is nothing to hold you back. The reason there is so much pain and anguish in the world is because people won't accept this fabulous nothing into their lives—that and they don't know how to use their words properly, of course. A void is not such a terrible thing after all; it only becomes oppressive when you haveta run endless miles just to fill it. Drugs alcohol sex fighting plastic money gambling fighting plastic sex money and then there's

… <u>nothing</u>.

Somebody today said: Trump is trying to divide us, so if you support Trump, please I don't want to be your friend anymore (the irony!). I said: It's not Trump that's trying to divide us, it's Democracy. Don't blame Trump, blame Democracy. Blame Democracy! For in fact, Democracy is the very thing that allowed people like Trump to get elected in the first place. You're fighting all the wrong wars!
I say: Wage War on the Television Set. Blow It Up! Kick the Radio in the Teeth. Murder the Commercials Beaming Materialistic Visions into Our Less-Than Interested Heads. Throw Rocks at YouTube. Bash Facebook with a Wooden Club.

Stab Mass-Produced Intelligence with Razor Blades and Steak Knives. Hurl Grenades into the Media. Bury the Clear Channel, Lynch the FCC, Lynch the DJ, Lynch the President, and Detonate the Pretty, Flowery Insight of Every Pop Philosopher Who Is Presently Waging War on All of Us, on Our Minds on Our Thoughts on Our Wills, Trying to Reduce Us to Mere Raisins Stomped On Forgotten About & Devoured by the Rich Government Officials.
Trust me when I say: <u>Nothing is worth fighting for</u>.

Because in the End We're All Just Slaves
anyway/
        slaves to our own
        minds

So fuck it!
        right?

Jaded Delicacies

Struggling

    I would not wish my guidance onto my own worst enemy

        i.e. myself

    because I've been struggling a lot as of lately

    and I just don't know what to do about anything

Faceless

I know nobody
and boy does it feel great
I can vanish between mobs
and no one knows my name

There's nothing to lose
when you've got no face
Be anybody you choose
because nobody cares what you do
at the end of the day

I can go anywhere do anything
be anyone and I've just got
nothing left to lose

Possessive

The most important thing in my possession is my mind, but if you were to strip me of that, then what would I have left? My body???? No, but that's boring.... My mind isn't a vacuum, but it might be a vacuum cleaner/// But my body?? What is that good for, anyway? other than the obvious: taking up space. Someone once explained to me that the body and the mind are interconnected; they're one and the same—well, fuck that! I have a tendency to neglect my body, but my mind ... well,,,, my mind withers as a result. But I guess that's the point, isn't it? Drive myself insane, push myself beyond reason, make myself lose it ... lose my mind, because, you know, when I lose my mind ... well, then I've gotta start taking care of my body to get my mind back into shape— well, fuck that! I mean, at least my art thrives in the absence of control, right? It thrives on insanity. I am Jeremy Void, after all. VOID! But my mind is not a vacuum, although it might be a vacuum cleaner///

Terminal

Sitting in misery
fidgeting with literally
every single miniscule
notion my brain disseminates
in times of extreme stress

Help me please///
Help me see
Help me get outta my own
way   living in dismay
twisted & bitter I'm hitting
every sinking, crispy slash that
I streak across my veiny wrists
in a fit of shitty belligerence
a game I play out of disintegration

It's a diluted fate///
It's a hopeless wait
Futile despair- - -rejected from
the tiger's lair/
I'm dejected &
oppressed
by evil midgets with knives
a politically-correct race
I'm running for my life
running only to die
I'm running outta time

Help me get out///
Help me   period
Help me get through
today

By God I'm living like///
a door-to-door obituary
delivering blasphemous truths
surrendering my soul for a pack of smokes
a bag of crack
a pound of hash I'm tumbling through
day&night searching for the past
Running from a
smashed-up future

slashing it up
crashing through
bashing my head
thrashing the mirror

The mirror it's nasty &///
mean >>>   sinister
I'm a screwed-up soliloquy
Shouting just to be seen
Looking through rose-colored glasses
Slashing my wrists on the thorns
Saying Kiss My Ass You Fascist Pig

& there I am///
back where I started
finishing a race I never wanted to
take part in
Look at the space between
my parted lips
& tell me
can you tell me   please
just one thing

Do you see me in the///
obituaries because I was supposed to
die today but God said no no no not yet
& I said what do you mean not yet?
& this ever-sought deity
that means absolute shit to me but
decides my entire unyielding fate
says to me through its shapeless maw
Son   wait your goddamn turn!

& I think God you bastard///
you did it to me again

& there I am///

Explosive

Do you ever just wanna
blow something up
because the mere sight of it
makes you feel small and
out of control

Shunned Bullied & Ignored

I'm just so sick of
being picked on by people
for not
fitting into their
precious little mold

Look at me
it's me
the guy who
took his shirt off his back
to help your starving
neighbor struggling to keep
his head up
as you projected and said:
The Homeless Are Mentally Unstable

But still
let's give to charity
let's give to causes
support the struggle
by standing in line

marching down crowded roads
holding signs alongside my
brethren
all the while turning my back
on the real struggling man
and woman
and saying: I'm Privileged
I Come from Privilege
I Got It Really
Really Good
so I march down crowded roads
singing chanting and shouting:
You Are Wrong
You're Not One of Us
Go Back to Where You Belong
Go Back to the Psych Ward
for all I care
Go to Back to Jail
Mr. Homeless Man
because you think differently
act differently
are different than us
in so many ways
and you just don't belong with
the chosen race
us who give a shit
about the state of
the world we live in
today
My Money Just Can't Go to You
because you have different views
than that of the chosen few
I'll blindly give my money
to blind charities
drop it in slots and never see it
again

because the sign says
That's What the Sign Says
it says that
the money
is going to a good
cause
and now I've done my part
and now I can go home
I'm a jackass and you know it
but I've done my part
and that's what matters
in the end
        right?

First off:
    I yelled at somebody
    today
    who supports an
    alternative cause
Secondly:
    I dropped money in a slot
    bearing a sign that said
    the money'll go to charity
and thirdly:
    I joined the mob as they
    shouted pointed and blamed
    everyone else
    for all the world's problems

Try taking some responsibility
for your actions, dick
        I'm not perfect but
        at least I can admit that
        I'm a sick person

It's more than
you've ever done with
your flapping, flying banners of
the self-righteous kind

So I guess now
that that's done
I guess I've done
my part
in making the world
a better place
and now I can go back to
being a jackass
like I was before
the herd lined up for a
march
so righteous and absurd

But then there's me
Me
who let the homeless man
into his house
to sleep on the floor or on
the couch
And then there's me
Me
who hangs out with the broke
the people who struggle
day in
day out
and yet
there's you
You
who shun bully and
oppress everyone

who you declare as a threat
to your own
self-righteous herd
You oppress
those who think outside the range
of the mass majority
of fakes

I'm sorry I won't stand behind
your self-righteous façade///

On the Fast Track

Everybody's life is on a track, and there's no getting off until you die. Which means your life is like a ride that moves circularly. Every event, every thought, every everything, it will all happen to you again.

Some people's tracks are more like the merrygoround variety, a steady flow of ups and downs, a course that is boring to people like me. There's not too much to see; and once it starts, there's no getting off until you die.
Other people, people who think similarly to me—well these people are on a track too, a fast track, a track that rips through the horizon a hundred miles per second, and soars like a hawk as it plunges straight downward and cuts an immediate right, rolling and tumbling as it tears a smoldering path through the blackened sky. This track is that of a rollercoaster, where the ups reach the sky and the downs cut deep into the earth. This is my track///the track that I'm on———————

——& i wanna get off of it—
— **now** —

Friends Not Fans

Sometimes someone will
come up to me and say:
I really like your writing.
I always say, Thanks.
Say: Hey,
what's your name?
They tell me; we shake.
So I guess I don't
really have fans
when I think about it.
      I have friends///
      is what they are
It might start with
intrigue for my writing
but in the end I always
reach my hand out and say:
Hey, what's your name?

On occasion I'll stumble
across an under-appreciated
poet that I myself will dig.
Self-published, just like me/
I'll shoot him/her a message
via Facebook.
Say: Hey,
I really dig your writing.
But I never usually hear back....
It's really quite a shame!

Nothing to Lose

A lot of people say they had lost everything.

Me, I lost nothing because I had nothing to lose.

My Brain Knows Best

I fell off my path when I listened to my dick instead of my own heart. But I fell off my path, too, when I listened to my heart. I'm impulsive, and intellectually I know the right way to go; but my emotions want it and my dick wants to fuck it; and while my head tells me to HALT! I end up chasing trains through jungles of death. I want it, and I want it now. I crave action and I'll go to the end of the line to get it. Just dive headfirst into the freezing cold water. Some might first test the temperature with their toes. But me, I say there's only one sure-fire way to know. Splash-splash-splash, crash&burn///that's the only way for me to go >>>

in luv

i think im in luv—so in luv

——w/ myself....

Break Her Neck

                                                Same shit, over & over again. Same shit different day.
Over & over again/

                                                                    When will it fuckin end??

I swear

                    the next girl who looks at me with anything
                          remotely resembling intrigue

                            I will break her fuckin neck!

                                                  Just you wait and see….

Curtains

Lumbering through the day like a boiling zombie. It's pointless to care, it's pointless to try, it's pointless to stay, it's pointless to cry, it's pointless I lie to the face in the mirror, to the wary nomad who glares furiously at the bold and blazing sun like a daytime coyote; I wait till the day evaporates and the night overtakes the earth and I can finally lay my head down and say goodnight to the town to the world to the whirlpool of turmoil caused by the moody maneuver I carried out in a fit of desperation and now I can sleep & sleep till I don't know, I just wanna sleep forever and don't bother waking me because the embers of life will already have faded from my eyes by the time you find me lying there in a pool of my own blood. It was a sacrifice that I needed to make—a happy ending awaits, when we take that final step into oblivion and say goodbye. Goodbye!

A Thorn in My Mind

Dissipating- - -let's start there

                                      - -
                                      - -
                                      - -

When life opens you up, run for cover. I'm under life's blundering spell. Clouded by rich judgment, a clutter of punches jabbing my ribcage. When you open up your eyes, the truth will make you go blind.
I've just got nothing to say. So strange how a murderous tantrum can drive you insane///

                                                Too much/
                                                           to say

                                                Too much/
                                                           to say

No more daydreaming
                    I'm fading
                                                                 away

Crossing many algorithms, many vengeful decisions, delivering myself through the web/

You can buy me   for the right price.

I'm tagged & bagged.

I'd sell you my soul   if you wanted it
but I doubt that
               you do/

I've just got nothing to say.
So start from
                the top:
For starters, my stomach aches, my eyes feel like they're being ripped through my own spine. I'm drawing a blank, seizing mentally, like disintegrating thoughts.

Where was I?
That's where::::
                Sold on broken ideas.

Food for thought.

But I'm not hungry.

It's all gone viral, anyway. Every last devouring gem- - -all of it, eradicated///

Broken.

Hopeless.

It's all just a hoax.

Unwinding my brain like a devastating spiderweb….

Yielding.

I'm jumping through hollow shields….

From the top:
In a room. Surrounded by a clamor of thought. Everybody writing.
      I can't sit still >>>

My stomach aches.
I need a cigarette.

The rantings of a desperate
            silencephobe.

Punctured in my aching gut///

Guess if I've just got nothing to say, I might as well kill the moment with comatose gibberish.

They screwed me
        again

Hold On!

My grip on reality is weak|||
It never seems to be
just what I need….

Here It Lies

Oh this racing mind
Oh this one-track line
I'm riding escalators
up through winding hills
like mazes of elevation
zeroing in on the zits
on my braces
the way my face looks
when I'm screaming at the
devastating mirror

It looks exasperated
so I shatter it with
my shadowy spit
Oh my destructive nature
only today I seek creation
I want to create explosions
uproars
and the thinnest shards
of stained-glass windows
splattered across bloody driveways
filled to the top with
human decay
Now
I'm back
where I started
back from the top
which is where I take it
when I'm home all alone
strumming my mental chords
Like a One-Man Band
Living in a One-Track Land
A Once-Said
Once-Destroyed
Possibly Deviated
Force of Defiant Nature
this man I had built
from the ground up
So follow me why don't you
Follow me down
endless rants
through ecstatic tirades that
I always kick in the nads
by an endlessly persistent accident
that follows me around
like a crass marching band
Now

watch me why don't you
Watch me wither away
delivered through entrails of
a mentally diluted
mess
I conjured up on my
insubstantial time
like a dirty algorithm
that offers me no such
peace of mind
and yet
I always go to sleep not knowing
although
I NEVER FUCKING SLEEP
it just never
seems
to be
and I find that I'm
never quite satisfied
gratified or relieved
and that is why
I go and write SKULLFUCK
on the golden toilet
amid Town Hall's silver palace
then flush
and the shit spirals outta sight
And then there's
My Future
Did I tell you about
My Future?
It disintegrates
It deliberates
It undulates through
swollen prostates
An epically sealed
and overly drilled

underachiever
I breach the swollen
brain of a
frequent performer
All in a Day's Wet
Dream
Show me the mirror please
cuz I seek perfection
What a Defective Lesson
I teach dissection
of the entire human race
I'll break my brain on
shattered bricks
but then miss and whine
that these fucking bricks
just don't fuckin care enough
to connect with skull and skin
But then
I'm just too thin
to really give a shit
Just a worthless dipshit
with a swollen——
Wait what??
Like putting my shoes
on the wrong feet
then walking around all day
knowing not the difference
And then there's
The Mirror
Did I tell you about
The Mirror
It always lies to my face
What a Useless Waste!
And now
I'm back
where I started

back from the top
screaming my face off
at the bluest, most convenient screen
It always makes me
just so blue in the face
What a Useless Disgrace
I make myself out to be
when the dancing flamingos
plastered across the walls
call out my name
through a distorted haze
But they don't really know
I mean how could they?

Untitled Poem

Have you ever had
such an outstanding
realization
that you knew
——Just Knew—————
that if you told it
to an ex-
lover of yours
he/she would love you
    again?

Moody

I'm in a good mood tonight
But I feel guilty for saying that
So now I'm in a bad mood

THE JOKE'S ON ME, I Guess

WHY ME? SEEMS TO BE THE QUESTION OF THE DAY—BUT I'VE GOT NO AN-SWERS FOR YOU, ANYWAY. BECAUSE I ASK MYSELF THE SAME EXACT QUES-TIONS EVERY FUCKIN DAY. SOMETIMES I THINK I'D BE BETTER OFF IF I JUST STUCK A LOADED GUN IN MY MOUTH—yeah what a laugh <u>that</u> would be! RE-CENTLY A FRIEND OF MINE DIED OF A HEROIN OVERDOSE—ME, I'M OVERDOS-ING ON LIFE AND THE END IS JUST NOT COMING FAST ENOUGH, NO MATTER HOW MUCH I DOSE MYSELF WITH IT. IT'S A USELESS JOKE, ANYWAY, ONLY I'M THE ONLY ONE LAUGHING. LOOK AT ME, I'M STRUMMING YET ANOTHER MIS-ANTHROPIC NOTE, I'M POUNDING OUT YET ANOTHER ANTAGONISTIC BEAT—ONE TWO FUCK YOU // ONE TWO FUCK YOU———IT'S A FUCKIN DISASTER-PIECE IF YOU ASK ME, AND YET I'M THE ONLY ONE LAUGHING, AND YES I LAUGH AS I CHOKE DOWN YET ANOTHER FUCKIN SMOKE AFTER I POUND DOWN YET ANOTHER CAN OF HEARTACHE AND YET ANOTHER BRAINSTORM OF WORTHLESS THEORIES THAT ONLY SERVES TO LOCK ME UP IN A HOLE. AND YET I FIND MYSELF LAUGHING BECAUSE IT'S JUST A STUPID FUCKIN JOKE.... SO LAUGH WITH ME NOW, WHY DONCHA.

worthless i'm so worthless..
hopeless it's so hopeless.......

AND I'M ASKING YOU, WHY ME? IT DOESN'T HAVETA BE THIS WAY, AND YET IT IS, AND YES I'M 29 AND ALONE AND LIVING IN A DIVE ALL ON MY OWN.... BUT DON'T YOU DARE ASK ME THAT BECAUSE I'M THE ONLY ONE WHO WONDERS

IT///not you but me! I'M THE ONLY MAN OR WOMAN THAT HATES EXISTENCE LIKE I DO I'M THE ONLY HUMAN BEING THAT JUST WANTS TO FUCKIN DIE ALL THE TIME—i mean, don't you? cuz i sure as hell do.

BUT YOU SHOULD NOT FEEL THIS WAY, I SAY TO YOU OVER COFFEE. I TELL YOU HOPEFUL THINGS, THE KIND OF OPTIMISTIC GARBAGE THAT MAKES ME HATE OTHERS WHEN THEY SAY IT TO <u>ME</u>. FOR BEING SO GODDAMN BUBBLY ALL THE TIME….

      TOO BAD I DON'T BELIEVE THE CRAP THAT I PREACH. TOO BAD I HATE OTHERS WHO SAY THIS KIND OF CRAP WHEN I FEEL LIKE CRAP MYSELF; AND IT'S ALL JUST STUPID CRAP AND MAYBE I HATE MYSELF FOR SAYING THAT, BUT THAT TOO IS CRAP BECAUSE EVERYTHING IS CRAP, AND IT'S ALL JUST STUPID CRAP, AND NOW WE CAN GO AND HAVE A LAUGH, WITH OUR MISANTHROPIC RIFFS AND OUR ANTAGONISTIC BEATS, AND YOU CAN'T FORGET THE CRAPPY BASELINES THAT ARE SO CRAPPY THEY JUST MAKE US CRAP OUR PANTS ALL THE TIME, AND NOW I'M SCREAMING WITH MY CRAPPY VOICE THAT CAUSES THE WHOLE CRAPPY WORLD TO BLEED CRAP OUT OF THEIR OWN CRAPPY EARS; AND YOU MY FRIEND ARE CRAP/// can't say that again….

useless i'm so useless..
running away i keep on running away…….

I ASK YOU, WHY ME? WHY DOES IT HAVE TO BE THIS WAY?

GIMME THE FUCKIN ANSWERS SO I CAN HATE YOU FOR HAVING THEM. GIMME SOME OPTIMISTIC WORDS OF WISDOM SO I CAN PASS THEM ON TO THE PEOPLE THAT I HATE, OR SO I CAN HAVE SOMEONE TO RESENT FOR THE REST OF MY FUCKIN LIFE, SOMEONE TO BLAME FOR ALL THE FUCKIN THINGS GONE WRONG BENEATH THE FUCKIN SKY, AND THEN THE SUN WILL EXPLODE AND I'LL SIT DOWN AND DINE IN ALL THE MADNESS—<u>oh my</u>!—BECAUSE IT'S ALL SO FUCKIN USELESS, ANYWAY. AND SO I LAUGH, AND I LAUGH LAUGH LAUGH; THAT'S RIGHT I FUCKIN LAUGH …

AND I LAUGH …
AND THEN I LAUGH …

AND THEN I LAUGH ...
AND THEN I PULL ...
AND THE GUNSHOT REVERBERATES THROUGHOUT THE NIGHT SKY ...
AND THE BULLET PUNCHES A HOLE IN MY RIGHT EYE ...
AND IT'S EJECTED THROUGH THE BACK OF MY SKULL ...
AND THEN THE HOSPITAL TAKES ME AWAY AND KEEPS ME ALIVE ...
AND I GO THROUGH THE REST OF MY LIFE BLIND AND MISSING HALF OF MY BRAIN AND I GUESS YOU CAN LAUGH ABOUT THAT BECAUSE I SURE AS HELL DO///

We Can Laugh About It Now—JUST LOOK BACK AND LAUGH AT OUR CRAPPY CIRCUMSTANCES;;;;   yeah what a laugh <u>that</u> would be, ya slimy fucks!

FOREVER AND EVER AND EVER I LAUGH .... UNTIL I DIE, ANYWAY.... I MEAN, IT'S JUST A USELESS LAUGH, RIGHT????
JUST A CAUSTIC JOKE THAT KEEPS ME LAUGHING..........

Regrets

When I'm in a good mood

I tend to do things that

when I'm in a bad mood

I regret

Ferocious Renegades

When you're a
nihilist
everything becomes
nihilism
this nothingness a
cure-all to the
everything that inspires
hope
I see no hope
To me hope is equivalent to
a dangling rope
that swings as the body
flounders
in a panicked surge of
adrenaline
seizing
Cease the day
Waste away
Frolic in dirt-encrusted alleyways
Run for cover
Run for cover
Blunder the wandering relic
the fumbling hellions
of a hopeless rebellion
When I open up the Bible
and turn the pages
I see blank lies
blank bindings
my faith is empty
Eternal bliss or
total darkness
it's all too frightening to
fathom correctly

so instead I laugh dementedly
When you're a nihilist
everywhere you look
nothingness spans its
massive wings and takes off
Nihilism replaces the maddening desire
for something anything everything
takes over that need for a higher being
and now you can release the rope
and run free
Just let yourself go
let yourself fly
let yourself be one without
hope
because hope'll only
drag you down
down
down
and the lack thereof
will lift you up
up
up
Liberating
tintelating
medicating
penalized by deliberate
insinuating
ferocious renegades
running through blank caves
The nothingness has got its
hooks in me
and everywhere I look
I see _____

Defective Characters

My goal is to pull out your defects, put them in the spotlight, and then kick em in the teeth. I will shame and humiliate you so badly, forcing you to tuck your defects deeper into your own subconscious. Then I will reach in and pull em back out again, and again ... I'll kick em in the teeth! Forcing you to tuck em even deeper into your subconscious. And then, when you least expect it, I will reach in and carefully pull em back out again, almost as though with a pair of needle-nosed pliers or a fine-toothed comb, hold em high up in the air for everyone to see, and again ... I'll kick em in the teeth! Forcing you to tuck em even deeper into your subconscious. Again and again we will repeat this process until your defects are tucked so deep into your subconscious, locked up and stored away so soundly that not even you have access to them, and as a result you act out and treat everybody like dirt because you can't face your own self in the mirror any longer than you can put up with the sight of someone smaller weaker and so much more grotesque than you; and you put them to shame with everything you got.

  ——and thus, the bully is born\\\

Give Up!

What would happen if I gave up?
   stopped fighting
   stopped trying
   stopped caring
Would the pieces then fall into place?

Like Me

Where am I?? What am I doing?? Feeling hopeless again! Feeling outta place! Tryin ta clean it up! Tryin ta be someone else! But in the end my old ways always catch up ta me again! Running outta time Im runnin outta time! People they grow up! Me I stay young an angry! I seek fun with every last ounce of misery I got trilling deep down inside of me! Life was easier one day! Take a hit blow a line be a man a man whos succumbing to addiction! A man whos lost himself to a throwaway world a throwaway society Ive been thrown away once again! Forgotten about! Seeking hope in a hopeless realm! It feels like hell the way I emerge from the boiling hot water an my skin is peeling an my heart aches an my brain doesnt ever stop racing around the sun 500 thoughts per second it aches! How did I ever live this long anyway?? How'd I ever get here?? Thought life was a joke! Yeah I laughed at everything an everyone an now everything an everyone are laughing at me! Life wasnt the joke <u>Im</u> the joke a phony tryin ta stay real in a world where nothing is real except for everyone else!

Help me! Im killing myself! I hear the cigarettes I smoke speakin in hushed tones the loads of caffeine I drink telling me war stories bout what this is doin to my heart what this is doin ta my mental state! Yeah I know it aint drinkin or druggin but still Im lumbering through life like a blundering zombie! Yeah I call <u>them</u> the Zombies! Yeah I say <u>theyre</u> the Losers an the Mindless an the Hopeless but its all jus projection cuz Im the Dejected the Rejected an the only thing oppressing me is my hatred for my oppressors!

So I gotta get a gun   Someday! So I gotta hit an run   One Day! So I gotta lose my mind   Everyday! Ive lost it now Im tumbling inta damnation its a losing battle that I/ll die tryin ta fight but I/ll survive it first because not even death can hold me down! Not even life can satisfy a dissatisfied freak like me!!!

Inconspicuous Vibes

It's amazing these delusions
we convince ourselves
to be true
And just like that
something new
bubbles up
to the surface
Love turns to
rage
Rage turns to
despair
Despair turns to
disgust
and finally the wanton bandits
disguised thoroughly as
lust
devour your fears
And fear turns into

Overdose

No Wonder drugs will
grant you death
Beats the alternative

Fear Inventory

I am afraid of

People
What people think of me
How I act in public
Sexual relationships
Romantic relationships
Maintaining a platonic relationship with someone for an extended length of time
Losing friends
Running out of things to talk about
Emptiness
Nothingness
Overbearing silence
Too much counterproductive noise
Losing control
Being out of control
Being so in control that I feel like I'm being controlled manipulated or per-suaded by outside parties
Being possessed
Being obsessed
Being misled
Remaining so unmovable that it feels as if there's led in my shoes
Haunting ruminations
Too many hopeless fabrications
Powerful sensations
Love
Lust
Commitment
A lack of imagination
Getting lost in so many fantasies that I lose touch with what's real
Reality
The real reality

People who hate me for no reason
People who love me. Period
Attachments
Detachment
Brash reactions
A lack of satisfaction
Action that comes to me much too readily and easily
Dissatisfaction
Success
Failure
Injustices
Violence
Peace & order
People who enforce the rules
Disorder I can't control
Control I can't disorder
The need to forfeit or submit to established law
Lacking the proper discipline to stop fighting my oppressors and just simply give in to their restrictions

Defective Dream Catcher

Yesterday this guy said I have a lot of wisdom. Well I'm really glad I could offer him some reprieve, but what about me? where's my reprieve? Nothing can shake this rattle from my depraved soul: I'm doomed to seek what cannot be sought and reject what wants to be found. I dream, I envy ideas, I see flaming clouds in a world where the mutant inhabitants frolic bashfully and yet I'm determined to remain dilapidated. I wonder if I'm just ahead of the times, or perhaps too far behind to possibly catch up—I'm being lapped by society and I can't seem to catch up—I'm being eaten by commercialized visions and I try to climb out but do I really want to? I hold on to late night schemes like they're made of gold; I carry early morning thoughts as if they keep me grounded and help me stay whole—but then what's on the ground but rotten vegetation and vile animals who think they know a thing about a thing about a thing? There's nothing no one no place no heaven no hell no race no world no nothing no nothing but a defaced paradise where I lay my head down to die....

Girl

aren't you tired of dating deuchbags?

by no means am I telling you this cuz I think I'm any fuckin better
                                                                                   cuz I'm not I realize

<u>but the fucker cheated on you too</u>
                                  you know

I mean **<u>come on</u>**   you deserve better

                                                                      just give me the word
and I will take care of him for you///

Relapse Report

A drink does seem
kind of appealing
right about now
Drown my sorrows
Maybe burrow into a
plastic bag
and never come out
again
I mean I'll never have to
once that first hit
sets in and I'm off running
again
Floating
Drifting

Becoming one with
my surroundings
Lying in a bed of bloody
roses
Pounding my head through glass
picture frames framed over slanted
alleyways where the sun shines
through
at the dead of the night

My Guide

My guide says, "You're wrong." I say shut your pie-hole.

My Guide (cont.)

I say go to hell! My guide says, "Been there done that." Then what are you doing following me around? "I've been to hell and back," my guide says; "that's why." I say I don't follow. "Be-cause," he says slowly, drawing out the words to make sure I hear him clearly this time. "Because I've been there and don't wish for you to make the same mistakes as me, don't you see?" I stare at my guide, perplexed. "So," he continues. "So I've seen a side of life most people don't ever see; I've seen true evil on my journey; I've seen things most people would never, <u>could</u> never, understand, and I wish no one a fate like that. Please," he adds. "Please think about this."

Busybodies

I feel like I just don't
belong
    <u>any</u>where!
albeit that if I did
I'd be a total failure
      don't you think?
seeing that I've made it my
entire vocation to not
belong
    anywhere!

So I sit here and I
      watch
the
everyday busybodies
talk and mingle
amongst one another
these happy couples
holding hands
smiling and
smooching
beneath the
glittery sky
up above\\\

I just find I'm
so easily
being immersed by
the activity of
my fellow man and woman

shrouded with
their relentless, giddy voices
just
talk-talk-talking it's so
incessantly sad and alien
to me
to see such an outright
display of
futile intermingling

whereas I'm stuck here
all alone
without a place to go to
without a place I can call my
own
      a place I can call my home

So I sit here and I
      watch

Familiarity

Everywhere I go
I see somebody I know
But it doesn't matter anyway
because I wish that just for once
somebody I didn't know
would see me///

Only She

I will never tell you
about the man
I really am
An image
A façade
shattered by years of
neglect &
abuse
But only she can see through
the disguise
that took me years to build
It was protection
A defense mechanism
A way to mislead intruders
away from my heart
because all that's left of me there
a part of me I will never share
is empty and battered
Plastered on every lamppost
and telephone pole
scattered throughout my soul
Scabbed and beaten by
decades of neglect and mistreatment
are flyers shredded around
the edges
that hold secrets
that hold indecencies
that hold vulnerabilities
that hold the key to my
Golden Mask
which I had bolted shut
so that no one can see the man
that I really am

Only she/
only she can see behind the scars
The tears
The years of rejection
The rotten intentions
The blasted ill-directions
My own messy inflexion
She could make out my voice
She listened to
the words that I sung
picking up on every note
and the meaning behind
what I wrote
listening to my
strangled cry
bellowing out from somewhere
in the labyrinth of time
where giants stomp and stagger
smashing and grabbing
everything in sight
A calamity
A catatonic cataclysmic
cacophony so epic
no one can hear
the sound of my mumbled wails
But she understands the pain
painted across my dungeon
She has seen it
evident in her own years
of torment
I have seen it too
in her eyes
The tears
The years of rejection
The rotten intentions
The blasted ill-directions

Her own messy inflexion
I hear it in her voice
as she howls from afar:
"I'm coming!"
I shout back, from deep
in the depths
of the darkest corners where
I was tucked away in the shadows
so that no one can see me
or hear me, ever again—
I shout: "I'm waiting!"
She listens for my voice
I listen for her own
Only she/
only she can hear me
Only I/
only I can hear her
The words that we speak
because only she understands the pain
I feel
and the reprieve
that I seek
I seek her
Only she
seeks me

Power Struggle

Put Down the Rock, they say

I put it down/

Put Down the Fuckin Rock,

they spit at me

and I'm lost|||

in a lucid power struggle

devouring me whole

All-Fools Parade

I hope they
hate me
I hope they're spreading
rumors about me
I hope they're talk
talk talking shit
gossiping like parrots
I hope they look
the other way when
I come walking down
the street

I don't trust anybody
who gets along with
everybody

because only chameleons
change their skin to match
that of their surroundings

How do people
not pick up on
the fact that their friends
are narcissists??
        dirtbags
        losers
        bloody rags
        bag em stamp em & send em
away
        Oh That's Why:
those people are narcissists
too

and being cool
isn't all what it's
cracked up to be

I'd rather stay a loser
than earn the acceptance
of fools

Feeling the Despair
A Letter

Dear Despair,

Here's a brick to wear, a flame to share, a blaring silences resonating behind hateful eyes. Glaring hard through lines of denial, powdered lies, a pinprick to help me decide. You hold me here, but forever I will wear you like Spartan gear. Oh Despair, go shit on someone else's life, why doncha. You are a demon of obscurity, a dirty fit of immaturity—sometimes I go berserk, and wrestle you down the sliding scale, all flailing limbs, we tumble and wail; and my luminescent ruminations drive me to ... stop!

In Flux

The problem with
friends & family
is

They keep on mistaking me
for an
actual human being

I don't even know
what that really means

<u>They box me in</u>
<u>personify me</u>
<u>say I'm something</u>
<u>when really I'm</u>
<u>nothing</u>

They try to classify me
tie the ribbon around
my constricting throat
sign their names on
the card
and tape it to my side
then send me off >>>
to someplace else
to
rot
      I'm someone else's problem
          now

Someone else's
that's right!
      The Court's
      Society's
      Doctors & Nurses
      who are really just scientific Drug Dealers
          always mistaking people for
              words in a
              book
              with a blue cover
              written by other doctors
              wearing blue coats and
              ugly gray slacks\\\

They all pressed my back against
the wall
when I was a child
and as a result
I felt like I had
nowhere left
to turn/
      no escape route
      I could see

other than that of
con
form
ity

So you see
I was stuck
        in a bit of a
         reformative rut

So I said Sure
I was really just
biting my tongue
I hated where this conversation was
heading/
afraid of where it might be
going
for they had no reason anymore
to preserve my existence any
longer
        I was just a menace
        to their jurisdiction

The life I lived was——

The life I lived??
I was only a kid!
while their lives
pressed up against
my own/
I was completely cornered
forced into
    compromise
with no place left for me to

hide
nowhere left
for me to run to
                <u>Check Mate</u>!

So I said Sure
even though what I
was really thinking was: *Go Fuck Yourself*
       <u>*Please*</u>!

I mean
this is Your Society
    Your Culture
        Your Customs
           Your Social Order/

                              just another way
                              for you to reap
                              control
                              on the freakish minority

You're all just forcing me
to conform
      over time/
But still I rebelled

You pushed your own
brand of structure
into my own
free-flowing, haphazard pathway
I jumped left ducked right
spun around this
new obstruction
I'd been presented with/
      which only represented
      Your Fascist
      Regime
          in the end———

those whacky impositions
you used to dictate
my current state of being
      which is subject to change
      at any given moment
of course

What a tacky prostitution
those public school systems
brought us up to
be///
    Their Will
    Not Mine,
              they pushed
upon me

They pushed
but I pushed back
            ... End of story....

So I said Sure
and that turned into the
beginning/
the beginning of
something new
My Brand-New Beginning

Something had happened to me
then
Something had finally clicked
inside my head
Or maybe it really
unclicked///
      came undone like a
      seatbelt———

and for once
    in my life
I felt somewhat
                        <u>free</u>
freer than I'd ever been/
        Free
from all my previous fears and
worries
    My Will
    Not Theirs

                                          … and so it was >>>

Finally
I saw things
clearly///
        for once ___

               — — — —

But today people think
I'm so much better than that
boy
I used to be

You see
I'm not drunk
    anymore
I'm not high
        anymore
I'm a good boy
now
who always tries to
push
positive vibes onto those
who do not have it///

      and yet I push
      negative vibes
      onto those
      who live
in a reality deemed
positively clean
of all freaks like me
          ———*Yuck!*———

But fuck em though!
They deserve the
negative heat
    I'm dishing out
    at them

You see
    basically
          (although I know I've
          digressed
          quite a bit)))
just because I drink
a lot of coffee
    throughout the day
does not in fact mean
that's the only thing
I drink///
    because I do in fact drink
    Monsters and Red Bulls
    too
just so you know ____

People
they perceive me as
something else—

        <u>something I'm not</u>
        and will never choose to
           be///

But
I'll tell you
experience has shown me
    <u>time & time again</u>
that I'm bound to disappoint///
    (I'm just not gonna argue
    this fact
with you
any time in the near future
though
        because I do believe it was
        what I was meant
        to do
        in the grand scheme of
        things
           just hardwired
            to disappoint
              since
                the first day
                  I was
                    born
and I presume
it'll always be the case
        until the day I'm
        no more
But on another,
much happier note
            I think I can
            live with that
            inevitable outcome
for now
anyway

            Because a Fact is a Fact
            and how can you argue
            that?)))

Or maybe it's just that
I'll surprise you
in the end///
        (Oh what a
                fantastic change of
                    events
that had turned out to
be)))

Either way though
I won't always be
the same exact Jeremy Void
you saw me as
            today
            yesterday
            and the day before
because really
I'm actually an
    interchanging
    constantly fluctuating
    destructive/creative
        force of
defiant nature

I'm apt to change
        <u>one day</u>
                        at a time
and I'm not prone to stay
completely the same
        all the time/

It's just so easy to
stamp on a label
and give it a price
in a world where our parents
      <u>have the right to</u>
get fed up and then
send us off to
the next

You see
tomorrow you'll be astonished
by my flux of
human emotions
    I guarantee
But if you shut me down
before giving me the chance
to impress you with
      <u>something else</u>
then you'll miss out on the opportunity
to know a man
    to love a man
        to hate a man
who carries around with him
a heart scarred with
passionate desires
and a mind that seeks
      constant
exploration///
          This desire of mine
          is a
<u>Terminal Elation</u>!
if I were to
   give it a
          name

But then
     I won't!
because I refuse to satisfy
your perpetual need
to put
a price tag on
<u>everything</u>
         Put it on his toe
         and it'll stay there
         forever

So just don't mistake me
for a civilized being
because later you'll see
I'm much more intricate
than such a thing
Because later you will be
rather fascinated
by my outward display of
potential/
         how it can turn me into
         a whole other thing
               in a matter of
seconds minutes hours and days

<u>So sit back and enjoy</u>
         <u>the ride</u>! >>>>>>

Bottled Courage

running with wolves
is a rather difficult task
when the flask is empty

A Fallen Angel

Somewhere
Someplace
Sometime
Somehow
I messed up bad
and now I'm nowhere good
wandering the boring streets.
My eyes are slipping as my head
dips deeper
and I listen for their voices but
they never seem to come to me
not ever—forever walking
this lonely road
of stolen hope.
I pray to the sky, but he or she
or it I don't know
seems to have forgotten about me
or holds me to higher regards
than the rest of the flock
and now my head hurts;
it throbs with an aching pain
that pinches and pulls
me right apart.

I kick a stone and it
fades into the bleak nothingness
spread out before me.

Where did I go wrong?
What the hell
did I ever do wrong??
Hoping and wanting and needing
relief salvation and to rid me of these
miserable tears that drip and dissipate
as I stare out yonder
and the liberated birds tweet
and the flittering bugs chirp
and howl and buzz forlornly—
it makes me so sad.

I walk the cobble stones seeking
answers on this nefarious path
where the nighttime steals the light
and the daytime steals the night
and my head is a mess
broken and holding faith that seems to fade
as eternity breaks   and I seem to be
stuck
in a dream

This isn't real——
It can't be—what happened
to my grace??
It faded and evaporated.
I sift through my memories which seem
to be diminished
as the softly ticking clock breaks apart
and my hardly beating heart takes me far
and the whole wide world comes undone.
Slowly unfolding it sheds moonlight
across my face/

A turtle falls and it can't get up.
I've fallen and my wings are gone.
The stars in the sky explode with remorse—
where did it all go wrong??
I'm a dirty beast defeated and my legacy is
deleted and the whole wide world is
too damn seedy to take
anymore of///

It's a hopeless battle >>>
Standing up for what's right …
Lost and rattled because the fight
and the challenge was just too dastardly
and sad
so sad they said
that they just had to let me go….

I'm just so beaten and alone.
Lost and troubled there's just
no hope anymore\\\
I'm just a fallen angel with
nowhere left to go.

Modern Love Affair

That girl is just so sweet
That guy is such a twit
      I wonder what
         she sees in him….

Walking Home

This is torture
walking thru the
sunlit bliss
This is forever
I walk along
the lonely road
of mental coffins
I play in madness
outta sight danger
I bite the moon
The sun breaks apart
I walk the tainted
traffic jams
of forlorn & lonely hearts

Where am I?
I'm here
the grass-stained overalls
blissfully falling into
her arms
She catches me & I
look into her eyes blindly
She doesn't know me
She has a face I've seen before
in smoky dreams
But her aura
forever broken
Our eyes meet
We stare
finding salvation in
a shared insanity
together twisted & mangled
It's a wildcard

I played
& this stranger
holds me
till I evaporate

Who am I?
How'd I get here?
on this road
alone
walking a thousand miles
just to get home....

Broken

Everything is broken! Where's my head when I need it! That's right, it's fuckin broken! I'm holding on to this insanity like a life vest! I will not let go cuz I know what's there and what's here is broken! It's all so broken! I can barely keep my eyes open! I see flashing lights and mirages and flittering dots! Where's my head when I need it! It went off somewhere without me so I can disintegrate in solitude without a brain to latch onto! It's a hopeless concept! Where's my soul when I need it! It's rotting from the inside out! Fuck you all, I'm going to sleep now! To find reprieve from all the broken objects! Thank you for not caring! I always appreciate all the GET WELL SOON cards I have never gotten! Because the world is rotten and I've forgotten the point of this awful things I'm throwing up on the screen through a blue screen of convenience and if I could only fall asleep I might find relief! But everything is just so broken, and I find life is just so hopeless! I promise you, Officer, I'm not on dope! I'm just an insomniac who has no hope in a sparkly, glittery non-reality that was born from a liar called God! Goodnight!!! Sleep poorly, and please, oh please, let the bed bugs bite! Because then they won't be biting me anymore!   Bye!!!

ARTistic Endeavors

Oh
the joys of being nothing
no one
and going nowhere
rejected by
yet another magazine
just another failed endeavor
just another something that comes
crashing down
on me
like
a shattering pane of glass/

Oh
the joys of being a
struggling artist in today's world
so hungry & broke
so alone & hopeless
is this life worth it?
is it worth it
to be tossed out the window
like a measly heap of trash
wasted like water
taken for granted
like a coiling trail of smoke
as it swirls upward
and fades
away in a puff/

Oh boy
don't you just love
this existence
Oh the joy of suffering

Oh oh, struggling to get by
Oh oh oh, losing a rat race that I
never wanted to run
in the first place
it's hopeless
I'm hopeless
going nowhere
I'm going nowhere
the smoke drifts away
and

Oh
I'm happy
really I am....

Poetic Suicide

I wanna fuckin
kill myself
Maybe then
I'll be recognized
All the best poets die young
right
so what the hell am I
waiting for
I mean I'm only getting
older
I hate this stupid culture!

Time's Up

I'm spent. The day's up. I'm lost and wound up. I'm looking for answers. I punch the clock—tick tick tock: a senseless rattle. I'm jittery and annoyed, tired and so damn self-absorbed. I'm lost, and I just don't know anymore. I watch the clock/// The second hand jumps, and I jump. The minute hand flinches, and I flinch. When will my time be up?? It's a relentless cycle, senseless and so damn psychotic. I watch the clock the hour hand winks at me; sweat stings my eyes. I'm waiting I'm waiting I'm waiting waiting waiting >>> The second hand jumps, and I jump. It's just not enough—not enough not enough not enough! The minute hand flinches, and I ... I ... I—— I tear open the top drawer of my desk, shuffle through random sheets of paper, grab my gun. It feels nice in my grip, nice and firm, like pure fuckin power. Just squeeze the trigger and see where it gets you. I stick it against my head|||

The hour hand winks at me, and ... fuck you, time!——   I pull >>>>>>

My Friend the Junky

the scene was set with beaten lies
a tormented backdrop for everything that went wrong
in your eyes shone a lustfulness that made you a spirited orb
seeking romance and destruction was your only crime
crying for mercy all night shoving the spike in your arm
you squandered the hellish rut in search of that next piece of fun
running from yourself while trekking beautiful clouds
clad in golden cobwebs of joy you sank lower and lower into the ground
floating away on the thickest wisps of madness
it was your only ploy to find satisfaction in a world shrouded with sadness
all play and no hope are the magical ingredients that made up this terrible rem-
        edy

shake it up and sprinkle in a tad-bit of fear—flick the wand and say your most
    magical prayers
and watch as your whole life ebbs away
and your mental health melts quickly into fading tears as the spell washes away
    your pain
the prior angst and frustration you felt on a day-to-day basis
fades away with no required bat of the eye
you my friend are stuck on a life-devouring ride
a black hole that grows and grows—getting bigger and bigger—wider and
    wider—and more and more sinister—until—your———untimely de-
    mise
washed away in a seizing ethereal experience as your pupils shrink
and you blink away the tyranny of numbness that swallows you up
erratically gasping for that next but rather hopeless breath that never seems to
    come
your frothing mouth drying up as your eyes shut forever

just a kid on the skid seeking that next radical hit—on just another mission
    from God to make things right in your life, to become instantly grati-
    fied but the gratification never lasted but sadly that last one did
permanently eradicated—just a 20-year-old kid who will be forever tied to
    tears and remorse———intensely interested he was
but nothing ever seemed enough to satisfy this kid's ever-fascinated mind

and now his friends and family are crying as they pick up all the crumbs

tell me my friend, was it worth it to be so intensely amused by everything in
    sight? so passionate about life and death and everything in between?
    so caring yet so care-free was your only curse, was it worth the burden
    of being so fun-loving and loveable that you just had to bite the dirt
I'm so glad we were friends because you went where no one else would, stood
    by me when no one else could—but so sad we had met because now
    all that is left are memories of regret

I'm so sorry this had to be the case..........

An Eye for an Eye
A Love Story

Now
you got me in

A Web of Lies
    A Web of Lies
        A Web of Lies
            A Web of Lies
                It's just the story
                of
    my life....
A fate that haunts me
torments and
    degrades me
holds me still
and beats me till
I'm ill in the face
decked with black-
and-blue splotches
that shine hot like
a thumb caught in a
sliding car door
        There just seems to be
        no escape
        from your gargantuan
        tug
You see
the way I felt about you
then
and the way I feel about you
now
it's like I never ever felt it
in the first place

They say that love is real
They say that hate is only based in
fear
But I'll tell you
I got stuck in your
Web of Lies
and girl
you sucked me dry
every single time
with every little twitch of
your rueful tongue
and I hope I'll never have to
go back to that place
again
I'll never have to feel that same
way
again
        Never again
will my emotions hold me
hostage
like that
so that you can destroy me
from the inside out
Never again will I be
victimized by
a girl that I despise
I cannot stand the sight of you
so I will scribble over your image
with loads of whiteout
hoping that you
just simply evaporate
        So Why Don't You Just
        Go Away!
because today it's my turn
to have a say
to shut down

compartmentalize
and reject
the normal flow of
human emotions
that hold me in place
as I try to break free from
their nefarious ways
Now It's My Turn
to Be Cold
and
Emotionless
Now it's my turn to
DESTROY
and I will
destroy
        every last one of
        you
if it's the last thing
that I do....
I will neglect you
and treat you so badly
leaving you baffled and
confused
wanting nothing more than
to be my lover
my fucker
my leashed succubus
a beaten slave shunned
by the diseases
she carries
around with her from day
to day
Because what I really want
is for you to
want me
to love me

to see me as the man
I've always wanted to be
but what I always get
is just a clusterfuck
of useless
human emotions
and I will kick you down
until you realize
it's me
that you want
and when you do
I promise you
I will be gone
for good
    because only I
    hold the truth
    in my hands:
        1. Love Is Dead
        2. Hate Is Alive
           and
                Fed
    and 3. the fastest way
for me to get you
to love me
in return
is by devaluing
your life and your
existence
and I will watch you
suffer
I will watch you
blunder
curl up into a ball
and cry for me
to stop the torment
the pain

the madness
all of it winding down
to the finale
What Do You Want
from Me??
you'll ask me
in dismay
and I'll say to you
then
through the most jaded
grin
you've ever
seen
      I Just Want You to Feel
      What I Feel
and See What I See
   <u>In the end I just</u>
      <u>want you to be</u>
         <u>there for me</u>
in the end....

The Humanoid Contract

This is not what I signed up for when they asked me if I wanted to be human!

Mediocrity

They might be happy with
mediocrity
    just being a nobody till
        the day that they die

But Me—
    I guess I need
        <u>something</u>
something more than
what I'm getting

But what I always get
what I will always get
what I've always gotten
    is a big heaping pile of
        nothing—*nada*

I'm mediocre
don't you see!
and I will always be
just another nobody lost to
    just another
futile effort a succession
of failed endeavors

But it's useless
    anyway
        and I swear to you
I will die trying to
prove myself wrong/
I will die trying to rise
above the self-degradation >>>
    that keeps me
        in chains——

these nefarious impositions
that belittle my fate
But it's useless
    anyway
        so why bother
at the end of the day///

Loner on the Run from Reality

It's a lonely night
devoid of noise
and
activity

Or could it be in fact
that I'm the one
who's lonely
That I'm the one
merely placing blame
on the inanimate sky's
brooding source of light
that goes out like a defused candle
when the time is right
Maybe I'm the lonely one
      lost without a home
      without a base to go to
      without a set of arms to
      catch me
          next time I
            fall
and I do fall
hard///———
            Next Time Will You
            catch me??
                !! PlEaSe !!

Sure I can say
the night is cold
and dark and
bold and frightful
and sure I can see through the black
ness as though I possess in my hands
an X-ray telescope that passes
blame through mighty storms
of self-righteous divisions
Sure I can sell you some of my
poisonous wisdom spawning from
logically flawed algorithms like
lopsided cobwebs

I sit on the curb and ponder
the whatfors
of a distorted past
and hope for a restored future

as I walk on a lonely path
through
mental backwash
like paddling a rowboat up white-
water rapids
Better have your tantrum now
before the boat flips over
and your existence gets flooded with
turbulent foam just fizzing and
popping and spraying
and bubbling over to
eliminate you
      entirely/

But now you're immersed in
sheer hatred for
all your fellow mutants

Me I haul my mind back up to
the streets unloading drunks
bums and freaks
and I try to communicate but instead
I can only disseminate my
blatant distaste for drunks bums and
        freaks
with bitter resentments
building up like bile
stuck to the back of my
mind

It's a lonely night
devoid of noise
and
activity as I

sit on my stoop
and chain-smoke
with great hopes that I
only knock another five minute
off of
my life
with every smoke devoured

It's a lonely night
devoid of noise
and
activity

and now the streets are
awash with darkness
with a great nothingness
absorbent like an impulsive
plague
that embraces me I

stare off yonder
and wonder
> Where the hell did it all
>> go wrong??
>>> What the hell had happened to
>>>> the swarming mobs??
>>> that had enveloped me yesterday
>>> with its toxic fervor

excitement romance adventure and
passion and devotion and
action action action
for we were devoted to
action
> back then/

And so I ask you
as another ignored tear
and another neglected sorrow
and another dejected yearning
goes unnoticed and discounted
through the devouring maw of time:
> Why the hell
>> did they all feel the need to
>> leave me behind?

and now they have vanished and
  their sins had
    vaporized in gushing tears
      with which to dissolve their
        boredom///
> just another reason for me to Hate

my dimming condition as the
flaming, enthusiastic light
dwindles even quicker now

It's a lonely night
devoid of noise
and
activity and

I sit here and unwind
feeling just so devoid of
noise and
activity

It's a hopeless fight
and I just feel so goddamn lonely
tonight

Let Me Hate (if I want to)

Let me hate if I want to! I'm not hurting anyone but myself. Let me be a liar, let me beat my head against the wall, let me run wild & free. Let me scream the world is on fire. Let me be delivered through space & time. Let me write FUCK on the walls, let me scribble words on the toilet bowl, let me scrawl penises on your face while you sleep. I'm not hurting anybody but myself. Don't cry when I die; don't cry let my memories fade. Let me see red when I close my eyes, let me see the madness before I say goodbye. I'm not hurting anyone but myself. I'm standing in the sirens' flare. Don't be scared, my child. Don't be afraid of the chaos. Jump into the fire, leap into the flames, be the maniac the Big Bang had programmed you to be. Just remember, only in death shall you surrender your soul to the overwhelming light of an empire. So set the world on fire…. It's your last chance to radiate in waste & desire.

The Rebuttal

I feel quite guilty sometimes.
I get restless and I
need to write or this
anxiety will take over
and that's something I don't want
to have happen to me.
In fact it's a hazard to everyone I touch.
So I write relentlessly
I write endlessly
I write manically—that's
a bit of an understatement, don't you think?
I'm outta control
the pen my machine gun
the paper my target
and I'm gunning down lines
with pen ink and rhymes
but fuck it, for me it's write
or die—and frankly
I'm too fuckin young
to die///
maybe tomorrow but today
I write
and I write with my heart dangling
in between my bright blue eyes
beneath my spikey, jet-black hair
I write without a care >>>
and what's an artist without an audience
to share his art with.
——<u>if a tree falls in the forest</u>
<u>& theres nobody there to paint its descent</u>
<u>to describe the sound it makes</u>
<u>as it racks the leafy ground beneath it</u>
<u>& the heavy **whump!** reverberates</u>

<u>throughout the ominous mountainside & yet
nobody cares enough to listen,,,,
what good is the trees defiant trajectory
of terror as it topples straight downward?</u>——
not good at all, worthless and messy that's what/
No beauty to be found in
the absence of the artist.

So I feel quite guilty
at the amount I post in groups on Facebook.
I've already been kicked out for such
transgressions against the sinister group
conscious it's devious is what it is.
But I understand their point too; really I do::::
If I clutter the walls with my own junk
there will be no room left for
the likes of others, and that they cannot have.
But fuck em anyway, I've been 86'd enough
in my short-lived life
to know where I'm not wanted
to know where I'm despised/
been thrown to the wolves time
and time again it's getting old.
But still

I feel quite guilty….
I just can't help it though///
this is just something I've gotta do
to survive the tumultuous webs
my mind spins around me and if
I'm not careful enough the greedy, hungry little spider
will suck my thoughts out through my spine.
But still I feel quite guilty
and that's something I can't deny///

on-the-prowl——

i-mean--its-fairly-easy-to-read-my-emotional-state-from-just-a-glance—its-the-soul-reason-that-my-old-friend-andrew-wud-explain-to-me-that-when-i-was-actively-looking-for-a-fight-i-cud-never-find-one———they-knew-i-was-on-the-prowl--&-they-knew--too--that-if-they-tried-anything-at-all--theyd-fuckin-go-down———i-was-that-bus-w/-the-cut-brakelines-buzzing-down-the-wrong-side-of-the-highway--only-the-current-driver-wanted-to-ram-it-into-something-so badly———i-mean--most-people-only-try-to-fuck-w/-me-when-im-feeling-rather-low-myself-&-whatever-fight-i-wud-normally-have-inside-of-me-was-curled-up-limp-&-deflated-inside-of-my-aching-heart///

The Power of Suggestion

Everyone I know is joining hands in a magical death dance down the center of awestruck faces and flashing lights. Me, I avoid the lights and step out into the night. The night doesn't flash me except with entrancing wisdom that only the social elite possess, from a lifetime of cars doing donuts around planet earth. Stay strange, stranger than whacky America with its unification, with its corporate conformity—and yet I find myself feeling quite depressed because I don't seem to fit into their Master Plan. **The power of suggestion///the hour of death.** When everyone you know is falling neatly in line like cattle, where do you go? I'm dying from irony; it's a twisted joke and I'm the punchline. I say defy everyone, defy the system, defy God while you're at it, because he's the one who created this MASTER PLAN in the first place. Go against The Flow or you'll lose yourself to a faux-existence. The Thought Police?? <u>No need</u>! They got a dresscode and if you don't submit, your peers will turn against you. I run away, I avoid confrontation, I do everything in my power—— But what power???? My peers got the whip: just another victim of inculcation—again & again I've got no choice. Voices like thunder; left-wing hudu tying me up in chains. **The power of suggestion///the hour of death.** Peer pressure is tearing me up, and soon I'll get married >>>

The end.

Nothing Matters Anymore

Self-destruct
fuck shit up
    Play it safe
    make no waves
Live on the sly
get real high

Too many indecisions
too many lonely opinions
Fuck it all
because nothing matters anymore

I'm a hopeless romantic
waiting for something more
than what I'm getting
I'll bathe in chemicals
because nothing matters anymore

Haha, it's all just a joke….

Dead Flowers

        Have you ever stared into a mirror so deeply that the glass just shattered, like just spontaneously crashed into a billion little pieces, and the sound of clattering glass on the tiled floor beneath you startled you out of your stupor—simply because there was no way you could have safely predicted such an outcome??
Well I know I sure have\\\

They say that Self-Destruction is a curse a burden on everybody who encounters you throughout the course of your life. They might come across my inflicted intuition, my lack thereof reality, my seemingly nonexistent self and my fate that's going nowhere because Nothing is my god my savior and the very thing that's killing me so as to harvest my soul when I'm dead & gone because Nothing's the only thing I got left to cherish when all the bets are down and the crazed, rabid bookie holding the ticket to my soul is presently pointing the barrel of an AK-47 assault rifle against my inner eardrum and I feel like I might fall tumble or worse, maybe go splat and crumble against the tall, looming brick walls of last year's padded cell >>>||| but besides, Nothing's already got a long list of buyers waiting for me to die in vain—and in pain—and insanely deviate from the fair range of human emotions and decency because they know that that day—(((the day of my untimely demise]-|-[the day I step on a crack and break my mother's back and my dad snaps and breaks down bawling—or I was not supposed to go that way at all)))—will come soon enough; but then again, it will come so much sooner than anyone could have ever expected because it always comes way too soon and too soon I'll be choking on my own vile it isn't pretty at all—it just ain't pretty to die like that///trust me I know———or I suppose they could discover that phony sensation I portray so frequently which derives from Nothing and thrives on Nothing and I suppose I strive to live by the code of Nothing too—which is just so cold and dark and desolate and will only bring you nothing in the end because now you won't amount to nothing ever again———but then again, Nothing is worth fighting for worth dying for||| Nothing is all I live for in the end///well, until the sun explodes in a smoldering swelter of blazing hellfire, that is....

So this morning I find myself standing on the shattered glass littering my bathroom floor, scratching my head and analyzing the veins that pop out of my arms like open wires; and the fact that I have no muscle mass whatsoever, shouldd serve to frighten me but it doesn't....
The only memory of mine that comes to mind easily, without straining too hard to access it, is from last night when I was walking down the street brooding, with a head hanging and wobbling on a limp neck as I gazed at my feet, and i passed this beautiful garden which really caught my attention for some rea-

son—I'd never actually seen it before. It was just so magical the way it was brimming with sparkling glitter, colorful, mesmerizing dots that were blooming great big pedals wobbling in the easy breeze; and I took a brief, cautious gander, as if the gods would strike me dead if they knew, into the direction of the unfamiliar, glowing sea of greens and reds and pinks and blues and it drew me in completely I just started walking toward it walking closer like I was floating and when I stood in the center of the billowing garden my initial reaction rolled over me and I suddenly felt as if the flowers were mocking me like maybe this was a sign a sign from something that is so much more powerful than me and I knew that this was a sign it had to be. And I knew just what I had to do….
I hobbled and kicked and chopped and snipped and cut and beat and wobbled and ripped until I was standing in a big heaping pile of nothing but dirt and dead flowers.
I figured if this had been a sign it must have come from Nothing after all ____

So I snap back to the here&now and suddenly I remember the mirror and how it shattered when I looked at it———but no that can't be right that can't be it just can't be right at all: I look down at my knuckles and they're stained with blood. My knees wobble and I just don't know what to fuckin do with my life about my life anymore. Nothing doesn't fuckin care about me in the end!…

The Anniversary

He's dead now
died from a heroin-
induced stupor
He's dead now
the drug having burrowed
into his head
It's been almost
a year now
since the junky died

He was my friend
      my brother
      a kid who lost himself
      to the depth of
self-destructive circumstances

A heathen seeking relief
A boy lost to wretchedness
and waste
It was His Only Cure
for the relentless boredom that
plagued him daily
A Conniving Burden
But what's it worth
to die like that
to be lost
      forever
            in tears
of remorse

It's Our Loss!
    not his

So
he's dead now
and everywhere I look
I see dipping heads
with needles stabbing into
their eyes
      Everywhere I look
      I see reminders
      of Him
No word carries
the right amount of
power to describe
such a kid

Today
doing heroin is almost like
smoking cyanide
    It'll kill you
    you can be damn sure of it
Like playing a game of
Russian Roulette where
there's only one bullet
for every six chambers
        Today there's
        <u>five</u>
        explosive tablets
        for every six chambers
Just Pull the Trigger >>>
    and see
        where it gets you///

It's been almost a year
since I'd seen him
He bit the big one
and now he's
forever traipsing dreams
    forever & ever
What a wasted thing that he is!
A brat who would just not
grow up
let alone
        !WAIT!
for that salvation
to come

and now all his best mates
hold their heads in dismay

He's dead now
and there's not a thing
anyone can do
about it///
        He's dead now
        and now
        all that we can do is
pray that maybe
THEY GOT REHAB IN HEAVEN

The Fate of an Artist

1. No friends
2. No friends
3. Some friends
4. More friends
5. A lot of friends
6. Too many friends to know what to do with
7. No friends
8. Suicide

30

Life has brought me nothing but pain. Now I'm jaded. As of twelve minutes ago I'm 30. Yes, jaded. I always said I'd kill myself when this day came. When I turned 30. And I want to so badly. But I'm jaded and I've got nothing to say. I don't care one way or another. Live or die, it's all the same to me. Pain! I don't mean to sound melodramatic, but that's not the case at all. I'm done trying to explain myself. See you on the other side.

Table of DisContents

Manic Nihilism/Absurdism/Call It Whatever You Want It Makes No Difference in the End ... XI
   An Introduction

Manic/Depressive Monuments

29 ... 1

Vindictive Arrogance ... 1

Artistic Expression ... 3

Sober-X ... 3

Tied to Remorse ... 4

I don't know ... 5

Burn Out ... 6

Safe House ... 7

Fake ... 7

Existential Angst ... 9

People Places & Things ... 9

A Rebel's Paradise ... 9

The Crazy ... 11

Love & Death ... 12

Today or Nothing ... 13

Harmful Determination ... 13

Pushed! ... 14

Into My Heart ... 15

Baby ... 15

HOPE ... 16

Misunderstood ... 16

Untitled Poem ... 16

Lonesome Loathing ... 17

Unpredictable ... 17

Why Do the Good Always Leave Such Feasible Scars on Our Hearts? ... 18

Racing Thoughts ... 19

A Hopeless Cry ... 19

Insanity Is In ... 19

Mental Oppression ... 20

Control ... 21

Timeless Indecisions ... 21

Misplaced Rage ... 23

Fire-Starter ... 24

Just Swell!- - -☺ ... 24

no such thing ... 25

On Gratitude ... 25

Everybody ... 26

Collateral Damage ... 27

Dynamite ... 33

lost ... 34

Anxious Qualities ... 34

a drug called life ... 35

No Misgivings ... 35

Down the Tubes ... 35

Is this love? ... 37

Beat the Devil ... 40

Decomposed Compositions

Caustic Reality ... 43

My Void ... 47

Experimental Poem ... 48

You are loved ... 49
    (or) Journey to the End of the American Dream

Nihilism Is Everything ... 59
    said he

United We Divide ... 60

Broken Sunshine ... 63

The Genius in Failure ... 63

Breaking Down ... 65

Horrorscope ... 66

I begin to notice ... 68

Come Be Androgynous with Me ... 70

I can't sleep ... 73

Fixer-upper ... 73

Glittered Romance ... 74

About a Boy ... 75

Darker Things ... 75

tantric excursions ... 76

Untitled Poem ... 77

Never have I ever ... 79

Don't go into the light! ... 83

Insomnia ... 87

Taking Flight ... 88

Untitled Poem ... 88

Looking into it ... 89

Untitled Poem ... 90

Oblivious Discontentment ... 94

You & I ... 95
    and Anyone Else Who Wants to Join Us on Our Ride

Can't Take the STRAIN ... 97

Let me dream if I want to ... 98

everything I need to say ... 99
    in only a few words

round&round&round ... 100

Document, Recovered ... 100

The Show Must Go On ... 101

A Pet Called Projection ... 103

A Method to My Madness ... 105

Flight ... 111

Untitled Poem ... 112

Staggering to the Blues ... 113

Untitled Poem ... 114

Sifting through dreams ... 114

So Out of Place ... 117
    RIGHT NOW

Untitled Poem ... 117

Days of Brutality ... 118

Wounded ... 120

Untitled Poem ... 121

A Vague History of the Wheel ... 122

The Bush Burns Brightest at Night ... 122

Dotted Lines ... 123

Nighttime Blunders ... 123

A Pain in My Diction ... 124

Exponential Interpretations

Friendship ... 127

Blind Submissions ... 130

Divide- -Unite- -Crucify ... 130

Untitled Poem ... 134

Generation Z ... 135

Taken by Delusions ... 135

Animosity ... 136

Caring ... 138

Liberal Mythology ... 138

The Good ... 139

CaSe-SeNsItIvE ... 140

All-American Dinner ... 140

Sometimes: ... 141

Blind Hatred ... 141

When the Dominos Fall ... 141
    You can always count on this

Fuck Society! ... 142

It's Party Time, Dude! ... 142

In the Loop ... 143

Talking to God About Ethics ... 144

Fuck Art, Let's Dance! ... 144

Love Is the Monster Beneath My Bed ... 145

Hate the Closet Case ... 145

Overboard ... 146

The Foundation ... 146

When I say jump ... 147

Live Free &—DIE HAPPY! ... 150

For Sure ... 151

Blacklisted ... 151

LOVE ... 153

Fuck Sadness ... 154

Pick ... 156

LISTEN.. to me, please! ... 157

Pander Division ... 158

The Night Sky >>> ... 159

Mommy, I think I wanna be androgynous when I grow up! ... 159

Pillage! ... 162

A naked man showers in the spray of a hunchback whale ... 163

Identity Crisis ... 163

卐 ... 164

Exclusive ... 164

PC ... 164

In the Big City ... 165

Lifeless America ... 166
    Flip the Channel I'm bored

The Popular Opinion ... 168

Revolting Sensitivity

Never … 169

Liberty … 169

Searching for the Present Ending of a Delirious Mirage … 171

Lovelife … 172

Cause & Effect … 173

PANIC || a t t a c k … 174

Killing Time … 184

I'm Fine! … 185

The Story of My Life … 185

Untitled Poem … 188

On This Warm, Sunny Afternoon … 189

Haunted Reflection … 190

A Travelling Companion … 191

On the Edge … 192

The Last Void Standing … 193

On the Offense … 193

Customer Service … 194

Live Fast Die Young … 194

Pedestal People … 194

I CAN'T … 195

Gratitude … ? … 195

Restless Body Syndrome … 196

Untitled Poem … 197

More … 197

Self-Destructive Tendencies … 197

Untitled Poem ... 202

Transcend ... 203

Withdrawn ... 205

Untitled Poem ... 205

Sip Hit or Fuck ... 206

Giving Up ... 207

What's the Big Deal? ... 208

Stimuli ... 209

L.O.S.E.R. ... 209
  once again I felt the cold, sharp, brutal sting of rejection

Soundly I lie awake ... 214

Untitled Poem ... 218

To love me ... 219

Thought Police ... 220

What I Get Back ... 220

Stupid ... 221

Illegal ... 221

I don't know how to be ... 222

Structure ... 224

In This State ... 225

Time! ... 225

My Love & Deceit ... 226

To Hearts Unknown ... 227

Sorry ... 229

My Apologies ... 229

Untitled Poem ... 229

Hysterical Resolutions

The Sky Tells No Whys ... 231

On My Mind ... 232

Wretched Neon ... 232

A Sick Mind—— ... 236

Phantoms ... 240

On the Road ... 241

Pop'd ... 242

tainted tapestry ... 242

Bed Time ... 243

The Sky Speaks ... 244

Deep-Fried Love ... 244

Useless ... 245

Pedantic Ransom ... 249

Evacuate! ... 251

Untitled Poem ... 252
    with Anonymous

Bible Stories ... 252

Conversation ... 257

Royally Fucked ... 257

When in Doubt ... 258

Ode to Chaos ... 259

Untitled Poem ... 261

Anti-Hero ... 262

Stupid Questions ... 264

Reprieve ... 265

the siren's song ... 266

Incompletion ... 268

Livestock ... 268

Independence Day ... 269

Wordplay ... 270

my shadow ... 271

Deface Me Like Cubicles Made of Stone ... 273

Untitled Poem ... 275

A Poetic Threesome ... 276
    with Melody Fair and Emily Lopez

The Ghost Robber ... 277

Did It My Way ... 277

Girls ... 278

Pulp Fiction ... 278

AK47 ... 279

Order ... 279

7 Words ... 281
    splattered, burst, platter, torn, bent, laced, knuckles

Antipathy ... 281

A Clusterfuck—— ... 283

The Mirror of Youth ... 283

i hurt ... 285

Inspired ... 286

Of Unknown Origins ... 288

i hear her now ... 290

5 Words ... 291
    logical, steamed, moved, believed, considerate

Prayers of the Lonely ... 292

A Race to the Top ... 293

The Darkness, Afraid of Humanity ... 294

Haikus of the Future ... 296
       personal goals & ambivalences

That which shall not be named ... 297

Esoteric Demonstrations

Perfection ... 299

conditioner ... 299

Untitled Poem ... 301

EgO ... 301

DISempowerment ... 301

AWKWARD Not Asocial ... 302

Why not dream?? ... 303

Radical Deception ... 304

Untitled Poem ... 306

Controversy ... 307

I am! I was not! ... 308

Forced Ejaculation ... 308

Opinionated Friends ... 309

To Heaven & Beyond ... 310

Nostradamus ... 312

hooRAH ... 312

Formalities ... 314

Terminal Cases ... 314

Performance Art ... 316

When ... 317

Incorrect Thoughts ... 319

445

Punk Rock in the Modern World ... 320

Dilapidated Derelict & Devoid ... 320

what for ... 320

Malfunction ... 321

LIKE this! ... 322

Sign on the Dotted Line ... 322

The Devil's in the Details ... 325

Disorder NOW! ... 326

Personification ... 326

The Big Picture ... 328

Untitled Poem ... 328

Categories ... 329

The Jaded Soldier ... 330

Prayer & Meditation ... 332

Ask Yourself: ... 332

Ask Yourself: ... 333

The Meaning the Purpose & the Deity ... 333

Like Clockwork ... 333

Black Sheep ... 334

21st Century Artists ... 335

Kid with the Replaceable Head ... 335

Dead Rockstars ... 337

The Inferno ... 337

"I am smart" ... 339

He Said ... 341

Artists— ... 342

Optimistic Nihilism … 343

Unjustified & Irrational … 344

Divide & Conquer … 344

Barred from the Garden of Eden … 344

Heaven … 348
 Beyond the Legend

A Germ … 348

Unity … 351

in a way … 351

Bad … 352

TV Junkies … 352

SOBRIETY!—A Deviant's Drug of Choice … 353

Free Speech … 353

The Best Way to Win the Game … 354

Filthy Abrasions … 355

Jaded Delicacies

Struggling … 357

Faceless … 357

Possessive … 358

Terminal … 358

Explosive … 361

Shunned Bullied & Ignored … 361

On the Fast Track … 365

Friends Not Fans … 366

Nothing to Lose … 367

My Brain Knows Best … 367

in luv ... 367

Break Her Neck ... 368

Curtains ... 368

A Thorn in My Mind ... 369

Hold On! ... 371

Here It Lies ... 371

Untitled Poem ... 375

Moody ... 376

THE JOKE'S ON ME, I Guess ... 376

Regrets ... 378

Ferocious Renegades ... 379

Defective Characters ... 381

Give Up! ... 381

Like Me ... 382

Inconspicuous Vibes ... 383

Overdose ... 383

Fear Inventory ... 384

Defective Dream Catcher ... 385

Girl ... 386

Relapse Report ... 386

My Guide ... 387

My Guide (cont.) ... 387

Busybodies ... 388

Familiarity ... 389

Only She ... 390

Power Struggle ... 393

All-Fools Parade ... 393

Feeling the Despair ... 395
    A Letter

In Flux ... 395

Bottled Courage ... 406

A Fallen Angel ... 406

Modern Love Affair ... 408

Walking Home ... 409

Broken ... 410

ARTistic Endeavors ... 411

Poetic Suicide ... 412

Time's Up ... 413

My Friend the Junky ... 413

An Eye for an Eye ... 415
    A Love Story

The Humanoid Contract ... 419

Mediocrity ... 420

Loner on the Run from Reality ... 421

Let Me Hate (if I want to) ... 425

The Rebuttal ... 426

on-the-prowl—— ... 428

The Power of Suggestion ... 428

Nothing Matters Anymore ... 429

Dead Flowers ... 429

The Anniversary ... 431

The Fate of an Artist ... 434

30 ... 434

www.ingramcontent.com/pod-product-compliance
Lightning Source LLC
Chambersburg PA
CBHW020728160426
43192CB00006B/146